Political Candidate Selection

The "secret garden of politics", where some win and others lose their candidate selection bids, and why some aspirant candidates are successful while others fail have been enduring puzzles within political science. This book solves this puzzle by proposing and applying a universally applicable multistage approach to discover the relationship between selection rules, selectors' biases, aspirants' attributes, and selection outcomes.

Rare party and survey data on winning and losing candidates and insider views on what it takes to win a selection contest at multiple selection stages are compared and used to reveal the inner workings of the secret garden. With a primary focus on the British Labour party over several elections, the findings challenge many long-held assumptions about why some aspirant candidate types are successful over others and provides real-world and controversial solutions to addressing women's and other marginalised groups' descriptive underrepresentation. As such, it provides a much-needed fresh look at party selection processes and draws new conclusions as to why political underrepresentation occurs and should inform policies to remedy it.

This text will be of key interest to scholars and students of gender and ethnicity in politics, political parties and candidate selection, and more broadly to the study of political elites, comparative politics, sociology, labour studies, gender, race, and disability studies, and to practitioners.

Jeanette Ashe is Chair of the Political Science Department at Douglas College, British Columbia, Canada.

Routledge Studies on Political Parties and Party Systems
Series Editors: Ingrid van Biezen
Leiden University, the Netherlands, and Fernando Casal Bértoa, University of Nottingham, UK

This new series focuses on major issues affecting political parties in a broad sense. It welcomes a wide-range of theoretical and methodological approaches on political parties and party systems in Europe and beyond, including comparative works examining regions outside of Europe. In particular, it aims to improve our present understanding of these topics through the examination of the crisis of political parties and challenges party organizations face in the contemporary world, the increasing internal complexity of party organizations in terms of regulation, funding, membership, the more frequent presence of party system change, and the development of political parties and party systems in under-researched countries.

Party System Change, the European Crisis and the State of Democracy
Edited by Marco Lisi

Do Parties Still Represent?
An Analysis of the Representativeness of Political Parties in Western Democracies
Edited by Knut Heidar and Bram Wauters

Leaders, Factions and the Game of Intra-Party Politics
Andrea Ceron

Informal Politics in Post-Communist Europe
Political Parties, Clientelism and State Capture
Michal Klíma

Political Candidate Selection
Who Wins, Who Loses, and Under-Representation in the UK
Jeanette Ashe

For information about the series: www.routledge.com/Routledge-Advances-in-International-Relations-and-Global-Politics/book-series/IRGP

Political Candidate Selection

Who Wins, Who Loses, and
Under-Representation in the UK

Jeanette Ashe

Routledge
Taylor & Francis Group

LONDON AND NEW YORK

First published 2020
by Routledge
2 Park Square, Milton Park, Abingdon, Oxon OX14 4RN

and by Routledge
605 Third Avenue, New York, NY 10017

First issued in paperback 2022

Routledge is an imprint of the Taylor & Francis Group, an informa business

© 2020 Jeanette Ashe

Publisher's Note
The publisher has gone to great lengths to ensure the quality of this reprint but points out that some imperfections in the original copies may be apparent.

British Library Cataloguing in Publication Data
A catalogue record for this book is available from the British Library

Library of Congress Cataloging in Publication Data
A catalog record for this book has been requested

ISBN: 978-1-03-240093-8 (pbk)
ISBN: 978-1-138-03951-3 (hbk)
ISBN: 978-1-315-17580-5 (ebk)

DOI: 10.4324/9781315175805

Typeset in Times New Roman
by Apex CoVantage, LLC

For my Mum and Dad

Contents

List of tables   viii
List of figures   x
Acknowledgements   xi
List of abbreviations   xiii

1   Study overview   1

2   The selection process puzzle and ideal candidate types   22

3   Data and initial supply and demand tests   42

4   Centralisation and the Labour party's candidate selection process   61

5   Assessing centralisation in the British Labour party's
    selection process   85

6   Assessing early stage selector preference for "ideal" candidates   110

7   Do local party members select "ideal" candidates?   154

8   Conclusion   180

Appendix: British Labour party candidate survey   189
Bibliography   204
Index   214

Tables

1.1	Factors influencing the selection processes	11
3.1	Labour party candidate selection process results (2001, 2005, 2010)	46
3.2	Labour party's selection process	50
3.3	Labour party selection process filtering (sex)	54
3.4	Labour party selection process filtering (race)	55
3.5	Labour party selection process filtering (physical ability)	56
3.6	Filtering by sex, race, and disability (2015)	57
4.1	Key reforms to the Labour party candidate selection process	69
4.2	2010 General Election 12-week selection timetable	74
5.1	Labour candidate selection process: key participants and rules	88
5.2	Multistage assessment of the Labour party selection process (women)	98
5.3	Multistage assessment of the Labour party selection process (BAME)	100
5.4	Multistage assessment of the Labour party selection process (disabled)	101
5.5	The effect of centralisation on women	102
5.6	The effect of centralisation on BAME	104
5.7	The effect of centralisation on disabled aspirants	105
6.1	Independent variables and associated categories	112
6.2	Survey data from aspirant candidates (2005 and 2010 selection processes)	122
6.3	NPP approval: variables, descriptive statistics, and relationship tests	125
6.4	Shortlisting: variables, descriptive statistics, and relationship tests	131
6.5	Model 2 logistic regression predicting likelihood of being shortlisted	133
6.6	Shortlisting: descriptive statistics and relationship tests for open seats	136
6.7	Model 3 logistic regression results for shortlisting in open seats	138
6.8	Descriptive statistics and relationship tests for open and winnable seats	139
6.9	Model 4 logistic regression results, shortlisted (open and winnable seats)	142

6.10	Regression model summary	143
7.1	Selection contests	157
7.2	Model 5 regression results (selected)	161
7.3	Selection contests in open seats	163
7.4	Model 6 regression results (selected in open seats)	165
7.5	Selection contests in open and winnable seats	167
7.6	Model 7 regression results (selected in open and winnable seats)	170
7.7	Selection contests in AWS seats	172
7.8	Model 8 (AWS seats)	174
7.9	Regression model result summary	176
8.1	Regression modelling summary	183

Figures

1.1 Legislative recruitment, selection processes, and
    candidate selection   6
1.2 The British Labour party's ladder of selection   8
2.1 Three levels of legislative recruitment   27

Acknowledgements

Political Candidate Selection: Who Wins, Who Loses, and Under-Representation in the UK results from years of support from Joni Lovenduski, my senior doctoral supervisor, whose legendary scholarship propelled me to explore why some aspirants are selected as candidates over others. Joni's mentorship keeps me forever focussed when thinking about the critical links between parties' selection processes and legislative descriptive representation. I also owe a huge debt to Rosie Campbell, my second supervisor, whose friendship continues to mean so much. My debt grows still with Sarah Childs, who has been so generous with her time and insights into parties and representation, and whose work, including *The Good Parliament*, has been so inspiring. I am deeply grateful to have these women in my life. Thanks too to Edwin Bacon and Yvonne Galligan for their invaluable feedback and encouraging words, as well as to the many conference discussants who read earlier chapter versions. And many thanks to the doctoral students at Birkbeck and UCL who read really, really early versions of my work – thank goodness for the many pubs nearby where we'd find ourselves after evening classes. I made many good friends in London whilst undertaking this research whose input kept me on the right track and whose company kept me going – a special shout out to Elizabeth Evans, Gita Subrahmanyam, and Simon Thomson. A generous Birkbeck scholarship made it possible to do this research, as did the British Representation Study with Joni Lovenduski, Rosie Campbell, and Sarah Childs. While I was at Birkbeck, many people gave time to me – including the faculty and administrative staff – thank you. This book would not have been possible without the support of the British Labour party and officials, who, for over ten years has been providing selection process data and explaining how the process really works. A special thanks to Roy Kennedy, Melanie Onn, and Fiona Twycross for opening your doors. Thanks to all the aspirant candidates who participated in the surveys and to the candidates and MPs who agreed to be interviewed. I'd also like to thank officials from the Conservative and Liberal Democratic parties for their time, especially the late Shireen Ritchie as well as Jo Swinson. The ongoing support from my colleagues at Douglas College and generous funding has been invaluable. Thanks to Marjorie Griffin Cohen for helping with the book proposal, and to Libby Davies, Kim Elliot, Patricia Losey, Fiona MacDonald, and Patrick Smith for cheering me on. A big thanks to Sophie Iddamalgoda for her patience while I worked on an election or two and readjusted to related life changes while updating the manuscript. Any errors in the book are mine alone. Lastly, thanks to my parents and sisters, to my Stewart clan, and to my dearest Kennedy for everything all the time.

Abbreviations

All Black Shortlists	ABS
All Women Shortlists	AWS
Black, Asian, and Minority Ethnic	BAME
Branch Labour Party	BLP
Campaign for Labour Party Democracy	CLPD
Constituency Labour Party	CLP
Executive Committee (of the CLP)	EC
European Parliament	EP
General Committee (of the CLP)	GC
General Secretary	GS
Lesbian, Gay, Bisexual, Transgender, Queer	LGBTQ
Labour Women's Network	LWN
Inter-Parliamentary Union	IPU
Members of the European Union	MEP
Member of Parliament	MP
National Assembly of Wales	NAW
National Executive Committee	NEC
National Parliamentary Panel	NPP
Operation Black Vote	OBV
One Member One Vote	OMOV
Parliamentary Labour Party	PLP
Prospective Parliamentary Candidate	PPC
Quasi-autonomous Non-governmental Organisation	QUANGO
Speaker's Conference	SC
Scottish Parliament	SP
Special Selections Panel	SSP
Trade Union Congress	TUC
United Kingdom	UK
United Nations	UN
United States	US
Women's Action Committee	WAC

1 Study overview

There is no shortage of highly publicised stories retelling candidate selection contests as if they were made-for-Netflix dramas, replete with allegations of vote rigging, insider meddling, and unexpected endings. The British Labour party – a comparative star amongst parties in liberal democracies trying for the increasingly coveted part "most diverse candidate slate" – is no exception. Recent controversies include Vauxhall's selection for the 2019 snap election where social media has been alighted with heated exchanges over whether the central party should designate it an all women shortlist (AWS) seat or implement all black shortlists (ABS) to ensure a Black, Asian, minority, or ethnic (BAME) candidate replaces Labour MP Kate Hoey. Other standouts include Liverpool Walton, one of Labour's safest seats, where, following the selection for the 2017 snap election, six Labour officials resigned after the central party's candidate, a politically inexperienced Dan Carden, was selected over the local party's choice, Liverpool's mayor Joe Anderson. Suspicious sign ups prevailed as the theme in the lead-up to the 2015 General Election in Falkirk, where selection voting irregularities linked to trade union Unite's efforts to get Kate Murphy selected led to an internal investigation and eventually to Murphy standing down. Questions abound in Erith and Thamesmead, another safe seat, where local party members selected the relatively unknown Teresa Pearce as their 2010 candidate over the party-establishment-backed Georgia Gould and six other women aspirants on the AWS. This result, like other selection outcomes, left the losing aspirant candidates scratching their heads and wondering why they lost and, more to the point, why another aspirant won.

Selection process outcomes illustrate three important and connected points concerning representation and party selection processes explored throughout this study. First, even though some selected candidates go on to secure House of Commons seats, they sit in a legislature which does not reflect the demographic composition of the population from which it is drawn. As is the case with all liberal representative democracies, the British Parliament's elected lower house does not mirror population characteristics such as sex, gender, race, physical ability, age, or class. Rather, it is disproportionately composed of members belonging to social groups generally associated in the scholarly and popular literature with political success, and, as argued in this study, the ideal aspirant candidate type. From party selectors' choices, the ideal aspirant candidate type tends to be white, professional, middle-aged men and men without disabilities, and tends not to be women, BAME, working class, young, or disabled people. Further, the ideal aspirant candidate type often possesses several other attributes similarly linked in the scholarship to political success. With this in mind, this study evaluates eight categories of variables commonly associated with the ideal candidate type: social background, party experience, political experience, political networks, personal networks, appropriate political attitudes, political ambition, and voter mobilisation methods.

Truly representative legislatures should be composed of the same proportion of social groups found in the population (Phillips, 1995). In other words, they should be a microcosm of society on the premise that policy decisions are not seen as legitimate unless voters from marginalised groups see themselves in the social makeup of their legislative bodies (Mansbridge, 2010; Phillips, 1995). Increasing the descriptive representation of social groups leads to substantive changes in public policies on grounds that they better represent members of the same social groups (Childs, 2007, p. 85; Lovenduski, 2005; Norris and Lovenduski, 1995, p. 135, p. 224). If a population is composed of 51 percent women, 12 percent BAME people, and 10 percent disabled people, there should be at least the same proportion of legislators elected from each of these social groups (Bird, 2005; Charlton and Barker, 2013, p. 324; Mansbridge, 2010; Phillips, 1995).

While many authors attempt to explain what causes unbalanced legislatures, answers remain elusive. However, as getting elected generally requires first getting selected as a party candidate, it would appear a close examination of party selection processes is the key to understanding the social imbalance in any legislature. Party selection processes are the focus of this study, given the potential influence they have upon the final candidate pool presented to the general electorate. Party selectors' quest for the so-called ideal aspirant candidate described earlier is influenced by the homo politicus model, leading to a system

> designed to select a standard model candidate who is articulate, well-educated and typically employed in a professional career, in business as an executive or manager, in education as a school teacher or university lecturer or in the law as a practicing barrister or lawyer. . . . By defining the appropriate qualifications for a career in politics in such a way then certain types of candidates will tend to be successful. As a result, women, working class candidates and those from the ethnic minorities will tend to be consistently disadvantaged.
> (Norris and Lovenduski, 1989, p. 94)

It is proposed here that the homo politicus model and selector preference for the ideal aspirant candidate type disadvantage aspirants from marginalised groups such as women, people who identify as BAME, and people with disabilities.

Secondly, a complete picture of a party's selection process must not only portray who wins but also who loses. For example, Pearce's and other candidates' wins only become intriguing and counterintuitive when other aspirant candidates are included in the story. Using the logic presented earlier, a party's aspirant candidate pool – comprised of all individuals who put forward their names for candidacy and either won or lost their bids for candidacy – should proportionally reflect the social characteristics of its final candidate pool – comprised of individuals who are selected as candidates. For example, if a party's aspirant candidate pool is composed of 30 percent women, 10 percent BAME people, and 2 percent disabled people, its final candidate pool should be at least the same proportion of aspirant candidates who came forward from each of these social groups. Any disproportionality between the aspirant candidate and candidate pools suggests the presence of structural or intentional biases either toward the standard, ideal aspirant candidate type or against the non-standard, non-ideal aspirant candidate type (Phillips, 1998, p. 229).

Third, selections such as Erith's and Thamesmead's also demonstrate how selection processes are multistage. While being chosen as the candidate by party members at the final selection meeting receives the most attention, aspirants win candidacies only after submitting their curriculum vitae to the Party, applying for seats, acquiring nominations from key party organisations, and making it onto the party's final shortlist. They must not only survive the final selection vote, but they must also survive several other elimination rounds of the selection process. In this sense, the social imbalance in candidate pools is not solely determined by the party's selection rules and selection participants at the final selection stage; it is also influenced by the rules and participants at preceding stages. For example, if an aspirant does not receive the nominations required to get onto the local party's shortlist, their name is not considered by party members for candidacy. The selection process, then, is a multistage filter with ideal aspirant candidates potentially being more successful than non-ideal candidates at different stages throughout the process.

At its core, this study seeks to better understand the representational imbalance by developing a methodology toward explaining why some and not other types of aspirant candidates secure party candidacies. Women's underrepresentation is highlighted throughout this study for several reasons. Concern with women's underrepresentation has exponentially grown in prominence amongst the academic community, interest groups, the media, and the public, not least because recent viral campaigns such as #MeToo and #SheShouldRun are reinforcing the link between women's political presence and women's social justice. Further, the suggestion that women candidates offer parties an electoral advantage has led many parties to track more closely this group's progress over others' (Kenny and Verge, 2016; Russell, 2005, pp. 111–112). Given this incentivization, if parties collect any data on aspirant candidates, they are more likely to first collect it on sex, resulting in more robust data on women aspirants than, for example, on lesbian, gay, bisexual, transgendered, and queer (LGBTQ) aspirants. Considerable attention is also given to the underrepresentation of two other marginalised groups, BAME people and people with disabilities, whose underrepresentation, although gaining attention, is relatively underexplored within the context of party selection processes.[1]

This study uses the well-established framework of supply and demand and a multistage approach to test the extent to which party rules and party selector preferences impact selection process outcomes using a diverse range of data on almost 20 years of Labour party selection processes. These include rare Labour party census data on all aspirant candidates for the 2001, 2005, and 2010 General Elections, party data on aspirant candidates for the 2015 General Election, original survey data of aspirant candidates for the 2005 and 2010 General Elections, interviews with party officials and aspirant candidates from 2010 to 2017, and analyses of parliamentary selection rule books. 'Given the expedited nature of the 2017 snap election, the central party did not systemically collect usable selection data and thus they are absent from this study (but see Campbell, Childs, and Hunt, 2018). In addition, this book was at press when the 2019 snap election was called, making data analysis impossible for this election.' These available data sources from elections held between 2001 to 2015 help illuminate an underexplored yet critical part of the larger legislative recruitment process concerning the micro-steps individuals take at the beginning of their parliamentary careers (Norris, 1997a, p. 1).[2] In doing so, this in-depth and intensive examination of a single party within a single political system over four general elections uses a wide range of data to shed light on the immediate case at hand and also to test the validity of long-held theories and provide generalisable methodological advances.[3]

There are several reasons to focus on the British Labour party. For some time the party has been considered an exemplar within liberal democracies with majoritarian single member plurality electoral systems and a party that has a "contagion effect" upon other parties (Seyd, 1999, p. 387). While it has a long tradition of internal party democracy, only in the early 1990s did Labour extend the right to select parliamentary candidates to all party members. There have since been many reforms to its selection process. Over the last 30 years, Labour has exhibited a higher degree of commitment to increasing the diversity of its candidate slates than any other party in the United Kingdom (UK) as well as any other party in countries with similar electoral systems, such as the United States (US) and Canada. The British Labour party is the only party in the UK using equality guarantees for women in the form of all women shortlist seats (AWS) and equality quotas for women and BAME aspirant candidates.[4] These reforms contributed to the party having a higher percentage of women and BAME candidates and MPs than other major parties, including the British Conservative party, Liberal Democrats, and Scottish National Party.[5] Thus, this study offers a fresh look at the Labour party's selection rules and the way they influence the behaviour of selectors and the success of aspirant candidates at multiple stages of the selection process. Additionally, not only does this study seek to better understand the internal workings of the Labour party but also to use the lessons learned as a starting point by which to better understand the internal workings of other parties' candidate selection processes and outcomes in the UK and in other countries.

The remainder of this chapter introduces the study and its key components. After a brief justificatory and definitional section, the chapter outlines the various steps in the selection process. It then explains how others have sought to understand why some and not other types of aspirant candidates successfully move through the selection process to secure candidacies, with special emphasis on detailing the dominant supply and demand framework and associated approaches and testing regimes.

Legislative imbalance and candidate selection

Understanding why legislatures do not currently reflect their host populations is one of the enduring mysteries in politics. From a normative perspective, this imbalance is of critical concern as a matter of democratic justice. According to Phillips (1998), it is "patently and grotesquely unfair" for any one group to "monopolise representation" (p. 229). Many studies on this topic draw attention to longstanding patterns of persistent descriptive underrepresentation of women and other social groups, such as BAME, disabled, young, and LGBTQ people, with some using explicitly intersectional analyses to do so (Bird, 2011; Childs and Dahlerup, 2018; Evans, 2012; Everitt and Camp, 2014; Freidenvall, 2016; Norris and Lovenduski, 1995; Phillips, 1995; Shah, 2013; Tolley, 2019; Wagner, 2019).[6]

The underrepresentation of women remains a significant problem despite scholarly efforts to understand why it occurs and the corrective efforts of some political parties and legislatures. While the percentage of women legislators is higher than it was 20 years ago, recent gains have been small. Current data indicating women still comprise under 25 percent of MPs in lower houses demonstrate the widespread and persistent nature of their political underrepresentation (IPU, 2019).[7] In 39th place out of 193 countries, the British Parliament's standing in the Inter-parliamentary Union's ranking of women in national parliaments has improved since the last election; still, there is a long way to go before women achieve sex parity in the House (see The Fawcett Society, 2019).[8] In the span of nine years, the overall percentage of women MPs has increased by 10 percentage points from 22 percent in the 2010 General Election to 32 in the 2017 snap election. However, this historic high is only a 3 percentage point increase from the 2015 General Election, suggesting progress has stalled on this front and diminishing the symbolic effect of a woman prime minister, Theresa May, at the helm (Campbell, Childs, and Hunt, 2018).

In terms of BAME peoples' representation, cross-national research, although increasing, is rarer than on women's representation (Black, 2017; Bird, 2014, 2011; Norris and Lovenduski, 1995; Ruedin, 2013; Shah, 2013; Tolley, 2019).[9] A 2006 study reveals there is at least one BAME legislator in 75 percent of all democratically elected national legislatures (Ruedin, 2009). Another study shows BAME legislators exceed 5 percent of legislators in only 2 of 15 established democracies despite comprising a much higher proportion of the general population (Bird, 2005).[10] By 2019, BAME MPs in the British Parliament comprised 8 percent of all MPs – still, this falls short of their 13 percent representation in the general population (Operation Black Vote, 2019; Office for National Statistics, 2019; Squires, 2012).[11]

No equivalent comparative or national data sources exist with which to track the representation of legislators with disabilities, and the data that do exist are imprecise. In terms of the British Parliament, Judith Squires (2012) notes "only a handful of MPs identify themselves as disabled", with the 2017 snap election increasing the number of MPs identifying as having a disability from three in 2015 to five (One in Five Campaign, 2019).[12]

Overall, the British Parliament is more diverse than it has ever been, with a record number of women and BAME MPs, and people living with disabilities, elected. It is also more diverse in terms of sexual orientation, with 45 (7 percent) of MPs elected in the 2017 snap election identifying as LGBTQ, touted as the highest in the world (Reynolds, 2017).[13] Still, even despite a lack of data on a wider range of characteristics, it is not unreasonable to argue that non-standard model candidate types are still more likely to be underrepresented than their counterparts in liberal democratic legislatures (see Squires, 2012).

In terms of explaining demographic underrepresentation, research suggests legislative social imbalance often results from parties forwarding unbalanced candidate pools during elections rather than from, for example, electoral system irregularities or bias within the electorate (Gallagher, 1988a). The underrepresentation of women and other groups, then, is not due to the fact that being from these groups is in itself a barrier to doing the job of a legislator. It is most likely caused by party selection rules and selector preferences, making it more difficult for some aspirant candidate types to succeed in their pursuit of candidacy.

Before moving on, it is useful to clarify the various terms used in this field of study and to make an easily overlooked distinction between "legislative recruitment", "the selection process", and "candidate selection," and, in turn, between corresponding "legislative recruitment studies," "selection process studies," and "candidate selection studies". As shown in Figure 1.1, *legislative recruitment* is a rubric term referring to all successive steps undertaken to gain parliamentary office, from party attempts to recruit new candidates to an aspirant candidate's decision to pursue political office, through to being selected as a candidate,

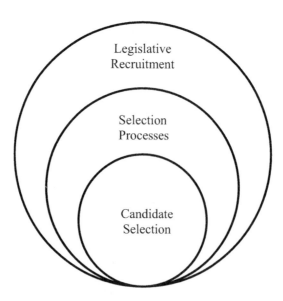

Figure 1.1 Legislative recruitment, selection processes, and candidate selection

winning elections, and even being promoted to the level of minister or prime minister (Norris and Lovenduski, 1995, p. 1; Norris, 1997a, p. 1).

The topic of this study, party *selection processes*, delineates the period during which aspirant candidates formally indicate to a political party their intention to stand for office until the point when aspirant candidates are selected or rejected by party selectors as candidates (Holland, 1987, p. 54). Thus, this study does not include an analysis of potential aspirants, for example, party members who have not formally indicated their intention to pursue a political career (Lawless and Fox, 2005). *Candidate selection* refers only to a very small but important sub-phase of legislative recruitment and subsequently selection processes, when party members select a representative from often a set of competing aspirant candidates through a pre-election voting process (Holland, 1987, p. 54).

Even using the narrowed scope of *selection processes* to explain legislative imbalance, it is still far from clear why parties put forward unrepresentative candidate slates and why certain types of aspirant candidates succeed more than others in securing party candidacies. Despite rich normative and empirical contributions, party selection processes and the main question explored in this study, why some and not other types of aspirant candidates are more likely to secure party candidacies, have been long-held in the literature as the "secret garden" and "enduring puzzle" of legislative recruitment (Gallagher and Marsh, 1988). It is important to peer inside the secret garden not only to describe what happens during the selection process but also to explore the dynamics of selection processes and how different groups fare as they pass through multiple stages.

Selection processes: multiple stages, multiple rules, and multiple participants

Aspiring candidates eventually become candidates by surviving a series of evaluations by various central and local party selectors. Parties play a key role throughout the selection of candidates, acting as "primary screening devices" to reproduce their organisations in public office, with scholars long linking the descriptive underrepresentation of social groups to these functions (Katz, 2001, p. 1; Seligman, 1961).

Party selection processes in liberal democracies always have at least two distinct stages: 1) *party application* – where aspirant candidates forward their names to a party, and 2) *candidate selection* – where aspirant candidates are formally selected by a party selector or selectors. However, parties often add additional hurdles for aspirant candidates to overcome. In this sense, the selection process is a multistage ladder with each rung representing a different filter in the process (Lovenduski, 2016; Norris and Lovenduski, 1995, p. 15).

Figure 1.2 shows the British Labour party's selection process as having seven distinct but connected filtering stages for the 2001, 2005, and 2010 General Elections: 1) party application; 2) NPP application; 3) NPP approval; 4) seat application; 5) nomination (sometimes referred to as longlisting); 6) shortlisting; and 7) candidate selection.[14] During 1) *party application*, the participant pool includes

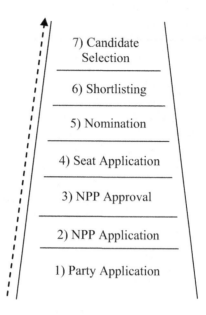

Figure 1.2 The British Labour party's ladder of selection

aspirant candidates who have indicated their willingness to pursue political office by submitting their curricula vitae and applications to the central party's National Executive Committee (NEC). During 2) *NPP application*, aspirant candidates apply to the NEC for a second time, this time for a position on the National Parliamentary Panel (NPP). During 3) *NPP approval*, aspirant candidates who are granted a position on the NPP receive endorsement from the NEC. During 4) *seat application*, aspirant candidates apply for seats as they become available. During 5) *nomination*, aspirant candidates secure nominations from eligible local party units and affiliated organisations.[15] At the penultimate stage, 6) *shortlisting*, aspirant candidates are placed on a shortlist by a general committee (GC) made up of local party officials. The final stage, 7) *candidate selection*, involves shortlisted aspirant candidates facing their last set of selectors at a meeting where local party members cast their votes, with the contest winner declared the party's candidate for the next general election.[16]

The selection process for the 2015 General Election has four stages, a result of the central party's decision to eliminate the NPP: 1) party application; 2) nomination; 3) shortlisting; and 4) candidate selection.[17] This is the only formal rule change to the selection process since 2010, and while the participants and rules are the same as for 2010, the NEC's decision to forgo the NPP has implications beyond reducing the number of selection stages, as is discussed in subsequent sections and chapters.

As with any party's selection process, the multiple stages involve a number of rules and participants. Generally, selection process rules and participants (e.g., selectors and aspirant candidates) are found within a party's constitution. Often the rules and participants differ from one stage to the next, with, for example, central party agents acting as the key selector at one or two stages, whereas local party agents are the key selector at other stages. Typically, the central party implements the rules, which, to varying degrees, restrict local selector and aspirant candidate behaviour. Such central party rules range from slightly to extremely intrusive with most political parties falling somewhere in-between the two poles (Hazan and Rahat, 2006; Norris, 1997a). For example, moving from the least to most intrusive, the central party sets clear eligibility rules for candidacy, such as being a member of the party in good standing for a minimum period of time. The central party can also implement rules of conduct to which local party officials and members as well as aspirant candidates must adhere or face disqualification. As well, the central party can implement equality rules to increase the representation of various social groups. Such equality rules restrict selector behaviour by limiting choice to women and/or BAME aspirant candidates and restrict aspirant candidates belonging to these groups by limiting the seats to which they can apply. Moreover, the central party can bypass the selection process altogether and appoint candidates. Looking again to the British Labour party, the central party has in place clear rules that govern all selection process stages, even those where the most active participants are found at the local party level (Labour's Future: NEC Guidelines for Selection of Parliamentary Candidates, 2006).

Describing and explaining underrepresentation during selection processes

One practical first step found in most legislative recruitment studies is to determine whether there is legislative imbalance within a particular political system and, if so, the extent of the imbalance. In the UK, women, BAME, and disabled people, as well as other marginalised social groups, are underrepresented in the House of Commons relative to their representation in the general population. For example, in the UK women make up 51 percent of the general population yet only 32 percent of MPs. This ratio shows significant imbalance between the general population and the legislature and indicates further study of party selection processes is needed to determine whether this disproportionality is reflected in party aspirant candidate and candidate pools. However, further investigation would be unnecessary if women held 51 percent of the seats available in the UK's House of Commons (Ashe and Stewart, 2012).

Supply and demand is the dominant theoretical framework used by scholars to understand selection process outcomes. Most famously applied by Norris and Lovenduski (1995) in the influential study *Political Recruitment: Gender, Race, and Class in the British Parliament*, supply and demand has emerged as the "leading theoretical framework" and the "main paradigm" used to explain selection process bias (Patzelt, 1999, p. 243; Lovenduski, 2016).[18] The framework suggests supply and demand factors interact to determine the composition of the pool of candidates eventually presented to the general electorate. Definitionally, "supply" refers to inputs, or "the supply of applicants wishing to pursue a political career", with factors such as party rules or aspirant candidates' political resources and ambitions used to explain why some and not others seek candidacy (Norris and Lovenduski, 1995, p. 15). "Demand" concerns selection process outputs, or when party "selectors choose candidates depending on their perceptions of the applicants' abilities, qualifications, and experience" (Norris and Lovenduski, 1995, p. 14). Generally, party selection processes are low information events where party selectors have little time to get to know aspirant candidates. As a result, aspirant candidates are "rarely well known to most selectors", thus their perceptions "may be colored by" discrimination "for or against certain groups" (Norris and Lovenduski, 1995, p. 14). Like supply, selector demand can be influenced by central party rules designed to counter selector discrimination.

There is disagreement among scholars as to the extent to which underrepresentation results from supply or demand, or from supply *and* demand, and in the case of the latter, more or less from supply or more or less from demand. Until relatively recently, it has been in vogue to explore and support undersupply explanations, for example, claiming too few women come forward to stand for office due to their traditional sex role and lifestyle constraints and lower levels of political resources and motivation (Lawless and Fox, 2005). Not downplaying the important influence supply-side factors have upon selection outcomes, other scholars argue the imbalance is due more to demand with, for example, unbalanced candidate pools reflecting selectors' preferences for those who most reflect the *ideal aspirant candidate type* (Lovenduski, 2016). Yet not since Norris and Lovenduski's 1995 study have both supply- and demand-side factors been rigorously tested at all stages of a party's candidate selection process.

It is most useful to view selection as a filtering process whereby the total number of aspirant candidates gets smaller as the party moves deeper into the process. An initial assessment of how supply and demand affects this filtering of the many to the few may be achieved by comparing the proportion and number of aspirant candidates from different social groups at different stages of the selection process. For example, comparing the percentage of eligible women aspirant candidates (e.g., party members) with aspirant candidate pools at one or more stages of selection is an established way to measure supply (Ashe, 2017; Ashe and Stewart, 2012; Holland, 1986; Niven, 2006; Norris and Lovenduski, 1995). Consider a scenario where party X needs to fill 100 candidacies in a country where women comprise 50 percent of the population and 1 percent of party X's membership. The proportionality test on potential aspirant candidates reveals a 49-percentage point difference between women's proportion in the population and party membership – a measure of candidate eligibility – and indicates an extreme case of undersupply. Although proportionality tests provide an initial assessment of whether a group's underrepresentation is due to supply, raw numbers provide a more accurate measure. For example, raw numbers reveal 1 percent of party X's 30,000 members is 300: three times the number of women needed to fill the 100 available candidate positions, and thus rejects the supply-side explanation for women's and potentially other groups' underrepresentation (Ashe, 2017; Ashe and Stewart, 2012, p. 691; Childs, 2008).

Descriptive work can further identify whether underrepresentation can be linked to supply and demand and at what selection process stages unfair filtering occurs. In this study, supply is first assessed by looking at the *actual* supply of aspirant candidates, measured as individuals who formally indicate their willingness to pursue candidacy, rather than the *potential* supply of aspirant candidates, measured as individuals who are eligible to pursue candidacy. The supply-side explanation of underrepresentation is greatly diminished if the number of aspirant candidates at the first filtering stage – party application – is equal to or greater than the number of available seats (Ashe, 2017; Ashe and Stewart, 2012; Childs, 2008). In this sense, if 300 women submit their curricula vitae to the central party in hopes of becoming a candidate for one of the available 100 seats, a 200 surplus, a lack of supply of women aspirant candidates does not fully explain their underrepresentation. On the other hand, if women aspirant candidates make up 20 percent of those at the second filtering stage – NPP application – but only 2 percent of the final stage – selection – the problem is likely more one of demand, where local party selectors have disproportionately screened out women aspirant candidates over men aspirant candidates. In this sense, if disproportionate screening of underrepresented groups is suspected, other simple descriptive tests can help narrow the cause and location of the problem (Ashe, 2017; Ashe and Stewart, 2012). These measures are explained in detail in later chapters.

Once undersupply or lack of demand during any particular candidate selection process stage has been identified and statistically described, then the investigation should move to explaining these deficits. It is important to expand upon the approaches employed by various legislative recruitment scholars. Fowler (1993) and Conway (2001) suggest theoretical approaches used to broadly explain patterns of political participation and here, multistage selection process outcomes include institutional, such as party rules, and behavioural, such as selector demand. As depicted in Table 1.1, some scholars explore the extent to which *institutional* factors explain undersupply or lack of demand during selection processes,

Table 1.1 Factors influencing the selection processes

	Supply	*Demand*
Institutional	Rules encouraging or discouraging aspirants	Rules advantaging or disadvantaging aspirants
Behavioural	Aspirants willing or reluctant to come forward	Selector bias for or against some aspirants

with feminist institutionalism "gendering" selection processes and exploring the interplay between gendered rules, practices, and outcomes (Mackay, Kenny, and Chappell, 2010, p. 574; see Erickson, 1993, 1997a; Caul, 1999; Kittilson, 2006; Norris, 1997a; Norris and Lovenduski, 1995, pp. 9–10). On the supply-side, in most liberal democracies central party leaders determine who can and cannot run for office, thus institutional features might work for or against certain types of aspiring candidates (Conway, 2001, p. 232). Regarding demand, formal rules directly advantage or disadvantage those with certain characteristics during selection, with, for example, equality guarantees such as party quotas and reserved seats artificially increasing demand for aspirant candidates from underrepresented groups (Lovenduski, 2016).

Other authors rely on mainly what are described here as *behavioural* factors to explain underrepresentation (Niven, 1998; Norris and Lovenduski, 1995). In terms of supply, members from certain aspirant candidate groups may be more or less motivated than those from other groups to step forward during the different selection process stages. On the demand-side, party selectors in some processes prefer aspirant candidates who resemble the ideal aspirant candidate type over aspirant candidates who do not. Each of these approaches to understanding supply and demand is discussed in what follows.

Institutional approach

A more detailed review of the authors pursuing institutional explanations shows these scholars test the extent to which party organisational structures hold the key to explaining why some but not other aspirant candidates are selected. The long accepted maxim "whoever controls selection – whether central or local party organisations – controls the party" has led many authors to explore the degree to which *centralised* as opposed to *decentralised* selection processes increase or decrease the extent to which women and other social groups participate and succeed in party selection processes (Caul, 1999; Kittilson, 2006; Gallagher, 1988a, p. 1; Ostrogorski, 1902; Rahat, 2001; Schattschneider, 1942, p. 64). As can be expected, centralised processes describe those in which decision making power is concentrated in the hands of national party leaders who, where there is a will for equal representation, may take the lead vis-à-vis various rules to ensure the supply of and demand for underrepresented groups at successive selection stages (Lovenduski, 2005; Childs, Lovenduski, and Campbell, 2005). In such centralised systems, selection rules tend to be standardised and formalised; rules are made explicit in party constitutions and rule books and transparent to all participants. Centralised processes are thought to make candidacy more appealing to individuals who may otherwise feel disadvantaged by non-standardised, informal processes that tend to advantage political insiders, such as men, who can rely upon their stronger political networks to navigate their way through the ins and outs of the process (Caul, 1999; Rahat, 2007). Thus, on the supply-side of the institutional coin, party rules can either encourage aspirant candidates from underrepresented groups to participate in a selection process stage or, of course, discourage such participation (Caul, 1999; Rahat, 2007). On the demand-side, the nature of party rules, whether non-mandated soft equality targets or mandated strong equality guarantees determine the demand for non-ideal aspirant candidates amongst party selectors by restricting their choices.

One of the major problems with studies using the institutional approach, however, concerns the inaccurate classification of selection processes. The tendency to focus on the final candidate selection stage overlooks the fact that all selection processes are multistage. For example, as discussed, the Labour party's selection process has several steps. As such, the focus upon the final candidate selection stage does not clearly explain the impact earlier stages have upon who is ultimately selected. For example, a selection stage as a whole may be classified in the literature as decentralised on the basis of final selection stage activities where local party members choose a candidate from a list of short-listed aspirant candidates. However, the shortlist of aspirant candidates from which local party selectors must choose may have been determined by central party selectors and/or local party officials during preceding stages. Thus, their choices impact the supply of aspirant candidates who move from one stage to the next as well as the demand amongst local party selectors. In this sense, the particular selection process as a whole is not assuredly decentralised; rather it is more accurate to view some stages as centralised and some as decentralised. Moreover, party rules may be in place to increase the demand for some aspirant candidate types, such as women, but not others, such as BAME and disabled people. Thus, multistage classifications are useful for taking such selection process nuances into account.

Institutional rule change is an ongoing process with rule changes in one selection stage potentially impacting how party selectors and aspirant candidates participate in subsequent stages. The decision to implement equality rules reflects a party's willingness to address underrepresentation in response to internal and external pressures to present a more diverse candidate pool (Bille, 2001; Russell, 2005). Not surprisingly, such rule changes normally coincide with attempts to democratise a party's selection process by, for example, opening up participation to all party members in the final candidate selection stage vote (Hazan and Rahat, 2006; Rahat, 2007; Rahat and Hazan, 2001). However, this is not always reflected in selection process classifications.

While broadening selection participation to include all local party members at first appears to decentralise the process, it often paradoxically leads to centralising some selection process stages. If the central party assigns local party members the task of choosing candidates, it must simultaneously ensure that they select a sufficient number of aspirant candidates from marginalised social groups to meet demands for greater descriptive representation. As noted, such demands require the central party to implement what may be observed as rules that constrain selector and aspirant candidate choice. This position is reflected by a British Labour party official who explains why the party re-implemented equality guarantees in the form of all AWS for the 2005 General Election: "We need AWS, without them local members tend to go with men. . . . In 2001, when we couldn't use AWS, they were ruled illegal, it was a disaster. We lost ground there".[19] This scenario reinforces a need to assess the institutional features at multiple stages of a party's selection process.

Behavioural approach

In terms of behavioural factors, many researchers suggest formal party institutions matter less than selector and aspirant candidate behaviour (see Gallagher and Marsh, 1988; Patzelt, 1999). On the supply-side, resources and motivations of potential participants can affect the extent to which aspirant candidates from underrepresented groups participate in any selection process stage. Concerning demand, attitudes and opinions of those who select can affect what type of aspirant candidates move from one selection stage to another. Both supply and demand aspects of the behavioural approach are discussed in the following.

Some authors investigate the impact ambition and motivation have upon outcome. For example, Fox and Lawless (2004) draw upon US data to understand the process by which women and men emerge as candidates, finding that women possessing personal and professional characteristics similar to men hold lower levels of political ambition. They conclude this variation in political ambition is due to women receiving lower levels of encouragement from party leaders than do men and seeing themselves as less qualified to run than men. In a similar style, Niven (2006) finds women aspirant candidates in the US have more negative selection process experiences than men, for example, they receive less support from party leaders and are more frequently placed in unwinnable seats. Niven (2006) further argues these factors contribute to higher withdrawal rates amongst women, which affects their overall supply. From a different perspective, Norris and Lovenduski (1995) more precisely compare the characteristics of British party members and aspirant candidates at the party application stage (filtering stage one) to assess the influence of supply to reveal that some groups are less likely to come forward than other groups (pp. 120–121). The authors find women are less likely to come forward in the Conservative party, whereas those with lower educational levels are less likely to come forward in the Labour party.

The behavioural approach to understanding demand-side outcomes involves capturing party selectors' preferences by comparing the characteristics and experiences of the aspirant candidates whom they do and do not select. Doing so reveals whether there is a greater demand for aspirant candidates who fit the ideal aspirant candidate type. As noted, in a short period of time, central and local party selectors must sift through hundreds of applications and curricula vitae to decide who stays behind and who moves forward, often drawing on minimal information.[20] Norris and Lovenduski (1995) suggest party selectors choose aspirant candidates according to their judgments about an aspirant's suitability (p. 107). Selectors' evaluations of aspirant candidates are affected by a wide array of factors, including assessments of character, formal qualifications, and political experience that, for example, may entail whether the aspirant candidate is articulate, persuasive, electable, hard-working, loyal, and competent with judgments given different weight by different selectors (Norris and Lovenduski, 1995, p. 107). Reflecting on this, one aspirant candidate notes, "a group of people who have very little access to proper political interactions decide what is the best criteria for a MP. . . . there is a perception of what a MP should be like and the selection process I went through allows this perception to be reinforced".[21] Thus, with only a few chances to make an impression, aspirant candidate success depends upon party selector perception of their qualities (Norris and Lovenduski, 1995, p. 14; see Gallagher, 1988b, p. 276). The large number of aspirant candidates to judge, compounded with the little time to get to know all but the party insiders and locals, leaves selectors to "rely upon background characteristics as a proxy measure of abilities and character" (Norris and Lovenduski, 1995, p. 14).

Selectors' perceptions and judgments are therefore often shaped by direct discrimination against certain types of groups or individual aspirant candidates and by indirect discrimination where selectors have a personal preference for a certain category (e.g., we need more women in office) or type of aspirant (e.g., the BAME aspirant candidate was the best speaker), but in practice do not select them because they fear they would lose votes.[22] According to a Labour party official:

> There are different kinds of people who run. The first are serial CV'ers. They keep sending in their CVs, but they'll never get through. *They're just the wrong type.* The second are hanger-on'ers. They've been around a long time and keep applying. They have a better chance of eventually getting in, probably to an unwinnable seat at first, then maybe a winnable seat. The last kind just get in on their first try. *They're the right fit* (emphasis added).[23]

Returning to Erith and Thamesmead, aside from being a woman, Teresa Pearce partially resembles what is sometimes seen in British politics as the ideal aspirant candidate type. Being white, local, middle-aged, and with party and political experience perhaps in part explains why party members chose Pearce as their candidate. However, focusing only on the attributes of the winner leaves unanswered many questions about why Pearce was selected, and, more directly, why party selectors preferred Pearce over the other aspirant candidates. Comparing attributes of winning *and* losing candidates helps shed even more light on the Erith and Thamesmead case.

First, while being a man is often cited as an ideal candidate attribute, this characteristic is eliminated in the Erith and Thamesmead case as the NEC designated this seat as AWS, thus no men aspirant candidates were eligible to contest the race. Second, the runner-up, Gould, possessed many other so-called ideal candidate attributes: non-BAME; non-disabled; strong central party networks (e.g., her father, Lord Gould, was the "polling guru" to former Prime Minister Tony Blair, and Minister Tessa Jowell endorsed Gould during the selection process); an Oxford education; political experience gained by working on US President Barack Obama's election campaign; and a well-oiled campaign with slick campaign materials (Harris, 2009). However, Gould had comparatively less political and party experience than Pearce, and being an "outsider" (e.g., she did not reside in the constituency), Gould had fewer local party connections. These findings suggest central party rules explain why a woman was selected, with aspirant candidate experiences offering a plausible explanation for Pearce's success over Gould. It may have been the case that local party members simply preferred the aspirant candidate with deeper local roots and greater party and political experience, Pearce, to the aspirant candidate who was not local and did not have this experience, Gould.

This explanation, however, is somewhat muddied when taking into consideration the other aspirant candidates who were rejected by the local party gatekeepers. It is possible to glean from the scant amount of publicly available information that the shortlisted pool included a former minister who was defeated in the 2005 General Election, several councillors, a union official, and a charity worker. Although the two shortlisted aspirant candidates who identified as BAME made it through to the final selection stage, they appear to be at a disadvantage given the alleged preference amongst local party members for non-BAME aspirant candidates.[24] Information on aspirant candidates' other attributes, such as party experience, educational background, and age, is incomplete. A fuller explanation requires more information on competitors to accurately assess whether other factors thought to be associated with success matter beyond being a man, and a non-BAME person, and a person without disabilities.

Such an approach, while an improvement upon comparing selected candidates with other selected candidates, selected candidates with MPs, MPs with other MPs, and MPs with the public, comes up against similar problems. Comparing aspirant candidates who make it to the final selection stage with other aspirant candidates who make it to the final selection stage is still comparing winners with other winners. Moreover, this approach says little about the rules and preferences of national and/or local party selectors at stages preceding the final candidate selection stage. Thus, for a deep dive exploration into political representation, a multistage approach is undertaken here to assess more than one stage of the selection process, more than one group of selectors (central and local), and more than one group of aspirant candidates (winners and losers).

Summary and book outline

In attempting to explore the dynamics of candidate selection processes and outcomes and to better explain legislative imbalance, this chapter introduces the study's main question regarding selection processes used by political parties to choose candidates, asking why some and not other types of aspirant candidates secure party candidacies. It is suggested ideal aspirant candidate types are more likely than non-ideal aspirant candidate types to experience success at all stages of the British Labour party's selection process. The challenge of addressing this question is demonstrated by discussing various approaches used to explain underrepresentation as applied to a British Labour party selection contest. While the supply and demand framework along with the institutional, feminist intuitionalism, and behavioural approaches for explaining the social imbalance in legislatures provide a good starting point, more empirical research is needed to test why some aspirants are selected over others.

This study includes seven other chapters. Chapter 2 discusses the concept of descriptive representation in more detail and provides normative reasons for exploring this topic. It also outlines the main stages of the British Labour party's selection process and discusses the supply and demand framework, along with related supply- and demand-side hypotheses. It concludes by reviewing methodologies used by other authors seeking to explain legislative imbalance and settles on using a multistage approach to better understand why some aspirant candidate types are selected over others. Overall, a case is made to further explore supply and demand using a multistage approach, and in terms of demand, whether party selectors indeed prefer ideal over non-ideal aspirant candidate types.

Chapter 3 provides methodological information, including data collection details and the data sources for the statistical tests. Party selection data are often difficult to access; however, the British Labour party granted the author full access to its records on *all* aspirant candidates participating in the 2001, 2005, and 2010 General Elections and permission to survey these same aspirants. The party also provided the author with data on the 2015 selection processes; however, these data differ from those collected for previous elections and are therefore treated separately. Another implication of the party's decision to eliminate the NPP following the 2010 General Election is it no longer keeps a national list of all those who apply to the party; rather, local parties are responsible for maintaining lists of aspirants who apply to their seats, which they may or may not share with the central party.[25] The central party, however, fully monitors a small sample of these seats, and these data are used here to give a sense of filtering. This makes the census data for the 2001, 2005, and 2010 General Elections all the rarer and more unique. Together these data remove some of the mystery surrounding selection processes.

Chapter 3 further describes the Labour party data for the four general elections and uses these to show how most aspirant candidates who seek candidacy are filtered from the process to become a much smaller pool of candidates. As well, these data are used to describe how women, men, BAME, non-BAME, disabled and non-disabled aspirant candidates differently fare at multiple selection stages. In addition, supply- and demand-side tests are performed to explore the extent to which the Labour party's selection process is affected by supply and demand. The tests reveal any imbalance within the Labour party's final candidate pool results more from demand-side factors than from supply-side factors.

Chapter 4 elaborates upon the multistage approach to assess selection processes and describes in detail the Labour party's selection rules and participants. It elaborates upon the concept of centralisation and decentralisation and reviews how authors classify and categorise the party's selection process. Further, it traces the evolution of the British Labour party's selection process to find that it is more centralised than initially thought. In doing so, this review challenges some past assessments of the selection process as decentralised and suggests all stages of the selection process should be separately assessed before offering an overall classification. In addition, it sets up the testing parameters used to assess the extent to which centralised or decentralised selection process stages affect the success of three non-standard aspirant candidate types – women, BAME, and disabled people.

Chapter 5 draws upon the information presented in Chapter 4 to classify the selection stages and processes for each election year. It then uses party data to determine if the nature of Labour's selection process helps explain why some aspirant candidate types are selected over others. Tests reveal overall support for the centralisation theory and that women, BAME, and disabled aspirant candidates are *more likely* to be treated fairly by central party selectors at centralised stages and are *more likely* to be disproportionately screened out by local party selectors at decentralised stages of the process. This important finding is expanded upon and explored in later chapters.

Chapter 6 further tests the ideal aspirant candidate theory using data collected from 566 original surveys completed by British Labour party aspirant candidates for the 2005 and 2010 General Elections. Aspirants for the 2015 General Election were not surveyed and are not included in the regression analysis in this chapter or in Chapter 7. As explained, after the 2010 General Election, the central party stopped collecting data on all aspirants and all selection contests and ceased keeping a list of all aspirants' emails as it had done in the past.

In Chapter 6, regression analysis is used to determine party selector demand for aspirant candidates at two demand-side stages: Stage 3, central party approval on the NPP, and Stage 6, local party shortlisting. Stage 7, candidate selection, is assessed in Chapter 7. The models include 38 variables associated with selector demand and aspirant candidate success at these stages, with regression tests performed under various seat conditions, for example, in all types of seats, in open (non-AWS) seats, and in open (non-AWS) seats that are seen as winnable by the party.

The most surprising result of this regression testing in Chapter 6 is that so few variables have a statistically significant effect on aspirant candidate success during the first six stages of the party's selection process. Indeed, the findings reveal none of the variables have an effect whatsoever on central party selector demand at Stage 3, approval on the NPP. At the same time, however, local party selectors express a demand for ideal over non-ideal aspirant candidates at Stage 6, shortlisting. For example, local party selectors are more likely to shortlist aspirant candidates who are non-disabled than disabled, who have longer party memberships than shorter party memberships, who are local residents than non-local residents, and who are councillors than non-councillors. On the other hand, local party selectors are more likely to shortlist aspirant candidates who have lower than higher incomes, which undermines the ideal candidate theory. Unexpectedly, in open (non-AWS) and winnable seats, local party selectors are more likely to shortlist aspirant candidates who are women than men and who identify as more centrist than left on the left/right political continuum.

Chapter 7 performs further statistical tests using the survey data to explore why some and not other shortlisted aspirants are selected to become Labour party candidates in the final selection process stage, with the focus upon exploring local party member demand for aspirant candidates. In addition to the variables tested in Chapter 6, a new set of independent variables is added concerning campaign efforts to secure candidacy, with those spending more time and money on their selection campaigns and employing voter mobilisation methods expected to be more likely to win than their counterparts. Regression is used to determine the traits of those who are selected in various seat conditions.

Regression testing reveals a single statistically significant independent variable in all seat conditions: party members are more likely to select aspirant candidates who reside in the local constituency. Regression results in open (non-AWS) contests also reveal residing locally matters, but so too does sex, with party members more likely to select men than women as candidates. Regression testing in open (non-AWS) and winnable contests again reveals local party members prefer men and local aspirant candidates and aspirant candidates who have been local councillors. Lastly, regression testing in AWS contests shows only one variable is statistically significant: residing locally. Thus, party members are more likely to select women competing in AWS if they are local.

Chapter 8, the study's conclusion, reviews the chapter findings and their implications for candidate selection process and legislative recruitment scholarship.

Notes

1 While the initial focus of this study falls to exploring the underrepresentation of women, ethnic minorities, and people with disabilities, it is not proposed here that only these social groups are descriptively underrepresented or that their experiences are the same.
2 This study's focus falls upon the micro level factors of a party organisation's selection process by analysing actual aspirant candidates who have officially indicated their intention to seek a party's candidacy through to their selection as candidates.
3 According to John Gerring (2004), a case study, such as this in depth study of the British Labour party, allows the researcher to "elucidate features of a larger class of similar phenomenon" (p. 341).
4 Women on shortlists were first used in 1989, and AWS were first used for the 1997 General Election, and again for 2005, 2010, 2015, and for the 2017 and 2019 snap elections. Equality quotas for women were first used in 1996, and quotas for BAME aspirant candidates were used for the 2010 General Election. These reforms are discussed in much more detail in Chapters 4 and 5. See Drude Dahlerup (2013) for a detailed examination of the various types of quotas (e.g., party and legislative).
5 More to the contagion effect, the Conservative party reconsidered the use of AWS to increase the number of women candidates standing for its party in the 2015 General Election (see Mason and Watt, 2014).
6 In Hannah Fenichel Pitkin's (1967) 'The Concept of Representation', descriptive representation is defined as "the making present of something absent by resemblance or reflection, as in a mirror or in art" (p. 11).
7 In only three countries, Rwanda, Cuba, and Bolivia, is women's representation higher than men's (IPU, 2019). Regionally, at 42.5 percent, the Nordic countries have the highest percentage of women legislators in their lower houses. The Americas come in second with 30.6 percent, Europe third with 28.6 percent (excluding Nordic countries),

Sub-Saharan Africa fourth at 23.9 percent, Asia fifth with 20 percent, the Middle East and North Africa sixth at 19 percent, and the Pacific last at 16.3 percent (IPU, 2019).

8   As in previous elections, in 2017, the British Labour party elected the most women MPs (119), followed by the Conservatives (67), the SNP (12), and the Liberal Democrats (4).

9   This is due to the obstacles faced in collecting data, for example, defining who is an ethnic minority and definitional variation from one country to the next.

10 Although there have been recent gains in the number of BAME MPs, still they remain underrepresented relative to their presence in the general population.

11 In 2017, BAME MPs made up 8 percent of MPs, a two-percentage point increase from the 2015 General Election. Most BAME MPs were elected to Labour (32), followed by the Conservatives (19) and the Liberal Democrats (1).

12 At the same time, 18 percent of working age adults report having a disability (Disability Living Foundation, 2019).

13 There is little diversity within this group, with 36 white men and 9 white women identifying as LGBTQ, and none identifying as transgender. Reynolds, A. (2017) 'The UK Elected a Record Number of LGBTQ People to Parliament', *Pink News*, 9 June, www.pinknews. co.uk/2017/06/09/the-uk-just-elected-a-record-number-of-lgbtq-people-to-parliament/

14 This sequence is drawn from interviews with party officials and aspirant candidates, as well as from 'Labour's Future: NEC Guidelines for Selection of Parliamentary Candidates' (2006). The 2010 General Election was the last election for which Labour used the NPP.

15 The nomination stage is also referred to as the longlisting stage.

16 In cases where only one aspirant candidate comes forward, no selection contest takes place, and the sole aspirant candidate is "acclaimed" as the candidate.

17 This sequence is drawn from interviews with Labour party officials, 2016 and 2017.

18 No one theory alone explains legislative recruitment, for example, institutional, feminist, rational choice, and elite theories all contribute to understanding supply and demand (Fowler, 1993).

19 Interview with a Labour party official. In 1997, AWS seats were first used by the Labour party: 38 seats were designated as AWS, to which 35 women were elected (92 percent). As a result, a record 101 women Labour party MPs were returned, representing 24 percent (101 of 418 Labour MPs) of the parliamentary Labour party (PLP). This represents a 100 percent increase from the previous election in 1992, where women MPs represented 14 percent of the party's caucus (37 of 271). In 2001, in absence of AWS seats, due to an industrial tribunal ruling in which they were deemed illegal, the percentage of women Labour MPs returned decreased to 23 percent (95 of 412 Labour MPs). In 2005, with AWS seats ruled legal, the Labour party set aside 30 AWS, to which 25 women (77 percent) were elected. As a result, the percentage of women MPs returned to the party increased by almost 5 percentage points to 28 percent (98 of 354 Labour MPs). In 2010, with AWS still in use, the party set aside 63 AWS, to which 28 women were elected (44 percent). Still the percentage of Labour women MPs increased by 3 percentage points to 32 percent (81 of 256 Labour MPs) (see Ashe et al, 2010). For 2015, AWS were used for more than 50 percent of the Party's target seats, further increasing the number of women elected to the Parliamentary Labour Party.

20 The importance of opportunities to meet local selectors comes through in a selection contest in the Labour safe seat Wigan, which was described by a member as a "cock up". Aspirant candidate Barbara Roche's "polished speech" was cut short by five minutes compared to the ten minutes allotted to her five opponents. Some attendees say this put Roche at a considerable disadvantage by costing her votes (Tribune, 29 January 2010).

21 An aspirant candidate's open-ended survey comment.

22 In the case of direct discrimination, party gatekeepers make positive or negative judgments on the "basis of characteristics seen as common to their group" (Norris and Lovenduski, 1995, p. 14).
23 Interview with a Labour party official.
24 Some argue that BAME women aspirant candidates are disadvantaged in the British Labour party's AWS seats (see Ashe et al, 2010).
25 Interview with a senior Labour party official, 2017.

2 The selection process puzzle and ideal candidate types

Things need to be done if the standing of Parliament in public life is to be restored. One of those is to make sure that the House reflects much more closely the diverse society in which we live. Parliament can do its work effectively only if its Members are in tune with the experiences of the people they represent. At present, Members of Parliament are for the most part white, male, middle-aged and middle class. That is why the House formally and unanimously agreed in November 2008 to establish this Speaker's Conference. The House asked the Conference to look into the reasons why women, members of the black and minority ethnic communities and disabled people are under-represented in the House of Commons, and to recommend ways in which the situation can be improved.

—John Bercow, Speaker of the House of Commons
—Speaker's Conference on Parliamentary Representation, January 2010

The problem of descriptive underrepresentation in the British Parliament is widely recognised by groups that lobby parties and government for more women, BAME, and disabled people in politics, such as the Fawcett Society, Operation Black Vote (OBV), and Disability Rights UK, respectively, and as shown in the epigraph, by parliament itself. Complementing these efforts is Sarah Childs' report "The Good Parliament" (2016), which makes 43 recommendations toward making the institution more gender and diversity sensitive by removing barriers to women's and other underrepresented groups' full participation (p. 7).

This chapter moves toward developing a methodology with which to explore descriptive representation during the selection process so as to better understand why some and not other types of aspirant candidates secure party candidacies and whether party selectors prefer "ideal-" over "non-ideal-" type candidates. To do so, this chapter first explains the concept of descriptive representation and touches upon the normative reasons for pursuing this topic of inquiry. The chapter moves to discuss *supply and demand*, the core analytical framework used by many authors to help explain descriptive underrepresentation, as well as associated approaches used by others to identify and explain supply and demand surpluses and deficits. It then focuses on how authors portray the main selection process stages and key selection process participants. The chapter next reviews several studies to determine the extent to which their methods contribute to assessing supply and demand, finding a range of selection process data on selection rules and participant behaviour at multiple stages are needed to determine why some aspirant candidates are selected over others. It concludes by pulling together the various literatures to strengthen the case to further explore supply and demand, and with regards to the latter, to further explore whether party selectors prefer aspirant candidates who resemble an "ideal" aspirant candidate type.

The problem with legislative underrepresentation

A key normative premise by which legislatures are evaluated concerns descriptive representation, or the degree to which these elected bodies represent the population from which they are drawn. Descriptive representation, reasons Jane Mansbridge (2010), pertains to situations where representatives in their "own persons and lives [are] in some sense typical of the larger class of persons whom they represent" (2010, p. 201). The representational character of legislatures is a long-standing normative concern to theorists examining substantive representation. For example, Jeremy Bentham and John Stuart Mill proposed government should have both representative and representativeness qualities. The concept *representativeness* often supposes a link between descriptive representation (e.g., the composition of legislatures) and substantive representation (e.g., influence upon policies and upon legislative styles in the legislature). Mansbridge (2010) further notes that while descriptive representation can involve circumstances where "Black legislators represent Black constituents, women legislators represent women constituents, and so on", it extends to include not only "visible characteristics, such as color of skin or gender, but also shared experiences, so that a representative with a background in farming is to that degree a descriptive representative of his or her farmer constituents" (p. 201).

The normative literature further suggests descriptive underrepresentation has two initial dimensions to consider. The first has democratic roots: the extent to which legislative representation can be adequate if a significant proportion of the population is persistently excluded from positions of decision making. The second dimension applies to representational patterns in legislative assemblies insofar that the persistent descriptive underrepresentation of women and other groups reflects a systemic failure of liberal democracies to fully address political inequalities (Judge, 1999, p. 37).

The feminist literature provides three additional arguments concerning descriptive underrepresentation that can be applied to any social group: legitimacy, interests, and justice (Judge, 1999, p. 42). The first argument suggests women's underrepresentation undermines a political system's *legitimacy* as "political decisions made by all-male or predominantly male governmental processes can no longer serve this legitimising function" (Darcy et al, 1994, p. 18). The second argument arises when *interests* are inadequately represented by all-male or predominantly male political bodies and whether this affects its policy priorities and outputs.[1] A number of studies demonstrate descriptive and substantive representation are entangled insofar that there are sex differences in legislative styles, activities, and priorities across several legislative bodies (Childs, 2007, p. 85; Childs et al, 2005; Erickson, 1997b, p. 663; Galligan and Clavero, 2008, pp. 18–21; Norris and Lovenduski, 1995, p. 135, p. 224; Skard and Haavio-Mannila, 1985; Thomas, 1994; Tremblay, 2007; Wängnerud, 2015; Welch, 1985).[2] However, a clear causal relationship between women's presence and legislative outputs has been difficult to establish empirically, yet the two *are* related in that legislative activities are different and women are somehow a part of this difference (Childs, 2007, p. 86; Lovenduski, 2005).[3] Nonetheless, establishing a relationship between descriptive and substantive representation is not a critical pre-condition for further exploring descriptive underrepresentation or making a case to increase the number of women, BAME, disabled, and other underrepresented aspirant candidate (Phillips, 1998).

Perhaps the strongest argument against descriptive underrepresentation is *justice*. According to Anne Phillips (1998): "there is no argument from justice that can defend the current state of affairs: and in this more negative sense there *is* an argument from justice for parity" (p. 232). Phillips (1998) encourages exploring the institutional structures of discrimination through empirical assessments of party selection processes and their outcomes:

> If there were no obstacles operating to keep certain groups of people out of political life, then we would expect positions of political influence to be randomly distributed between both sexes and across all the ethnic groups that make up society. There might be some minor and innocent deviations, but any more distorted political distribution of political office is evidence of intentional or *structural discrimination*. In such contexts (that is, most contexts!) women are being denied rights and opportunities that are currently available to men. There is a *prima facie case for action*.
>
> (p. 229, italics added)

Thus, if it is shown women and indeed other groups are disadvantaged by a party's selection process, that is, if some aspirant candidate types are being denied selection over others, there is a case for policy action (Phillips, 1998, p. 229).

The case for descriptive representation, however, is not universally accepted, even within the democratic theory community, as demonstrated in Hannah Pitkin's (1967) widely cited *The Concept of Representation*. Here Pitkin (1967) defines descriptive representation as "the making present of something absent by resemblance or reflection, as in a mirror or in art" (p. 11). This suggests representation occurs when the socio-economic background of legislators "corresponds accurately to the whole nation" (Pitkin, 1967, pp. 60–61). In this sense descriptive representation takes place when legislators stand for the salient characteristics of the citizens rather than act for them. A political representative's ability to act for constituents on the grounds of corresponding characteristics alone is problematic for Pitkin (1967), as too much focus upon a legislator's characteristics takes away from what they do. For Pitkin, what a representative *does* is of greater importance: "think of the legislature as a pictorial representation or a sample of the nation and you will almost certainly concentrate on its composition rather than its activities" (1967, p. 226). Representation thus occurs in activities rather than in characteristics. True representation occurs when representatives are "acting in a manner responsive" to their constituents (Pitkin, 1967, p. 209).[4]

Other prominent scholars writing on descriptive underrepresentation find Pitkin's definition of true representation problematic (Phillips, 1998). Despite this disagreement, Pitkin's (1967) argument that there is no relationship between descriptive representation and substantive representation has been difficult to overturn, with debate occupying considerable scholarly space relative to that accorded to *why* descriptive underrepresentation occurs. Yet Pitkin's argument that an overemphasis upon "who legislators are" detracts from "what legislators do" has not stood the test of time.[5] Indeed, after Pitkin (1967), few scholars concerned themselves with descriptive representation, but after Phillips (1991, 1995, 1998), there are few scholars who do *not* concern themselves with descriptive representation (Childs and Lovenduski, 2013). Where the normative concern about underrepresentation appears widespread, this chapter now turns to empirical investigations of this problem.

Explaining underrepresentation: approach, framework, and data

A rare creature reared its head in the lead-up to the 2010 British General Election, *The Speaker's (6th) Conference on Parliamentary Representation*.[6] This sixth conference was instructed to consider and make "recommendations for rectifying the disparity between the representation of women, ethnic minorities, and disabled people in the House of Commons and their representation in the UK population at large".[7] The much anticipated final report first describes how many more men than women, non-BAME than BAME, and non-disabled than disabled candidates become MPs.[8] Then, drawing on interviews with Parliamentary candidates and MPs as well as evidence from a wide range of expert witnesses and organisations, the report determines this imbalance to be caused by a combination of supply- and demand-side factors: too few aspirant candidates from these underrepresented groups come forward to stand as candidates, and when they do come forward, too few are chosen as candidates by party selectors.[9]

To fix supply-side problems, the *Speaker's Conference Report* proposes policies directed at levelling the playing field between, for example, men and women by placing spending limits on selection contests to encourage potential women aspirant candidates put off by prohibitive campaign costs associated with seeking candidacy to come forward. On the demand-side, the Report recommends a measure perhaps as radical as the 1916 recommendation to give women the vote, namely that "Parliament should give serious attention to the introduction of prescriptive quotas ensuring that all political parties adopt some form of equality guarantee by the time of the next election" if they do not see an increase in the representation of women by 2010, and, notably, to extend this entitlement to include BAME and disabled people (The Speaker's Conference Final Report on Parliamentary Representation, 2010).

The Report suggests these dramatic demand-side remedies are necessary to counter local party tendencies to select aspirant candidates who fit the white, male, and non-disabled political norm or, in the language used in this study, the ideal aspirant candidate type. Aside from its dramatic conclusion, it is worth noting three important empirical aspects of the Report, including: 1) the *general approach* used to understand the problem of underrepresentation; 2) the *framework* used to explore this problem; and 3) the *data* upon which the research relies. In terms of 1) approach, the Report follows what is deemed here as a "micro level" approach to investigate underrepresentation by focusing on the general selection rules and behaviour of selection process participants. It largely forgoes "macro level" investigations of, for example, the electoral system, or "meso level" factors such as party ideology. The Report 2) frames its micro level investigation work using a *supply and demand* analogy. This metaphor has been used in this area of study since the 1960s and is almost universally seen as the best way to organise research on this issue. 3) Data used for the Report touch upon both the institutional rules constraining participants (e.g., aspirant candidates and party selectors) as well as the behaviour of participants themselves. However, it sheds light only upon the winning candidates in the final selection stage of the process rather than exploring the process in greater detail and looking at successful and unsuccessful aspirant candidates. Each of these three aspects is more fully explained in the following.

Approach: macro, meso, and micro

Empirical theorists approach the challenge of explaining underrepresentation using three types of studies, categorised here as macro, meso, and micro. This subsection explores the details of these study types and shows why micro level studies are likely the most useful approach to help explain why some types of aspirant candidates are selected over others.

Figure 2.1 shows three interrelated levels on which selection processes are analysed. Macro level studies examine the broad opportunity structures existing within society under which candidate selection processes operate, including legal, party, and electoral systems, and how these structures benefit or hinder different social groups (Rule, 1985). Meso level studies examine operational aspects of political parties, including organisational features laid out in party constitutions as well as party ideologies (Kittilson, 2006; Gallagher and Marsh, 1988; Katz and Mair, 1992; Norris and Lovenduski, 1995; Rahat and Hazan, 2001). Micro level studies explore the rules and participants specific to party selection processes as outlined in the party constitutions, procedures, and/or rule books (Holland, 1987, pp. 55–57; Norris and Lovenduski, 1995, pp. 183–184; (Norris, 1997a), pp. 1–3; Ware, 1996, pp. 257–278).[10]

Macro level studies are the most common, perhaps due to the wider availability of data on electoral and party systems (Patzelt, 1999; Gallagher, 1988b).

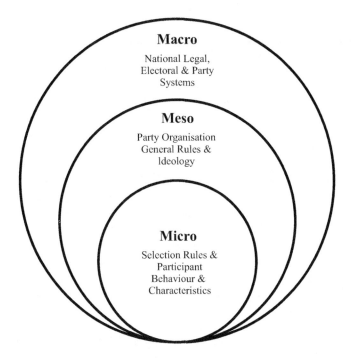

Figure 2.1 Three levels of legislative recruitment

Source: Adapted from Holland (1987, p. 56) and Norris and Lovenduski (1995, p. 184).

However, while electoral systems and party systems may indeed constrain selector and aspirant choices and opportunities, such studies overlook critical micro selection process factors (Gallagher and Marsh, 1988, pp. 257–258). For example, while proportional electoral systems are seen as more likely than plurality systems to provide greater opportunities for women through ticket balancing incentives, electoral systems on their own do not appear to adequately explain legislative imbalance (Norris, 1997b). According to Gallagher and Marsh (1988, p. 268), there is "too much variance from party to party and from election to election within one country" to produce robust explanations of underrepresentation (see Rule, 1985).[11] Moreover, while macro level factors such as term limits might lower incumbency levels and, in turn, create more opportunities for women and other underrepresented aspirant candidate types, term limits alone do not fully explain why women or other groups fail to secure adequate numbers of party candidacies and, ultimately, legislative seats.

Meso level studies are less common than macro level studies. These studies investigate factors having a more direct impact on selection outcomes than macro level studies, with the focus upon general rules governing the selection process, for example, whether the final selection choice is made by national or local party agents. Meso level studies, however, do not provide much, if any detail, on the specific rules governing the various stages of party selection processes or the range of participants involved. Thus, meso level studies are generally used to classify party selection processes as either "centralised" in the hands of national party participants or "decentralised" in the hands of local party participants (Caul, 1999). The centralised/decentralised classification has the potential to provide further insight into why some aspirant candidates are selected over others. Arguably women and other underrepresented groups do better in centralised party organisations where, for example, the national party can create opportunities for women and other groups vis-à-vis equality measures (Caul, 1999). The main meso level study weakness is those using this approach tend to focus solely upon final selection stage rules and participants rather than upon all selection process stages. This tendency potentially leads to imprecise classifications of party selection processes.

This study argues for using a *micro* approach to understanding selection: conducting multistage analyses of selection process rules and participants to more fully understand how different social groups are filtered out as they move through the selection process stages. This micro approach first requires identifying the selection process stages as well as the rules and actors at each of these stages. Second, it requires using the information on rules and participants to separately classify the party's selection stages as "centralised" or "decentralised" so as to develop hypotheses to assess, for example, whether an appropriate percentage of women, BAME, and disabled aspirant candidates pass through each selection process stage and the potential causes of underrepresentation.[12] Third, it requires using micro level data on aspirant candidates who win and lose their bids for candidacies to determine whether party selectors disproportionately screen out particular types of aspirant candidates.

Ultimately, explaining why some aspirant candidates are selected over others can only be determined by assessing micro level factors through collecting and comparing data on aspirant candidates who are selected and aspirant candidates who are rejected at multiple stages of the process (Holland, 1986; Marsh and Gallagher, 1988, p. 267; Niven, 2006; Norris et al, 1990, p. 223). Indeed, the rejected aspirant candidates are the "single most valuable people to understand" (Niven, 2006). Comparing winning and losing aspirant candidates reveals whether important differences exist between the two pools and is therefore a good measure of selection process neutrality (Niven, 2006, pp. 478–479; Holland, 1987). Norris and Lovenduski (1995) concur, arguing:

> [u]nless we understand micro level data – lifetime career patterns of individuals to see how some politicians move into elite positions while others fail – we will be limited to describing rather than explaining this phenomenon. We need to understand *who* the members of the legislative elite are, but, more importantly, *why* and *how* they got there.
>
> (p. 11)

Comparing those who fail with those who succeed at multiple stages of the selection process generates important information on patterns of recruitment at the micro level, specifically whether some aspirant candidate types are more likely to get rejected by party selectors.

Thus, micro level studies have the potential to provide a deeper understanding of legislative underrepresentation as they *directly* focus on assessing the micro-institutional rules of selection and, in turn, the supply of aspirant candidates willing to pursue candidacy and selector demand for these aspirants. As such, it is worthwhile to later explore what few micro studies exist in more detail. While crucial to understanding descriptive representation, few authors choose to explore the rules of selection *and* the supply of and demand for aspirant candidates at *multiple stages* of the process (Holland, 1986; Norris and Lovenduski, 1995; Patzelt, 1999). The next subsection more fully explains the supply and demand framework before moving to describe and evaluate several micro level studies.

Framework: supply and demand

As touched upon in Chapter 1, the vast majority of modern legislative recruitment scholars frame their investigations using the *supply and demand* metaphor (Judge, 1999; Patzelt, 1999), including those who operationalise Phillips' (1998) previously discussed structural discrimination theory (Holland, 1986; Norris and Lovenduski, 1995). The supply and demand has been commonly used to explain election outcomes and more precisely the social makeup of legislatures since the 1960s (Rush, 1969; Ranney, 1965). The model was used to explore women's underrepresentation first by Jill Hills (1983) and Vicky Randall (1982), and refined in the nineties to explore representation by gender, race, and class in the British Parliament by Pippa Norris and Joni Lovenduski (1995; see Lovenduski, 2016, p. 519). Their elaborated model of supply and demand is described as "a theoretical framework of considerable integrative power" and "the main paradigm for recruitment research" (Patzelt, 1999, p. 243). Moreover, Norris and Lovenduski's model *continues* to be the "the main framework for understanding the dynamics of the recruitment process", particularly in studies of gender and political recruitment (Kenny, 2013, p. 1; see Kenny and Verge, 2016). In essence it provides a framework with which to explore party selection processes and outcomes and to better understand *who* does and does not get selected as candidates and *why* some aspirant candidates get selected while others do not (Norris and Lovenduski, 1995, p. 2; for more on both theories, see Hunt and Pendley, 1972; Mishler, 1978; Niven, 1998).

Norris and Lovenduski's (1995) supply and demand framework draws upon a market analogy whereby selected candidates reflect the forces of supply and demand within the recruitment marketplace (see Lovenduski, 2016). The phrase "supply and demand" is not specifically tied to the economic law of supply and demand but is rather used as a loose metaphor for understanding selection processes and outcomes, and in this sense, it is a flexible framework that can be adapted by researchers to explore various aspects of political recruitment. As Lovenduski reflects, the supply and demand model, "for all its apparent simplicity has considerable capacity to carry ideas, concepts and methodological refinements. It was and is basically up to the researcher how to operationalise it" (Lovenduski, 2016, p. 519).[13] Some critiques of the model rest on a too literal reading of the economic model of supply and demand (see Krook, 2009, pp. 709–710; Lovenduski, 2016; Norris and Krook, 2014). In doing so, sometimes overlooked are the finer details of the framework which speak to its inherent adaptability to explore multiple selection stages and participants, as is undertaken in this study, and to explore the gendered ways in which party organisation rules and practices systematically disadvantage women, as is discussed later (Bjarnegård and Kenny, 2014; Lovenduski, 2016; Mackay, 2001).

In the supply and demand framework, supply-side factors affect who is eligible to come forward and/or who comes forward, while demand-side factors affect who is successful at one and/or multiple selection stages. The two dynamics interact: the supply of aspirant candidates willing to come forward may be discouraged by their perceptions of prejudice by party selectors, while aspirant candidates who come forward may not be selected by party selectors because they do not fit the ideal aspirant candidate type (1995, p. 15). In terms of explaining the under-supply of a particular group, some suggest resource factors (e.g., time, money, and experience) and motivational factors (e.g., drive, ambition, and political interest) influence who seeks candidacy (Norris and Lovenduski, 1995; Fox and Lawless, 2004, 2010). This line of reasoning suggests fewer women than men come forward because women have fewer political resources and lower levels of political motivation, ambition, and confidence than their male counterparts (Allen, 2012; Allen and Cutts, 2018; Fox and Lawless, 2004, 2010; Norris and Lovenduski, 1995; Pearson and McGhee, 2013). Indeed, some scholars suggest the underrepresentation of women in party candidate pools is due to an absence of party strategies and rules designed to increase the supply of women, such as financial assistance and training, and even equality guarantees (Campbell and Lovenduski, 2005).

Factors influencing demand include party rules and practices and party selectors' perceptions of aspirant candidates' characteristics and, as explored in detail in this study, the degree to which aspirant candidates fit selectors' pre-conceived "ideal" aspirant candidate type (Cairney, 2007; Durose et al, 2013; Murray, 2014; Norris and Lovenduski, 1995). Building on this, aspirant candidates' curricula vitae often only provide selectors with minimum information, and in the context of having to sort through hundreds of applications in a relatively short period, they rely upon "background characteristics as a proxy measure of abilities and character; prejudice functions as an information short-cut. As a result, individuals are judged by their group characteristics" (Norris and Lovenduski, 1995, p. 14). The implications of this are discussed in more detail in the following section.

Data: institutions, behaviour, and "ideal" candidates

Some studies of underrepresentation focus upon the institutional aspects of the selection process by limiting exploration to formal aspects as laid out in legal regulations, constitutions, and party rules specific to selection (Gallagher and

Marsh, 1988; Patzelt, 1999; Ranney, 1965; Rush, 1969). These type of studies tend to over-emphasise the influence formal rules have upon outcome, thereby eliding the role of informal practices (e.g., "constitutions may exercise *de jure*, not *de facto* authority") and participant behaviour (Norris, 1997a, p. 9). Other studies examine participant behaviour, seeking to understand selectors' and candidates' attitudes through surveys and elite interviews (Norris, 1997a, p. 9; see for example Bochel and Denver, 1983; Gallagher and Marsh, 1988). These studies often underestimate how formal rules often restrict behaviour. However, emphasising institutional factors over behavioural factors and vice versa is problematic. For example, it is difficult to fully explain the selection success or failure of certain types of aspirant candidates by examining only party rules *or* only participant behaviour *or* only demographics, given all likely combine to influence outcomes (Norris, 1997a, p. 9).

On their own, institutional and behaviourist perspectives inevitably fall short, as the former neglects participant preferences and the latter neglects how formal rules influence these preferences (Norris, 1997a, p. 9). Indeed, institutional and behavioural factors are entangled (Lovenduski, 2016; March and Olsen, 1989; Powell and Dimaggio, 1991; Norris and Lovenduski, 1995). As such, this study builds on Norris and Lovenduski (1995), who overcome the shortcomings of assessing the impact of one set of factors over another by considering institutional factors such as party rules *and* behavioural factors such as selectors' preferences. This "new institutional" approach suggests aspirant candidates' and selectors' behaviour may be more clearly understood within the context of a party organisation. In this sense, fuller accounts of why some aspirant candidates are selected over others ought to include analyses of both party rules and aspirant candidate and selector behaviour on grounds that this sub-set of legislative recruitment is also a "process of interaction" where the rules and procedures of party organisations structure behaviour in "predictable and orderly ways" (Norris, 1997a, p. 9).

Feminist scholars have gendered the new institutional approach by using the feminist institutionalism approach to assess candidate selection by "highlight[ing] the gendered aspects of the norms, rules and practices at work within institutions and the concomitant effect these have on political outcomes" (Mackay, Kenny, and Chappell, 2010, p. 573; also see Lovenduski, 2005; Mackay, 2001). By way of example, Elin Bjarnegård and Meryl Kenny (2014) find the local selection process operates differently for women and men when centralised party rules are not enforced, with "women positioned as gendered 'outsiders' to the process and therefore unable to gain access to political power" (p. 23). There is considerable room within the supply and demand framework to look at the way in which party rules and participant behaviour affect representation insofar as the persistent selection of some aspirant candidate types over others is influenced by a party's views on whether descriptive underrepresentation matters and in turn its willingness to address the problem (Krook, 2009, p. 7). Indeed, it is argued that the historic exclusion of women from positions of political power has meant party rules and practices favouring the success of men often evolve with little protest (Bjarnegård and Kenny, 2014, p. 4; and see Lovenduski, 2005; Kenny, 2013).[14]

Therefore looking at the influence of institutional rule change upon selector behaviour is critical to understanding the complexity of supply and demand and selection process outcomes.

In line with this, and as earlier raised, a party may choose to use equality guarantees in the form of quotas to manufacture demand for women, BAME, or disabled aspirant candidates by pinching off the supply of men, non-BAME, or non-disabled aspirant candidates and forcing selectors to choose a woman, BAME, or disabled aspirant candidate. Moreover, behavioural conditions, such as the preferences of party selectors, can also affect the demand for certain types of aspirant candidates. For example, party selectors may simply prefer men over women, non-BAME over BAME, or non-disabled over disabled aspirant candidates and choose accordingly at various stages of the selection process. In this light party rules constrain selectors' preferences and determine the aspirant candidate types that move through the successive filtering stages of a party's selection process (Lovenduski and Norris, 1989, p. 554; Tremblay and Pelletier, 2001, p. 161).

There is a large body of literature looking at the social background characteristics of the political elite to explain why it benefits from current legislative recruitment processes. Influenced by theorists such as Robert Dahl (1961), these studies begin from stratification hypotheses; the political chances of aspirant candidates are influenced by social characteristics and social statuses, and the best predictors of these include sex, ethnicity, age, educational attainment, occupation, and party and political experience, and networks, as well as a range of skills and traits useful for political office such as oration and confidence (Budge and Farlie, 1975; Cairney, 2007; Durose et al, 2013; Fox and Laweless, 2004; Hunt and Pendley, 1972; pp. 420–425; Murray, 2013; Norris, 1997b; Norris and Lovenduski, 1995; Saggar, 2013). On this basis it is argued that party selectors select aspirant candidates who possess the demonstrated accomplishments of those who have experienced past political success (Prewitt, 1970, pp. 28–29). In other words, party selectors disproportionately select aspirant candidates who *resemble* the group with a demonstrated history of past political success in their collective capacity as party candidates and elected politicians (Prewitt, 1970, pp. 28–29; see Campbell and Cowley, 2013, p. 2, pp. 6–13).

Given this tendency, it has been argued that party selectors' preferences are influenced by direct and indirect forms of discrimination. Notably, discrimination is used in a neutral sense to evaluate aspirant candidate group characteristics; discrimination can be for or against particular groups of aspirant candidates and candidates, for example, men or women, non-BAME or BAME, non-disabled or disabled, university educated or non-university educated, party workers or non-party workers and so on (Norris and Lovenduski, 1995, p. 107). Direct discrimination takes the form of judgments made about aspirant candidates on the basis of sex, race, and/or physical disability and occurs when party selectors make assumptions about the proper role of some aspirant candidates (e.g., politics is no place for women), which in turn count against some aspirant candidate groups' chances of being selected (Norris et al, 1990, p. 223). For example, when faced with a quick decision, selectors may choose men over women on the assumption that men are better suited to politics, as "women with a career and young family have little time to spend on party work" (Norris and Lovenduski, 1995). Indirect discrimination, on the other hand, occurs when selectors' choices do not reflect who they personally prefer. For example, selectors may choose a man over a woman or non-BAME over a BAME aspirant candidate even though they favour a woman or BAME aspirant candidate, but do not vote for them for fear they will cost the party votes (Bochel and Denver, 1983). In other words selectors may feel "we need more Labour women" or BAME candidates, but they fail to select them because they think the electorate will reject a woman or a black candidate (Norris and Lovenduski, 1995, p. 107; see also Bochel and Denver, 1983; Durose et al, 2013; Saggar, 2013).

This line of reasoning ties in with the stereotype theory tested in US election studies, which finds stereotypes are used as a low-information short-cut by voters who do not have enough information with which to evaluate a candidate (Dolan, 2010; Huddy and Terkildsen, 1993; McDermott, 1997, 1998; Sanbonmatsu, 2002; Sigelman et al, 1995).[15] The stereotype theory is relevant to selection contests insofar as it makes a case for further exploring the nature of demand and the idea of the ideal aspirant candidate type. Like elections, selection contests, as noted earlier, are often low-information affairs where party selectors rely upon whatever demographic information they have on hand to evaluate aspirant candidates. For example, sex can be determined by a name on the ballot and ethnicity and age can be determined by a picture on a leaflet, news story, or website (McDermott, 1997, 1998). Indeed, in the US psychology literature on candidate choice, it is widely accepted that electors often rely on stereotypes to judge candidates in the same way stereotypes are used by people to judge other people in everyday life (McDermott, 1998, p. 896; also see Campbell and Cowley, 2013). McDermott (1998) found "both political and social stereotypes of women and blacks influence how voters view women and black candidates, and as a result, influence voting decisions in races with such candidates running" (p. 897).[16]

The gatekeeper theory further complements the demand-side explanation of underrepresentation and feeds into the image of the ideal aspirant candidate (Cheng and Tavits, 2010; Niven, 1998, 2006; Tolley, 2019; Tremblay and Pelletier, 2001).[17] Party selectors act as gatekeepers and determine which aspirant candidates gain access to positions of political power and in turn determine the composition of the political elite. Thus, party selectors, be they national agents (e.g., the central party) or local party agents (e.g., party members), keep out aspirant candidates who lack the previously mentioned demonstrable accomplishments of historically successful politicians. Feminist scholars too have adopted the gatekeeping language to explain women's underrepresentation, arguing systematic bias against women aspirant candidates results from the institutionalisation of traditional masculinity within parties and in turn within party selection processes (Lovenduski, 2005, p. 56; Kenny, 2013; Tremblay and Pelletier, 2001).[18] Thus, a party's culture of masculinity is reinforced by party norms, which serve to reproduce traditional candidates and encourage the selection of aspirant candidates who possess the attributes of the ideal aspirant candidate type (e.g., white, professional, non-disabled men) (Lovenduski, 2005, pp. 56–58; Kenny, 2013; Kenny and Verge, 2016).

The explanatory power of micro level studies

This next section reviews the methodological approaches used in several micro level studies concerned with assessing representation by explicitly using the supply and demand framework.[19] The point of the review is to illustrate that many supply and demand assessments of selection processes rely upon incomplete supply and demand-side data – with few of the reviewed studies clearly assessing how party rules affect selection outcomes. Indeed, establishing whether or not party rules and selectors disproportionately screen out some aspirant candidate types over others is notoriously difficult without aggregate and/or individual level information on the winners and the losers of selection processes (Norris, 1997b, p. 221). There are several ways to do this. One way, for example, is to compare aspirant candidates' attributes, for example, sex, race, and ability at multiple stages of the selection process, to see whether they differ in any significant ways (Holland, 1987). If there are no differences between the pools of successful and unsuccessful aspirant candidates, institutional and selector discrimination is unlikely. Problematically, however, if the underrepresentation of aspirant candidates from one group is not clearly a demand-side problem, by default it is often explained away in the literature as a supply-side problem. For example, if more women came forward, more women would get selected (Bochel and Denver, 1983; Fox and Lawless, 2004; Niven, 1998, 2006; Tremblay and Pelletier, 2001). If, on the other hand, there are significant differences between successful and unsuccessful aspirant candidates at one or more stages of a party's selection process, institutional and selector discrimination is likely and reflects a demand-side problem, which should be further investigated (Ashe and Stewart, 2012; Niven, 1998, 2006; Phillips, 1995).

The methodological approaches used to understand the impact of supply and demand on candidate selection vary in at least two main ways. First, while all selection processes are multistage "ladders of recruitment" (Norris and Lovenduski, 1995, p. 16), most scholars choose to examine only a single ladder rung (Bochel and Denver, 1983; Cheng and Tavits, 2010; Erickson, 1997a; Hills, 1983; Mishler, 1978; Niven, 2006; Tremblay and Pelletier, 2001; Scarrow, 1964; Shepherd-Robinson and Lovenduski, 2002), with very few scrutinising the complete ladder (Ashe and Stewart, 2012; Holland, 1987; Norris and Lovenduski, 1995). Second, in terms of data, most studies include information from aspirants who successfully secure party candidacies (winners) (Bochel and Denver, 1983; Cheng and Tavits, 2010; Erickson, 1997a; Hills, 1983; Mishler, 1978; Niven, 2006; Tremblay and Pelletier, 2001), whereas very few collect information from those who fail to win (losers) so as to allow for comparisons of these two groups (Ashe and Stewart, 2012; Holland, 1987; Norris and Lovenduski, 1995; Scarrow, 1964; Shepherd-Robinson and Lovenduski, 2002).

Methodological considerations are extremely important, as it is clear study findings are greatly impacted by which data and stages are omitted, often leading to incomplete analysis. In terms of stages, some pertain only to supply (i.e., applying to a party to become a candidate) and some only to demand (i.e., whether or not party officials accept the application), thus focusing on only a single stage can leave analytical gaps and bias conclusions. In terms of data, Best and Cotta caution a lack of data on losing aspirants makes it much more difficult to evaluate demand for underrepresented groups than it is to assume their underrepresentation is due to supply (2000, p. 519). Understanding who loses and why is extremely important when evaluating fairness, but impossible to infer from looking at data only from winning candidates. Explaining why some aspirants are selected over others is best determined through collecting and comparing aggregate and individual level data on both winning and losing aspirants at multiple stages (Holland, 1987; Gallagher and Marsh, 1988, p. 267; Niven, 2006; Norris, 1997b, p. 221). Demand-side factors are unlikely the problem if there are no differences between winning and losing aspirants; however, demand is likely the problem if there are differences between the two and should be further explored.

Using a multistage approach to trace the fate of winning and losing aspirants during all stages of the candidate selection process allows for a deeper understanding of the process and reduces the chance of erroneous conclusions. Examples, however, are rare. Martin Holland was the first to use this approach to systematically examine the fate of women and other candidate types moving through the five stages by which parties select candidates to stand in the European Parliamentary elections (1987). Drawing on data from surveys on winning and losing aspirants, Holland finds that despite a robust supply of underrepresented candidate types, demand from party selectors favoured men over women, middle-aged to younger or older aspirants, highly educated to less educated, professional to working class, politically experienced to less politically experienced, and those with averse European Community attitudes to pro-European Community attitudes. While the data and method allows for a comparison between winning and losing aspirants at multiple stages and a conclusion which challenges supply-side assumptions, Holland does not use advanced statistical techniques – such as regression analysis – to test the significance of the variables or to control for their influence (1987).

Pippa Norris and Joni Lovenduski use a wide range of survey, interview, and aggregate data to compare how winners and losers fare during each stage through which aspirant candidates pass to be selected to stand in British Parliamentary elections for Labour (then a five-stage process) and Conservative (then a seven-stage process) parties (1995). They use regression analyses to test supply- and demand-side hypotheses to find both supply- and demand-side factors impact selection, with differences between the two parties in terms of who comes forward and who selectors prefer (Norris and Lovenduski, 1995). They expand the ladder of recruitment to include data on potential aspirants (party members) and test supply by comparing potential aspirants with actual aspirants (those who formally indicate their willingness to run by applying to a party), finding middle-aged professional men with property but without dependent children are more likely to come forward. Demand is tested by comparing aspirants with selected candidates to reveal selectors prefer white professional men under the age of 50 (Norris and Lovenduski, 1995, pp. 118–122). Overall the authors find aspirants and candidates to be relatively similar and on this basis conclude that the social bias toward younger, educated men more reflects the supply of aspirants coming forward rather than selector demand for certain types of aspirants (p. 122). It is likely their supply and demand conclusions would be different if Norris and Lovenduski compared actual aspirants (i.e., people who formally applied to a party for candidacy) with other actual aspirants at multiple stages, rather than with potential aspirants (i.e., party members) (1995).

Jeanette Ashe and Kennedy Stewart use a similar methodology to test selector bias during the three stages by which candidates are selected to stand as candidates in two parties during a provincial election in British Columbia, Canada. Using party, survey, and interview data with which to compare aspirant candidates with other aspirant candidates, they find that despite enough women and aspirants from other underrepresented groups coming forward to fill their fair share of candidacies, party selectors prefer men to women, white to BAME, and partnered to single aspirant candidates (2012). The study would benefit from more cases, perhaps by adding another election year.

Elaborated upon in subsequent chapters, this study draws upon the approaches used by Holland (1987); Norris and Lovenduski (1995); and Ashe and Stewart (2012) to further clarify and develop the multistage method by which supply and demand is evaluated during the Labour party's selection process.

Demand and the ideal aspirant candidate

The previously mentioned studies suggest standard, ideal aspirant candidate characteristics are not static, with some emphasising a variety of attributes common to candidates and MPs. As noted, despite some variation, it is possible to glean a list of purported ideal candidate characteristics from the supply and demand scholarship as well as from the more general political recruitment literature in which supply- and demand-side hypotheses are not explicitly tested. In the latter instance, selectors' preferences are often based on conjecture insofar as the scholars tend to work backward from who is elected and/or selected to develop a list of common ideal candidate features. As a whole, this approach reveals the characteristics shared by selected and elected aspirant candidates; at the same time, it reveals these will likely continue to evolve in particular with regard to occupation, sex, race, and residency.

In terms of occupation, the past literature on the professionalisation of politics reveals British MPs were disproportionately drawn from brokerage occupations, such as barrister, solicitor, lecturer, and teacher (Bochel and Denver, 1983, p. 56; Jacobs, 1962; Norris and Lovenduski, 1995; Ranney, 1965, p. 119; Riddell, 1993). More recent literature assessing candidates' multiple occupations – including the one immediately prior to seeking office – reveals candidates and MPs are increasingly drawn from instrumental as opposed to brokerage occupations (Cairney,

2007; Allen, 2012). Instrumental occupations include those related to the art of persuasion and publicity, such as journalism and public relations; providing an apprenticeship to politics, such as trade union officials, interest group representatives, full-time councillors, and MEPs; and having a clear connection to political decision makers, such as party workers, MP assistants, quasi-autonomous non-governmental organisations (QUANGOs), and think tanks (Cairney, 2007, p. 3). In this sense instrumental occupations and instrumental experiences likely offer "a clearer link to politics" and are "used as a steppingstone toward elected office" (Cairney, 2007, p. 3). This literature makes a convincing case that there has been a shift in the type of candidates coming forward and in selector demand.

In terms of women, BAME, and candidates from other underrepresented groups, recent, albeit small increases in the British Parliament are attributed to the shifting nature of supply and demand. On the supply-side, women and BAME candidates are forgoing the traditional pathway to parliament for a *new* pathway to parliament. The traditional pathway to parliament involved 1) exposure to politics, 2) joining a trade union, 3) becoming active or holding a position in a trade union, and 4) then standing as a MP. The new pathway, however, involves going to 1) university, 2) working for a national party, a political institution, or a campaign organisation, 3) having a successful professional career, and 4) then standing as MP (Durose et al, 2013, pp. 252–259).

On the demand-side, selectors are willing to choose candidates from minority groups perceived as being "acceptably different" insofar as they "tick off" some of the boxes associated with the ideal candidate type (Durose et al, 2013). Conforming to the ideal type in this way, for example, having a university education or instrumental occupation, "mitigate[s] against the perceived electoral disadvantage [held by local party selectors] of being from a minority group" (Durose et al, 2013, pp. 246–248, p. 258; Saggar, 2013). Indeed, some women MPs are described as acceptably different insofar as prior to candidacy and election they were political insiders, employed as parliamentary researchers and political officers to parliamentary parties (Durose et al, 2013, p. 261). Moreover, a number of BAME candidates/MPs in 2010 had strong backgrounds in political activism prior to their election. For example, Chi Onwurah, the first black MP in Newcastle, was active in the anti-apartheid movement, while many other BAME candidates/MPs were active in the student movement (Durose et al, 2013, p. 261).

Other recruitment scholarship reveals different ways of thinking about other candidate characteristics, such as education and residency. Although the studies mentioned earlier suggest aspirant candidates with university education are more likely to succeed than those with no university education, a recent study reveals the relationship may not be so straightforward. In an experimental study on electorate preference for hypothetical candidates for the British Parliament, Campbell and Cowley (2013) surprisingly found that "respondents seemed to noticeably prefer a candidate who had *not* been to university", and "a school leaver at eighteen is preferred to one at sixteen, but both are preferred to one with a PhD" (p. 11).

In terms of residency, it is suggested localism is increasingly important to selection and election success. In selectors' eyes, being local, that is, living in the constituency where a seat is sought, now trumps other candidate characteristics such as gender, ethnicity, age, occupation, religion, and activism (Campbell and Cowley, 2013; Evans, 2012). For example, Evans' (2012) research on by-elections in the UK finds in all three major parties there is a preference for local candidates over women candidates and political insiders (pp. 195–213).

Lastly, studies on the supply and demand for potential aspirant candidates offer valuable insight into the gendered nature of political recruitment and ambition. For example, mothers or women with other caring responsibilities, and women with similar educational and occupational qualifications as men, are less likely to be recruited by parties and are more likely to express lower levels of political ambition (Allen, 2012; Allen and Cutts, 2018; Bittner and Thomas, 2017; Fox and Lawless, 2004, 2010; Pearson and McGhee, 2013). In the US, Fox and Lawless' (2004, 2010) research draws on data from the *US Citizen Political Ambition Study* – a survey of over 2000 potential candidates – to find there is bias in the political recruitment process insofar as "highly qualified and well-connected women from both major political parties are less likely than similarly situated men to be recruited to run for office by all types of political actors" (p. 311, p. 322). They note that their findings reflect the stereotypical conceptions of candidates discussed earlier and reinforce other studies' findings, such as Niven's (2006), who argues party selectors more actively seek men than women to run for political office (Fox and Lawless, 2010, p. 322). Along the same lines, Pearson and McGhee's (2013) study of the US House of Representatives demonstrates a similar gender gap in political ambition, finding women wait to run for Congress until they have the self-perceived pre-requisite qualifications, resources, and credibility (pp. 256–257). Moreover, drawing on data from the UK, Allen (2012) finds women councillors are less likely than men councillors to pursue national politics.

Importantly, however, the pool of potential aspirant candidates is likely quite different from the pool of actual aspirant candidates who formally seek candidacy; therefore, these studies' findings do not fully address this study's main research question – why are some and not other aspirant candidates selected. Still, in terms of understanding the supply of potential aspirant candidates – which is not the focus of this study – when considering how to close the gender gap in legislatures it is valuable to take into account the disadvantages faced by potential aspirant candidates, particularly women (Fox and Lawless, 2010, p. 311).

From the wide array of research on candidate characteristics presented in this chapter and explored in the proceeding chapters, the ideal candidate type and, by extension, the *ideal aspirant candidate type* includes white, non-disabled men who are heterosexual and who speak English as a first language, as well as those who are middle class, middle-aged, university educated, and/or in professional, "politics facilitating – instrumental" occupations. Ideal aspirant candidates are also expected to have considerable party and political experience, strong political and personal networks, acceptable political attitudes, considerable political ambition, and/or use voter mobilisation methods.

Conclusion

This chapter discusses descriptive representation and the normative reasons for its exploration. It then outlines a theoretical framework for doing so: supply and demand. Multiple stages of selection are briefly discussed, as are the various agents participating in the process (e.g., aspirant candidates and selectors). A review of studies assessing selection outcomes is presented alongside a critique of the data needed to best analyse supply- and demand-side factors. Lastly, an updated list of ideal aspirant candidate characteristics is presented. This review illustrates the type of data collected shape our understanding about why the social imbalance in legislatures persists and more specifically why some aspirant candidates are selected over others. Many studies conclude the descriptive underrepresentation of women and other aspirant candidate types results more from supply- than demand-side factors; however, evidence is typically limited to one stage of multistage processes and to one type of aspirant candidate: winners. Studies that expand upon data to include multiple stages of selection and winning and losing aspirant candidates are more likely to find selection outcomes are at least in part determined by demand where selectors prefer certain aspirant candidate types over others. The next chapter discusses in more detail the data and methodology used in this study to investigate why some and not other aspirant candidate types are selected.

Notes

1 However, the argument for parity need not rest on an essentialist treatment of women's interests. As Phillips (1995) suggests: "the argument from interests does not depend on establishing a unified interest of all women: it depends, rather, on establishing a difference between the interests of women and men" (p. 68). This indeed has been the focus of recent feminist scholarship where the case for gender parity is strengthened by showing a relationship between the presence of women and their legislative activities and styles (Childs, 2007).
2 The critical mass necessary to enhance this difference, is, however, contested (Childs and Krook, 2008, p. 522; Lovenduski, 2016).
3 The difficulty in establishing this relationship is complicated by methodological concerns about how to know whether women have made a substantive difference (Childs, 2007, p. 85). The absence of sex differences does not necessarily mean women are not effecting change. An alternative way to measure substantive representation is the feminisation of the political agenda and legislation, which reflects an attempt to represent women through the articulation of their interests regardless of the impact on output (Childs, 2007, p. 86).
4 In this type of representation – "acting for" representation – the descriptive characteristics of a representative may differ from who they act on behalf of; however, this matters little given the following requirement: "there need not be a constant activity of responding, but there must be a constant condition of responsiveness, a potential readiness to respond" (Pitkin, 1967, p. 226). As such, representation cannot be guaranteed, leaving open whether it may be improved.
5 Indeed, as Sarah Childs argues (2008) "Pitkin herself chose to downplay the idea that elected bodies are determined to some [unsubstantial] degree by those who constitute them, even while she was aware that advocates of descriptive representation are

concerned about ensuring descriptive representation precisely because they expect the composition [of a political forum] to determine the activities" (p. 98). After all, this element of descriptive representation was influential in arguments for universal suffrage and the right to run for and sit in political office. Yet using Pitkin's logic, this would have been unnecessary given the legislators at the time (white, elite men) acted responsively.

6   "A Speaker's Conference is convened by the Speaker of the House of Commons following an invitation from the Prime Minister". To date there have been six Speaker's Conferences (UK Parliament, 2010).

7   "The recommendations of the first Speaker's Conference were subsequently embodied in the *Representation of the People Act 1918* 'which implemented the most sweeping electoral reforms since 1832.' The Act provided for the enfranchisement of women aged 30 and over and the introduction of a franchise" (UK Parliament, 2010).

8   The Report also describes how many more older than younger and professional than working class candidates are MPs.

9   While none of these factors are barriers to being a MP, the report views them as barriers to aspirant candidates' success in politics, with parties' cultures and selection processes combining to make it more difficult for women, BAME, working class, and/ or disabled aspirant candidates to get selected than others (*The Guardian*, Monday, 11 January 2010).

10 The political system, recruitment process, and supply and demand factors are "nested in a funnel of causality, so that supply and demand works within party recruitment processes, which in turn are shaped by the broader political system" (Norris, 1997a, p. 1).

11 For example, the dramatic increase of women representatives in the Norwegian Storting in the 1980s did not occur because Norway changed its electoral system, nor was the doubling of women in Britain's House of Commons in the 1990s due to a change in the country's electoral system (Gallagher and Marsh, 1988, p. 268).

12 The proportion is "appropriate" if the proportion of women, BAME, and disabled aspirant candidates is the same at each successive selection stage.

13 To address such critiques, one only needs to look at the way supply and demand have been used by other scholars to explore the underrepresentation of women and other groups across a range of countries, and by integrating the feminist institutionalism approach to explore the gendered natured of supply- and demand-side factors, and in particular the way in which formal selection rules and practices work to keep women out of political power structures (Ashe and Stewart, 2012; Bjarnegård and Kenny, 2014; Norris, 1997b).

14 For example, where the central party implements rules to address this, there is often a period of contestation (Bjarnegård and Kenny, 2014). As Bjarnegård and Kenny (2014) argue, "for every female candidate that wants to get in, another, often male, candidate has to go. The gendered power-struggle is therefore very real, and it is only rational for political actors to try to devise strategies to stay in power" (p. 4).

15 Although there is little evidence that voters in the US are biased against women candidates at the polls, there is evidence that voters use gender as well as race and other stereotypes to evaluate candidates. Kira Sanbonmatsu (2002) notes: "there are two distinct bodies of research on candidate gender. The first argues that voters are not biased against female candidates. These studies are usually based on aggregate analyses of the success rates of male and female candidates. The second body of research argues that voters employ gender stereotypes when they evaluate candidates. These studies are usually based on experiments which manipulate candidate gender" (p. 20). While sexism and racism may partially explain preferences, "logical guesses", which rely on information shortcuts, are not quite the same thing as selecting a man or non-BAME because they are unwilling to select a women or BAME candidate (Sanbonmatsu, 2002, p. 21). This research has revealed voter preferences are explained by gender and

race stereotypes about candidate traits, beliefs, and issue competencies (Sanbonmatsu, 2002, p. 20; see McDermott, 1998).

16 This literature further reveals that voters view women politicians as more compassionate and able to tackle education and family policy and women's issues, and found women politicians to be more liberal, democratic, and feminist (Dolan, 2010, p. 71). At the same time, voters perceive men politicians as strong, intelligent, and better able to tackle crime, defense, and foreign policy, and found men to be more conservative than women (Dolan, 2010, p. 71).

17 The gatekeeper theory is rooted in the field of communications. The term gatekeeping was first used by Kurt Lewin (1947) to show how the food that ends up on dining tables is decided by "the women of households" who shop for it, cook it, and feed it to their families. In this sense, the gatekeepers of food decide what passes through each "gated" section or stage on its way to dining tables from grocers' shelves, into shopping carts, through check-outs, through front doors, in and out of oven doors, onto plates, and into the mouths of families. Moving away from its application to the food chain, Lewin (1947) applied "gating" to describe the way news items move through various communication channels (e.g., from "sources" to reporters to the news editors to newspapers to readers). Although still a main theory in journalism, gatekeeping has branched out to other disciplines, including political science (University of Twente, 2014).

18 This happens when one sex dominates any institution's personnel, practices, and outcomes (Lovenduski, 2005, pp. 52–53).

19 The studies reviewed are restricted to liberal democratic countries using a single member plurality electoral system, the UK, the USA, and Canada, as the nature of selection to these countries' national legislatures restricts party selectors to one candidate per constituency. This influences the type of rules parties employ to bring about greater descriptive representation (e.g., it is more contentious to employ quotas when selectors may only choose one candidate) and selectors' preferences (e.g., they may feel more inclined to select a man over a woman on the assumption that the former are more electorally successful).

3 Data and initial supply and demand tests

This chapter explains the data sources and collection methods and provides an overview of the tests performed in this study. It also presents an initial investigation into the secret garden of candidate selection by providing a multi-year and multistage account of the British Labour party's candidate selection process with more selection stage details provided in Chapters 4 and 5. Descriptive statistics reveal the process by which thousands of aspirant candidates are filtered out of Labour's seven candidate selection stages and the extent to which participants are affected by supply and demand. The main finding of this chapter is that the imbalance within the Labour party's candidate pool is caused more by demand-side factors than by supply-side factors.

Data sources and collection methods

Where Chapters 1 and 2 establish the normative premise for this study and review relevant empirical work to date, the remainder of this study develops a method for using party data to test why some and not other types of aspirant candidates are selected to stand as candidates in elections. Five main sources of data are used in this study: census data, party data, survey data, interview data, and party rule book and constitution data. Census and party data are used to test supply and demand by comparing the sex, race, and the physical ability of aspirant candidates who are successful and unsuccessful at various stages of the selection process. Survey data are used to further test supply and demand by comparing the sex, race, and physical ability of successful and unsuccessful aspirant candidates as well as a wider-range of other attributes, such as party experience, political experience, political and personal networks, political attitudes, political ambition, and campaign strategies. Interviews with party officials and aspirant candidates help clarify selection rules and develop the hypotheses and survey questions. The British Labour party's constitution and rule books are used to assess the degree to which the selection stages and process as a whole are centralised and decentralised and, by drawing upon the census data, to test the centralisation hypotheses.

This study draws on almost 20 years of Labour party selection data over four elections, 2001, 2005, 2010, and 2015. As earlier raised, given changes in the data collected by the Labour party, there are different data for different years, making it impossible to perform some tests on selections for the 2001 and 2015 General Elections. While there are full census data on all aspirants for 2001, 2005, and 2010, there are limited party data for 2015, given the party's decision to do away with the NPP, the implications of which are discussed in more detail later. While there are survey data for 2005 and 2010, there are none for 2001 or 2015, as the party did not collect aspirants' emails for 2001 and did not keep a national list of all aspirants' names for 2015, again due to the elimination of the NPP. There are interview data with party officials and candidates in the lead-up to the 2010 General Election, with party officials before and after selections for the 2015 General Election and with party officials in the lead-up to the 2017 snap election. As earlier explained, selections for the 2017 and 2019 snap elections are excluded from this analysis. The next sections discuss these data and tests in more detail.

Census data

The Labour party granted the author access to a database recording a small set of details about all 4,622 aspirant candidates submitting their curricula vitae for consideration to the central party's NEC in the 2001, 2005, 2010 selection processes. Information includes, sex, race, and physical ability, and if the aspirant candidates applied or did not apply to the NPP, if they were approved or were not approved on the NPP, and if they were or were not selected as candidates. The 2005 and 2010 census data also include the aspirant candidates' email addresses. These census data were supplemented with interviews from party officials and aspirant candidates, data from the UK Electoral Commission, the British General Election Constituency Results Data Base (2001, 2005, and 2010), and online news sites and blogs. These never-before-analysed census data were released to the author after lengthy negotiations with senior central party officials.[1]

Labour party data

Following the 2015 General Election, the author met with party officials to request the most recent census data only to be informed the central party no longer collects or keeps these. Rather the party now only collects and maintains data on selection contest winners, in this case, prospective parliamentary candidates (PPCs) (i.e., aspirants who have been selected as the party's candidate) and on aspirant candidates in 164 seats it fully monitors.[2] In these fully monitored seats, the central party collects data on all winning and losing aspirants seeking candidacy, including information on 1286 aspirants' sex, race, ability, and unlike in previous elections, sexual orientation. Additionally, these data are on all four stages of the party's 2015 selection process: application, nomination, shortlisting, and selection. These data, however, can only be used to perform the surplus deficit/ supply-side tests and filtering tests in this chapter, and given the lack of survey data, are not used to perform regression tests in Chapters 6 and 7.

Changes to the data collected by the central party for selections after the 2010 General Election, as noted, are traced to the decision to forgo the NPP. Implications of this decision upon data collection were relayed during interviews with party officials who noted aspirants used to apply to the NEC's NPP, allowing the central party to keep a list of all aspirants seeking selection along with some demographic details and their contact information.[3] But now selections are "being done by the local constituencies – all CVs go to the local parties' procedures secretaries – so, to get a list of all that applied to seats, one gets this from each constituency procedures secretary, if they have it. So, there's no longer one central list of all aspirants".[4] The reasoning behind scrapping the NPP and ensuing problems with this decision are discussed in more detail later.

Labour party survey data

This study draws upon original online survey data from 566 aspirant candidates participating in the 2005 and 2010 Labour party selection processes.[5] The Labour party granted the author permission to email a secure online survey to all aspirant candidates for the 2005 and the 2010 General Elections and provided cover letters to encourage aspirants' participation. As noted, online surveys were not sent to aspirants for the 2001 or 2015 General Elections on grounds the party did not centrally keep records of all aspirants' email addresses. The survey data were supplemented with the party census data (2001, 2005, and 2010), interviews, election returns, blogs, social media, the Labour party's website, and newspaper reports. Once Labour party officials reviewed and approved the surveys, the author emailed the surveys to all aspirant candidates using information from the party's 2005 and 2010 census data.[6] Where email addresses were found to be invalid, the author searched for other contact details using a variety of online sources (e.g., websites, blogs, news sources, Linked-in, Facebook, etc.). In total, 566 of 3064 possible aspirant candidates participated, generating a response rate of 18.5 percent. The surveys asked a wide range of questions from demographic to selection experience to political experience.[7] Census and survey data were combined into a single SPSS dataset.

Interviews

The study also draws upon in-person open-ended interviews with 33 party officials and 2 aspirant candidates and an observation of a single selection contest.[8] The interviews were conducted between 2010 and 2017. Party officials varied from senior central party staff to regional directors. Most interviews with party officials were conducted at the party's headquarters located on Victoria Street in London and at cafes located throughout central London. Two interviews, however, took the author to Newcastle and Liverpool. The author contacted aspirant candidates who indicated their willingness in the survey to participate in an interview. The interviews with aspirant candidates were arranged through email and took place in central London. In addition to interviewing Labour party officials and aspirant candidates, the author interviewed a Conservative party official and two Liberal Democrat party officials at those parties' London-based headquarters.

While the Conservative and Liberal Democrat party officials discussed selection process rules and participants, they were unwilling to release data on aspirant candidates or grant permission to survey aspirant candidates.[9]

Rule books

The study draws upon information from Labour party rule books and the NEC Guidelines for the Selection of Parliamentary Candidates, which provide details of the rules and participants for the candidate selection process. Hard copies of these sources were provided to the author by Labour party officials. The rule books and guidelines make it possible to track changes in selection rules and participants concerning the selection processes under study. Together, the rule books and interviews relay the selection stages and participants are the same for 2001, 2005, and 2010, but, with the elimination of the NPP, differ in 2015.

Labour party selection processes

This section uses statistical information from the previously described census and survey sources to describe the Labour party's selection process. It provides a first look at all aspirant candidates who enter the selection process and how these initial entrants are filtered out of the process at each of the six subsequent stages. As noted in Chapters 1 and 2, the underrepresentation of women, BAME, and disabled people and other social groups in candidate and legislative pools is often presented as a supply-side problem with too few women, BAME, and disabled aspirant candidates coming forward. This conclusion is generally drawn from data on the final stage of the selection process where aspirant candidates are chosen as candidates. While data on the candidate pool reveal who is selected, they seldom reveal who is rejected in the preceding stages. The final selection stage, however, can only be understood as a filter if data on aspirant candidates who began the process (e.g., census data on all aspirant candidates) are compared to data on those who are selected (e.g., data on the final pool of candidates). Comparing aspirant candidate pools at various selection stages reveals how stages filter most aspirant candidates from the process.

Selection stages and filtering

Like all parties, Labour filters a large initial list of aspirants applying to participate in selection contests to a final, much smaller list of candidates to stand in elections. The party uses a selection process with seven distinct but connected stages during the 2001, 2005 and 2010 elections.[10] Each of these seven stages involves different participants and rules, with some stages focused on supply and others demand.

Table 3.1 uses data provided by party officials to provide an overview of Labour's selection process stages for the 2001, 2005, and 2010 General Elections,

Table 3.1 Labour party candidate selection process results (2001, 2005, 2010)

Stage	1 Party Application	pp/%	2 NPP Application	pp/%	3 NPP Approval	pp/%	4¹ Seat Application	pp/%	5¹ Nomination	pp/%	6¹ Shortlisted	pp/%	7¹ Candidate Selection	pp/%
Filter	(S)		(S)		(D)		(S)		(D)		(D)		(D)	
2010	1625	0/0	1580	3/3	1376	12/15	1274	7/22	1058	13/35	966	6/41	636	20/61
2005	1439	0/0	1430	1/1	1259	12/13	976	19/32	859	8/40	793	5/45	633	11/56
2001	1558	0/0	1558	0/0	1209	22/22	na	na	na	na	na	na	639	na/59
Total	4622	0/0	4568	1/1	3844	16/17	na	13/27²	na	10/37²	na	6/43²	1908	16/59²

Notes: Filter: (S) Supply-side filter, (D) Demand-side Filter

¹ = Figures in these columns estimated from 2005 and 2010 survey data. All other figures from census data.

² = These figures are based on 2005 and 2010 data as 2001 data were not available.

with selection process stages for the 2015 General Election discussed separately. Starting with 1) party application and ending with 7) candidate selection, the first row labels the seven selection process stages. The second row indicates the type of filter attached to each stage with stages labelled "S" for supply, where aspirants themselves determine to continue or drop out of the aspirant pool, and "D" for demand, where party selectors shape the aspirant candidate pool by eliminating aspirants from the process. Each stage has an associated pp/% column with the first figure indicating the number of percentage points (pp) by which the aspirant pool declines between each stage, and the second figure indicating the overall percentage (%) of aspirants entering the selection process in Stage 1 having been eliminated.

Stage 1, *party application*, concerns supply as aspirants formally indicate their willingness to seek candidacy by submitting their curricula vitae and applications to the central party's NEC.[11] Applicants must meet minimum statutory require- ments for national office, with the NEC setting clear eligibility rules for candidacy, such as being a member in good standing for 12 continuous months and a member of an affiliated trade union. In 2001, 1588 aspirants applied to become Labour party candidates, with this number decreasing to 1439 in 2005 and increasing to 1625 in 2010, for a total of 4622 aspirant candidates formally entering Stage 1 of the process for these three years. The pp/% is 0/0 as no aspirants have yet been eliminated from the selection process.

Stage 2, *NPP application*, also concerns supply as aspirants submit a second application to the NEC, this time for a position on the NPP, a centrally-screened and pre-approved list of aspirants who "meet an agreed standard, regardless of their gender or ethnic background" distributed to constituency Labour parties (CLPs) for their consideration.[12] As noted, the NPP contains the names of thou- sands of aspirants seeking candidacy.[13] These data are important to monitoring supply and demand by assessing if those who began the process differ in sig- nificant ways from those selected as candidates.[14] In 2001, all aspirants submitted their curricula vitae to the NEC's NPP. In 2005, just 9 of 1439 aspirants (1 percent of the initial aspirant candidate pool as indicated in the pp/% column) failed to submit this second application, with this number increasing to 45 (3 percent) in 2010, for a total of 59 (2 percent) dropping out for the years combined.

Demand-side filters begin with Stage 3, *NPP approval*, when aspirants either receive or are denied the NEC's formal stamp of approval to move forward in the selection process.[15] During this stage, in 2001, only 1209 of 1588 aspirants were approved by the NEC for the NPP – the 349 aspirants eliminated at this stage is a 22-percentage point (pp) drop from the previous stage, with a total of 22 percent (%) of the initial aspirant pool eliminated by Stage 3. In 2005, only 1259 of 1430 aspirants were selected by the NEC to the NPP. The 171 aspir- ants eliminated at this stage equates to a 12-percentage point (pp) decrease from Stage 2, with a total of 13 percent (%) of the overall aspirant pool being reduced by the end of Stage 3. The results were similar in the 2010 process. That the overall pool from both elections was reduced by 12 percentage points represents a considerable reduction of aspirants.

Supply is again a factor at Stage 4, *seat application*, where aspirants either apply for open or All Women Shortlist (AWS) seats as they become available or drop out of the process.[16] This supply-side stage demonstrates a high level of filtering.[17] In 2005, 1259 were eligible to apply for seats, but only 976 applied – a drop of 19 percentage points from Stage 3. The drop of seven percentage points was less dramatic in 2010 when the pool narrowed from 1376 to 1274 aspirants. The overall pool from both elections was reduced from 2635 to 2250 aspirants, a reduction of 13 percentage points, with the overall pool of aspirants reduced by 27 percent by this stage in the selection process.

During Stage 5, *nomination*, representatives from CLPs longlist aspirants at "mini-hustings" meetings. This stage includes equity rules designed to increase the number of included women and BAME aspirants. Rules vary between seat types and election years, with more robust equity rules in place for 2010 selections (Labour Party, 2003, 2006, 2008).[18] The overall aspirant pool drops by an additional 10 percentage points during this demand-side stage – 8 points in 2005 and 13 points in 2010.

Stage 6, *shortlisting*, also concerns demand as local party officials decide which longlisted aspirants make it onto the shortlists to compete in Stage 7 nomination contest votes. Various equity rules were in place during the 2001, 2005, and 2010 contests to increase demand amongst local selectors for women and BAME aspirants in open seats, and in 2005 and 2010 for BAME women in AWS seats.[19] As seen in Table 3.1, the aspirant pool was reduced by 5 percentage points in 2005 and 6 points in 2010, for an overall decrease of 6 percentage points when both years are combined.

In Stage 7, *candidate selection*, local party members vote to determine which shortlisted aspirants will stand as candidates during the general election. In 2005, the pool of aspirants was reduced by 11 percentage points, and 20 percentage points in 2010. The two years combined show a 16-percentage point drop – the largest combined percentage point reduction of the entire process. Overall, tracing the flow of all aspirants through the seven stages of Labour's process reveals the initial pool is reduced by almost 60 percent in the two years examined, from 3064 aspirants applying to become candidates to 1269 standing as Labour candidates in the 2005 and 2010 General Elections combined. These data further establish that the filtering process is closely related to demand-side factors, prompting three tests that are conducted and described in the next section. Before doing so, the selection process for the 2015 General Election is described.

Selections for the 2015 General Election took place without the NPP, the elimination of which is the only formal rule change to the process since the 2010 General Election.[20] Scrapping the NPP not only changed the type of data collected by the central party but also reduced the number of stages from seven to four: 1) party application, 2) nomination, 3) shortlisting, and 4) selection. Although there are no longer census data with which to trace the filtering process for all aspirant candidates, as was done for previous elections, the party data on a sample of 164 seats tells a story similar to the one played out in 2001, 2005, and 2010, with aspirant filtering taking place at the nomination, shortlisting, and selection stages and thus connected to demand-side stages.

By removing the NPP, Stage 1) party application now involves aspirants directly submitting their curricula vitae and application to the Procedures Secretary of the seat for which they are seeking. The Procedures Secretary meets with branch representatives to sift through the aspirants' curricula vitae and applications. At Stage 2) nomination, the branch nominations are boiled down to a longlist by the local Selection Committee.[21] As in 2010, there are equity rules in place at the nomination and shortlisting stages in both open and AWS seats; for example, in open seats they are required to nominate at least one man and one woman, but as a Labour party official notes, "they already know who they want".[22] At Stage 3) shortlisting, the Selection Committee reduces the longlist into a shortlist. According to another Labour party official, for 2015, "some committees in open seats make an effort to longlist and shortlist women but many don't. Most will only have the minimum number of women, one, on the longlist. They'll say 'we can't find more' – and this is where the NPP came in handy. It's a list of pre-approved women, qualified women".[23] Finally, at Stage 4), the shortlist goes to the membership for a candidate vote.[24]

Reasons for getting rid of the NPP include lack of resources – "it was time consuming and took too many people to properly implement".[25] Still, interviews with party officials following the 2015 General Election reveal concern with its removal and desire to bring it back on grounds it not only screened out "undesirables" but also provided a centrally maintained list or "supply" of pre-endorsed and qualified aspirant women from which local parties could choose, thereby weakening the argument "we'd like to select women but they don't come forward".[26] Without the NPP, the diversity of aspirants is no longer fully centrally monitored, making it much more difficult to assess if women and other underrepresented groups are getting passed up over men and if so at which stage, and, if needed, to recommend policies to address descriptive underrepresentation.[27]

Table 3.2 contains data needed to perform two tests: 1) the candidate surplus/ deficit test, and 2) the supply-side test for selections in the lead-up to the 2001, 2005, 2010, and 2015 General Elections. Column headings are explained before describing the tests and results. Data in the first seven columns are used for the candidate surplus/deficit test. The first column, *groups*, labels the main social groups explored in this study: women and men, BAME and non-BAME, and disabled and non-disabled aspirant candidates. The second column, *year*, indicates data on these groups are available for the election years under study. The third column, *actual candidates (#)*, is the number of candidates the Labour party fielded for each election year. For example, in 2015, 632 candidates were selected and 215 of these candidates were women. The fourth column, *actual candidates (%)*, reflects the percentage of all candidate positions held by each group. As shown, in 2015 women made up 34 percent of the party's candidate pool.

The fifth column, *expected candidates (#)*, calculates the number of candidacies each group would receive if they progressed on the basis of their representation in the general population.[28] For example, in 2015 women comprised just over

Table 3.2 Labour party's selection process

Groups	Year	Candidate Surplus/Deficit Test					Supply-Side Test	
		Actual Candidates (#)	Actual Candidates (%)	Expected Candidates (#)	Expected Candidates (%)	Candidate Surplus/Deficit	All Aspirants	Surplus Aspirants
All	2015	632	100%	632	100%	0%	1286	654
	2010	636	100%	636	100%	0%	1625	989
	2005	633	100%	633	100%	0%	1439	806
	2001	639	100%	639	100%	0%	1558	919
Women	2015	215	34%	322	51%	-17%	455	133
	2010	198	31%	324	51%	-20%	473	149
	2005	170	27%	323	51%	-24%	428	105
	2001	148	23%	326	51%	-28%	406	80
Men	2015	416	66%	310	49%	17%	831	521
	2010	438	69%	312	49%	20%	1152	840
	2005	463	73%	310	49%	24%	1011	701
	2001	491	77%	313	49%	28%	1152	839
BAME	2015	44	7%	82	13%	-6%	364	282
	2010	54	8%	76	12%	-4%	265	189
	2005	30	5%	63	10%	-5%	207	144
	2001	23	4%	51	8%	-4%	181	130
Non-BAME	2015	588	93%	550	87%	6%	894	344
	2010	582	92%	560	88%	4%	1360	800
	2005	603	95%	570	90%	5%	1232	662
	2001	616	96%	588	92%	4%	1377	789
Disabled	2015	5	1%	64	10%	-9%	57	52
	2010	14	2%	64	10%	-8%	68	4
	2005	7	1%	63	10%	-9%	36	-27
Non-Disabled	2015	627	99%	567	90%	9%	1229	661
	2010	622	98%	572	90%	8%	1557	985
	2005	626	99%	570	90%	9%	1403	833

Note: Discrepancy in figures due to rounding.

half of the general population, therefore their proportionate share of candidacies is just over half: 322 of 632. The sixth column, *expected candidates (%)*, calculates a group's proportionate share of candidacies as a percentage. Drawing again from the same case, in 2015, women would be expected to be 51 percent of the party's candidacies.

The seventh column, *candidate surplus/deficit*, is the first key test used in this study to determine whether a particular group is over- or underrepresented in the party's candidate pool in proportion to their representation in the general population. To do so, the percentage of actual candidates is subtracted from the expected percentage of candidates. For example, in 2015, at 34 percent, women fell 17 percentage points short of holding their proportional share (51 percent) of party candidacies.

The data presented in the last two columns of Table 3.2 are used to perform supply-side tests. The *all aspirants* column shows the total supply of aspirant candidates formally indicating a willingness to pursue a candidacy. In 2015, the total supply of women aspirant candidates is 455, whereas the total supply of men is 831. At first glance it appears the deficit of women in the party's candidate pool is due to supply, given there are almost two times as many men aspirant candidates. The last column, *surplus aspirants*, simply subtracts all aspirants from deserved candidates (#) to calculate whether there is an undersupply or an oversupply of aspirant candidates. Supply-side tests reveal, for example, that in 2015 there is a surplus of 133 women aspirant candidates. In other words, not only are there enough women aspirant candidates to fill half of the candidacies, but there is an oversupply. The test results for each group and all years are next explained, beginning with women aspirant candidates.

Turning to results, in terms of women, the candidate surplus/deficit test shows for all years women receive a smaller proportion of candidacies than proportionality suggests, but the deficit is declining, likely due to more robust equity policies from one year to the next. In 2001, there was a 28-percentage point deficit for women. In 2005 the deficit dropped to 24 percentage points, in 2010 it dropped to 20 percentage points, and in 2015 it dropped to 17 percentage points. These results show the selection process disproportionately filters out women aspirant candidates. However, these tests cannot determine why these deficits occur or whether they are due more to supply-side or demand-side problems.

The supply-side test shows that in all four years under study there was a surplus of women aspirant candidates and, with the exception of 2015, the surplus grew from one year to the next – from 80 to 105 to 149 to in 2001, 2005, and 2010, respectively. One possible explanation as to why fewer women threw their hats into the ring in 2015 is the growing perception that their best chance of winning is in AWS seats – given this, if only open seats are available within proximity to where they live, they are less inclined to put their names forward.[29] As explored in more detail in Chapter 7, open seats are increasingly perceived by women and men aspirants and by local party selectors as all men shortlists.[30] Overall, these results are extremely important, as they show the deficit of Labour women candidates is not caused by an undersupply of women aspirant candidates. More than enough women enter the selection process to fill more than 51 percent of the party's candidacies. The candidate surplus/deficit test results for men are mirror opposite of those for women, and the supply-side tests indicate almost a six- to ten-fold surplus compared to women.

In terms of BAME aspirant candidates, the surplus/deficit test for all years shows this group consistently receives a smaller percentage of candidacies than expected. In 2001, the deficit was 4 percentage points, in 2005 it dropped to 5 percentage points, in 2010, it returned to 4 percentage points, and in 2015 it hit a low of 6 percentage points. As is the case for women, these test results indicate the selection process disproportionately filters BAME aspirant candidates, but the tests do not determine if the results are due to supply- or demand-side factors.

Supply-side tests reveal a surplus of BAME aspirant candidates in all four years, with the surplus growing from 130 in 2001 to 144 in 2005, 189 in 2010 to a high of 282 in 2015. The remarkable increase in the supply of BAME aspirants in 2015 may be a result of the party's BAME equity quotas at the nomination and shortlisting stages as well as ramped up internal campaigns led by MPs such as Diane Abbott to implement ABS and external campaigns by Operation Black Vote to encourage BAME people to run.

Overall, the results reveal the deficit of BAME aspirant candidates is not due to an under-supply – in other words, there are more than enough BAME aspirant candidates to fill their expected share of candidacies. The candidate surplus/deficit test results for non-BAME aspirant candidates are mirror opposite of those for BAME aspirant candidates, and the supply-side tests reveal an almost six- to ten-fold surplus compared to BAME aspirant candidates.

In terms of disabled aspirant candidates, the surplus/deficit test shows for the three years for which there are data (2005, 2010, and 2015), they receive a smaller percentage of candidacies than expected. In 2005, the deficit was 9 percentage points, in 2010 it was 8 percentage points, and in 2015, it returned to 9 percentage points. The supply-side tests for disabled aspirant candidates are somewhat surprising. In 2005, there was a 27 aspirant supply deficit of disabled aspirant candidates – indicating a vast under-supply of disabled aspirant candidates seeking candidacy. However, in 2010 this supply deficit becomes a surplus of 4, and in 2015 the surplus of disabled aspirants jumps to 57. The candidate surplus/deficit test results for non-disabled are mirror opposite of those for non-disabled aspirant candidates, and the supply-side tests reveal an almost eight- to ten-fold surplus compared to non-disabled aspirant candidates.

These data and tests reveal two key findings: 1) women, BAME, and disabled aspirant candidates are disproportionately underrepresented in the candidate pool compared to men, non-BAME, and non-disabled aspirant candidates; and 2) with the exception of disabled aspirant candidates in 2005, the underrepresentation of women, BAME, and disabled aspirant candidates is not obviously due to supply-side factors. These findings provide grounds to further explore and test demand-side hypotheses associated with underrepresentation in later chapters. The next section provides filter tests to determine the degree to which women, BAME, and disabled aspirant candidates are filtered out as they pass through multiple stages of the candidate selection process.

Exploring filtering by sex, race, and physical ability

This section explores the extent to which this filtering may disproportionately affect the fortunes of women, BAME, and disabled aspirant candidates with later regression testing the influence 41 other independent variables have upon selection outcomes.[31] Selections for 2001, 2005, and 2010 General Elections are discussed first, followed by a separate discussion of selections for the 2015 General Election.

Sex

Starting with sex, Table 3.3 demonstrates how men and women aspirant candidates fare in each of the seven Labour selection stages for the 2001, 2005, and 2010 General Elections. "Total" is the total number of aspirants entering a stage in either 2001, 2005, or 2010. The number of men or women aspirants is indicated, along with the percentage of the stage aspirant pool. The +/- column simply subtracts the percentage of each category for the current stage from the subsequent stage to indicate the extent to which the group gained or lost during filtering. For example, in 2010, women were 29 percent of the aspirants and men were 71 percent of the aspirants in Stage 1, and respectively 29 percent and 71 percent of the aspirants progressing to Stage 2. This shows that while the overall pool of aspirants was reduced, it was reduced proportionally for each group in this instance. The final three columns show the overall trend by totalling data from 2001, 2005, and 2010.

In terms of the year by year picture, in 2010, women began the selection process by forming 29 percent of the aspirant pool but finishing with a 31 percent share and an increase of 2 percentage points. This indicates the process did not disproportionally filter women – rather the opposite is the case, especially during Stages 3, 4, and 5, where the central party exerts the most control over the process. The only stage in which women were disproportionately filtered out of the process was at Stage 7, where local selectors were more inclined to select men (+2 percent). The 2005 selection process tells a somewhat similar story, where women comprised 34 percent of Stage 6 participants, but they dropped to 27 percent of Stage 7 participants. Missing data for 2001 makes it difficult to exactly pinpoint where this reduction occurs – but it would appear to occur at the final selection stage. Overall, local party selectors were extremely punishing to women aspirant candidates in Stage 7, where their share of the pool was reduced from 34 percent to 27 percent – a drop of 7 percentage points.

Table 3.3 Labour party selection process filtering (sex)

Stage	Group	2010	%	+/−	2005	%	+/−	2001	%	+/−	Total	%	+/−
	Total	1625			1439			1558			4622		
1 (S)	Men	1152	*71%*		1011	*70%*		1152	*74%*		3315	*72%*	
	Women	473	*29%*		428	*30%*		406	*26%*		1307	*28%*	
	Total	1580			1430			1558			4568		
2 (S)	Men	1119	*71%*	0%	1005	*70%*	0%	1152	*74%*	0%	3276	*72%*	0%
	Women	461	*29%*	0%	425	*30%*	0%	406	*26%*	0%	1292	*28%*	0%
	Total	1376			1259			1209			3844		
3 (D)	Men	959	*70%*	−1%	884	*70%*	0%	887	*73%*	−1%	2730	*71%*	−1%
	Women	417	*30%*	1%	375	*30%*	0%	322	*27%*	1%	1114	*29%*	1%
	Total	1274			976			*n/a*	*n/a*		2254		
4 (S)	Men	883	*69%*	0%	665	*68%*	−2%	*n/a*	*n/a*	n/a	1548	*69%*	−2%
	Women	389	*31%*	1%	315	*32%*	2%	*n/a*	*n/a*	n/a	704	*31%*	2%
	Total	1058			859			*n/a*	*n/a*	n/a	1922		
5 (D)	Men	722	*68%*	−1%	573	*67%*	−1%	*n/a*	*n/a*	n/a	1295	*67%*	−2%
	Women	335	*32%*	1%	291	*34%*	2%	*n/a*	*n/a*	n/a	626	*33%*	2%
	Total	966			793			*n/a*	*n/a*	n/a	1818		
6 (D)	Men	650	*67%*	−1%	530	*67%*	0%	*n/a*	*n/a*	n/a	1220	*67%*	0%
	Women	314	*32%*	0%	266	*34%*	0%	*n/a*	*n/a*	n/a	598	*33%*	0%
	Total	636			633			639		n/a	1908		
7 (D)	Men	438	*69%*	2%	463	*73%*	6%	491	*77%*	n/a	1392	*73%*	6%
	Women	198	*31%*	−1%	170	*27%*	−7%	148	*23%*	n/a	516	*27%*	−7%

Note: Discrepancy in figures due to rounding.

Race

Turning to race in Table 3.4, BAME aspirants start as 16 percent of the overall pool in Stage 1 in 2010 (higher than this group's 12 percent share of the 2010 population) and remain at this level until Stage 7, where local selectors disproportionally filter BAME aspirants, prompting a decline of 7 percentage points from Stage 6 (UK National Statistics, 2014). In 2005, when the UK BAME population was 10 percent, BAME aspirants formed 14 percent of the overall pool (UK National Statistics, 2014). However, this proportion drops one or two percentage points during each stage – with BAME aspirants' share of the aspirant candidate pool dropping by nine percentage points, overall.

Physical ability

Table 3.5 moves to testing how disabled aspirant candidates move through the Labour party candidate selection process. Lack of available data did not allow for 2001 calculations.

The last column shows there is only slight disproportionately between disabled aspirant candidates at successive stages, and only then in Stage 7 when local

Table 3.4 Labour party selection process filtering (race)

Stage	Group	2010	%	+/-	2005	%	+/-	2001	%	+/-	Total	%	+/-
1 (S)	Total	1625			1439			1558			4622		
	BAME	265	16%		207	14%		181	12%		653	14%	
	Non-BAME	1360	84%		1232	86%		1377	88%		3969	86%	
2 (S)	Total	1580			1430			1558			4568		
	BAME	255	16%	0%	207	14%	0%	181	12%	0%	643	14%	0%
	Non-BAME	1325	84%	0%	1223	86%	0%	1377	88%	0%	3925	86%	0%
3 (D)	Total	1376			1259			1209			3844		
	BAME	201	15%	-1%	155	12%	-2%	109	9%	-3%	465	12%	-2%
	Non-BAME	1175	85%	1%	1104	88%	2%	1100	91%	3%	3379	88%	2%
4 (S)	Total	1274			976			n/a	n/a		2250		
	BAME	207	16%	1%	96	10%	-2%	n/a	n/a	n/a	303	13%	1%
	Non-BAME	1067	84%	-1%	880	90%	2%	n/a	n/a	n/a	1947	87%	-1%
5 (D)	Total	1058			859			n/a	n/a	n/a	1917		
	BAME	157	15%	-1%	67	8%	-2%	n/a	n/a	n/a	224	12%	-1%
	Non-BAME	902	85%	1%	792	92%	2%	n/a	n/a	n/a	1694	88%	1%
6 (D)	Total	966			793			n/a	n/a	n/a	1759		
	BAME	141	15%	0%	59	7%	-1%	n/a	n/a	n/a	200	11%	-1%
	Non-BAME	827	85%	0%	733	93%	1%	n/a	n/a	n/a	1560	89%	1%
7 (D)	Total	636			633			639		n/a	1908		
	BAME	54	8%	-7%	30	5%	-2%	23	4%	n/a	107	6%	-5%
	Non-BAME	582	92%	7%	603	95%	2%	616	96%	n/a	1801	94%	5%

Note: Discrepancy in figures due to rounding.

selection contests occur. As would be expected, 2010 and 2005 deviate little from the total column. However, it is worth noting that in 2010 the percentage of participants with disabilities is reduced by half from 4 percent in Stage 6 to 2 percent in Stage 7. Moreover, people with disabilities make up 10 percent of the population, but only 3 to 4 percent of the initial applicant pools and, as shown, between 1 to 2 percent of the final candidate pools. Thus, disabled aspirant candidates are disproportionately filtered out at the final selection stage, and they do not secure their expected share of seats.

In combination, these selections show that although most filtering occurs during Stages 3 (12 percentage point reduction of the overall pool over both years during NPP approval), 4 (13 percentage point reduction during seat application), 5 (10 percentage point reduction during nomination), and 7 (16 point reduction during candidate selection), those controlled by the central party (Stages 3 and 5) are fair when it comes to how women, BAME, and disabled aspirants are eliminated as compared to men, white, and non-disabled aspirants. As noted, this is likely due to the central party's use of equity rules at the nomination and shortlisting stages.

Table 3.5 Labour party selection process filtering (physical ability)

Stage	Group	2010	%	+/−	2005	%	+/−	Total	%	+/−
1 (S)	Total	1625			1439			3064		
	Disabled	68	4%		36	3%		104	3%	
	Non-Disabled	1557	96%		1403	97%		2960	97%	
2 (S)	Total	1580			1430			3010		
	Disabled	65	4%	0%	36	3%	0%	101	3%	0%
	Non-Disabled	1515	96%	0%	1394	97%	0%	2909	97%	0%
3 (D)	Total	1376			1259			2635		
	Disabled	49	4%	0%	28	2%	−1%	77	3%	0%
	Non-Disabled	1327	96%	0%	1231	98%	1%	2558	97%	0%
4 (S)	Total	1274			976			2250		
	Disabled	50	4%	0%	21	2%	0%	71	3%	0%
	Non-Disabled	1227	96%	0%	961	98%	0%	2187	97%	0%
5 (D)	Total	1058			859			1917		
	Disabled	42	4%	0%	15	2%	0%	57	3%	0%
	Non-Disabled	1018	96%	0%	854	98%	0%	1872	97%	0%
6 (D)	Total	966			793			1759		
	Disabled	37	4%	0%	15	2%	0%	52	3%	0%
	Non-Disabled	932	96%	0%	785	99%	0%	1707	97%	0%
7 (D)	Total	636			633			1269		
	Disabled	14	2%	−2%	7	1%	−1%	21	2%	−1%
	Non-Disabled	622	98%	2%	626	98%	1%	1248	98%	1%

Note: Discrepancy in figures due to rounding.

While the overall high level of filtering in Stage 4 can be attributed to some aspirants perceiving the application process as overly daunting, it can also be explained by aspirants feeling discouraged from competing against emergent local star frontrunners whose applications are touted by party leaders, activists, and local media. However, as shown, this drop-out rate is more or less even for the various groups, thus eliminating the need to further examine this supply-side stage for bias.

Data demonstrate the most filtering and imbalance between groups occurs during the selection process Stage 7, when local party selectors choose their candidate from a final list of aspirants. While imbalance between men and women is limited in 2010 and between BAME and non-BAME aspirants in 2005, women in 2005 and BAME aspirants in 2010 would seem at an extreme disadvantage. As such, Stage 7 is examined in more detail in Chapter 7.

2015 selections

Table 3.6 describes the selection process for the 2015 General Election by sex, race, and ability for each of the four stages: application, nomination, shortlisting, and selection. As a reminder, these party data are for 164 seats fully monitored by the central party.

Table 3.6 Filtering by sex, race, and disability (2015)

Stage	Group	2015 %	+/−	Group	2015 %	+/−	Group	2015 %	+/−
1 (S)	Total	1286		Total	1251		Total	1286	
	Women	455 *35%*		BAME	364 *29%*		Disabled	57 *4%*	
	Men	837 *65%*		Non-BAME	887 *71%*		Non-disabled	1229 *96%*	
2 (D)	Total	669		Total	662		Total	669	
	Women	264 *39%*	+4%	BAME	170 *26%*	−3%	Disabled	34 *5%*	+1%
	Men	405 *61%*	−4%	Non-BAME	492 *74%*	+3%	Non-disabled	635 *95%*	−1%
3 (D)	Total	509		Total	502		Total	509	
	Women	211 *41%*	+2%	BAME	99 *20%*	−6%	Disabled	23 *5%*	0%
	Men	298 *59%*	−2%	Non-BAME	403 *80%*	+6%	Non-disabled	486 *95%*	0%
4 (D)	Total	164		Total	157		Total	164	
	Women	104 *37%*	−4%	BAME	44 *28%*	−8%	Disabled	5 *3%*	−2%
	Men	60 *63%*	−4%	Non-BAME	113 *72%*	+8%	Non-disabled	159 *97%*	+2%

Note: Discrepancy due to rounding.

The overall 2015 findings presented in Table 3.6 are somewhat similar to selection outcomes for the 2001, 2005, and 2010 General Elections insofar that women, BAME, and aspirants with disabilities are more disproportionately filtered out at stages controlled by local party selectors than at stages where the central party exerts some influence. In other words, women, BAME, and aspirants with disabilities are not disproportionately filtered out at stages where the central party has in place equity rules – Stages 2, nomination and 3, shortlisting, rather, they are nominated and shortlisted in slightly higher proportions than men and white aspirants. However, compared to previous elections, women, BAME, and aspirants with disabilities are more disproportionately filtered at the final selection stage, where local members are the least constrained by the central party and its equity rules. For example, in 2015, the percentage of women aspirants was reduced by 4 percentage points between Stage 3, shortlisting and Stage 4, selection compared to 2010, when the percentage of women was reduced by 1 percentage point between the shortlisting and selection stages. This result could be connected to the removal of the NPP, which has made it more difficult for the central party to monitor all seats' selection process stages and to maintain neutrality or boost certain groups at all stages. In turn, local members are in a better position to select whomever they want with more leeway to disregard those aspirants they were obliged by equity rules to longlist and shortlist.[32]

Conclusion

Before proceeding, it is important to stress the extent to which these data undermine the idea that Labour has a supply-side problem when it comes to recruiting women and BAME candidates. In 2015, 455 women applied to fill 632 Labour party candidacies, and in 2010, 473 women applied to fill 636 Labour party candidacies – a surplus of 133 and 149, respectively, which is more than the party needed to ensure women secured 51 percent of candidacies equal to their proportion of the population. In 2005, Labour had a surplus of 105 women aspirant candidates. Instead of reallocating the women aspirant candidate surplus to ensure a gender-balanced candidate pool, Labour party selectors decided to let them go. This may provide some insight into why the Party did not reach its target of 50 percent women in its Parliamentary Labour Party (PLP) even after appointing half of its target seats as AWS seats.

The same holds true for BAME candidates. In 2015, 364 BAME community members applied to the Labour party candidacies, and in 2010, 265 BAME aspirants did the same. The Party only required 82 BAME aspirants in 2015 and 76 BAME aspirants in 2010 to be nominated so as to ensure the BAME aspirant candidate pool reflected its proportion of the population (12 percent) – whopping surpluses of 282 and 189 BAME aspirants. In 2005, Labour wasted a 144 BAME aspirant candidate surplus even though this social group was underrepresented in the overall candidate pool.

Labour had many more women and BAME aspirant candidates, and in 2015, more disabled aspirants than it needed to ensure these groups secured a fair proportion of candidacies.[33] If the selection process was re-structured to favour, as opposed to disadvantage, women, BAME, and disabled aspirants, Labour could ensure these two groups secured a fair share of candidacies without recruiting a single additional aspirant candidate. In other words, supply need not be a primary issue for Labour in terms of reaching its goal of running descriptively representative candidate slates. Instead, the party should focus more on demand-side problems, particularly in the final candidate selection process stage. With this in mind, the next chapters more deeply explore the Labour party's multistage selection process and demand-side dynamics.

Notes

1 The author agreed to protect the Labour Party's NPP data and received data protection authorisation to use Labour party data for the purposes of her research. The terms of the agreement are as follows: "This data is supplied for the sole purpose as agreed. To support ongoing research undertaken by the named researcher as well as data for the British Representation Study as allowed under the Data Protection Registration of the Labour Party 2012. You must ensure that you comply with your legal obligations in terms of handling and using this personal data under the Data Protection Act 1998. You must not: (a) supply a copy of this data to any other person or organisation, (b) disclose the information contained in it, or (c) make use of this information, otherwise than for the purpose you've been provided it for set out above. You must therefore: (d) delete this membership data after using it for this purpose; (e) if you use the email addresses, ensure you send any group email blind carbon copy to prevent inadvertently disclosing email addresses to the other recipients of the email".

2 It also fully monitors 27 key and retirement AWS seats, and 31 key and retirement open seats.

3 Interview with a Labour party official, 2017.

4 Interview with a Labour party official, 2017.

5 The 2010 survey was a part of the 2010 British Representation Study with professors Rosie Campbell, Sarah Childs, and Joni Lovenduski.

6 The surveys were sent using Survey Monkey, www.surveymonkey.com/

7 See the Appendix for the survey questions.

8 The author observed a selection contest in Liverpool Walton for the 2010 General Election.

9 The interviews ranged in length from one hour to three hours and were recorded and transcribed by the author.

10 The seven selection stages and the actors and rules at each stage were identified during interviews with Labour party officials and reviews of Labour's parliamentary selection rule books.

11 The NEC is the administrative authority of the party with the power to modify selection rules and procedures.

12 Interview with a Labour party official. A CLP is comprised of a General Committee, Executive Committee, Branch Labour Party (BLP), and organisations that affiliate to the BLP (trade unions and socialist societies), as well as a young labour group, ethnic minority's forum, and women's forum.

13 Aspirants are encouraged but are not required to apply to the NPP; however, most aspirants do apply. Those who do not apply have often left their applications too late in the process to go through this initial screening process. If this is the case, and they are selected, the Party can choose or choose not to retroactively endorse them (Interview with a Labour party official).

14 That the Party eliminated the NPP after the 2010 election makes these data all the rarer (Interview with senior Labour party official).

15 The NEC seeks aspirants with party experience, campaigning skills, and policy knowledge.

16 For the seat application, nomination, and shortlisting stages, examples are given for 2005 and 2010 as only estimates are available for 2001. Both men and women are eligible to apply to open seats; however, only women are eligible to apply to AWS seats. For the 2005 election, 30 of the Party's seats were AWS. This increased to 63 in 2010. AWS were first used for the 1997 General Election to create an artificial demand amongst local party selectors for women and have been used since, except 2001, due to an Industrial Tribunal ruling against them. This was reversed in 2002 when the Labour government passed the Sex Discrimination (Election Candidates) Bill permitting all parties to use AWS. To date, only Labour uses AWS.

17 To note, many aspirants apply to more than one seat, and some apply for as many as 10.

18 In open seats, local party branches make three nominations, up one from 2005, with at least one woman aspirant and at least one BAME aspirant where at least one woman and one BAME aspirant express an interest. In AWS, party branches submit the names of up to two women, up one from 2005, with at least one BAME woman if at least one BAME woman expressed an interest in the seat. In 2005, branches were not obligated to nominate a BAME woman.

19 In open seats, 2010 local party shortlists had a minimum of six aspirants (up from 4 from 2005), a minimum of 50 percent women aspirants, and if one BAME aspirant applied, at least one BAME aspirant was shortlisted (this was not a rule in 2005). In AWS, a minimum of six women are shortlisted (up from four in 2005), with at least one being a BAME woman where at least one BAME woman applied (this was not a rule in 2005).

20 Interview with a Labour party official, 2016.

21 The Selection Committee is made up of eight to ten members and the Procedures Secretary.

22 Interview with a Labour party official, 2017.
23 Interview with a Labour party official, 2017.
24 Interview with a Labour party official, 2017.
25 Interview with a Labour party official, 2017.
26 Interview with a Labour party official, 2016.
27 Interview with a Labour party official, 2016.
28 The numbers and percentages are drawn from the UK Office for National Statistics (2005, 2010, 2015).
29 Interview with a Labour party official, 2016.
30 Interview with a Labour party official, 2016.
31 The author is aware of the limitations of binary divisions between man and woman and white and non-white. Fulsome intersectional testing is limited by the party data collected which are "additive", for example, woman "plus" BAME people (see Bowleg, 2008). Although not explicitly intersectional, later regression testing controls for the effect of select sets of 44 variables.
32 Interview with a Labour party official, 2016.
33 Questions of merit do not come into play here as these pre-endorsed aspirants have already been vetted by party officials for a place on the NPP (Interview with a Labour party official; see Campbell et al, 2018; Murray, 2014).

4 Centralisation and the Labour party's candidate selection process

In the lead-up to any British General Election, the media and social media are awash with stories exposing central party interference in Labour party selection contests across the country. Falkirk and Liverpool Walton were already noted as examples. Others include Ashfield, where its Constituency Labour party (CLP) became publicly outraged when the party's NEC imposed AWS and parachuted in then Prime Minister Tony Blair's favourite TV personality, Gloria de Piero. The Ashfield case is far from unique, with CLPs frequently airing their discontent with central party intrusion in what they have long regarded as their area of sole jurisdiction.

Such cases suggest the type of aspirant candidate who survives the selection process to become the official candidate is influenced by the degree to which selection processes are *centralised*. Centralisation has two key components: *participants* and *rules*. The key consideration concerning *participants* is the extent to which central party agents (e.g., the party leader, the PLP, the General Secretary [GS], official party staff, and the NEC) as opposed to local party agents (e.g., CLP nominating bodies, GC, and party members) decide which aspirants candidates progress through the various selection process stages. On the other hand, the key consideration regarding selection process *rules* is the extent to which these rules constrain the choices of participants – mainly local party agents (Gallagher, 1988b, p. 236; Norris and Lovenduski, 1995, pp. 198–203; Rahat, 2001; Ware, 1996, pp. 261–288).

After explaining the concept of centralisation, this chapter reviews how other authors classify and categorise the party's selection process, then traces the evolution of the British Labour party's selection process in the lead-up to the elections explored here. The chapter treats each aspect of centralisation – participants and rules – as an independent variable and proceeds with the hypothesis that centralisation leads to fairer selection outcomes in that more centralised stages and processes reduce the likelihood that women, non-BAME, and disabled aspirant candidates will be disproportionately filtered out of the candidate selection process. British Labour party data are then used to test the centralisation hypotheses in Chapter 5.

The scholarship reveals two important findings. First, evaluations of centralisation tend to focus on participants and ignore how rules constrain choice. Second, as has been stressed in earlier chapters, many authors examining the British Labour party's selection process also tend to overlook early selection stages. Rather, some classify the entire selection process in terms of evaluations of the final selection stage where local party members choose their candidate from a shortlist. As noted, using only data from the final selection stage to classify the entire system and focusing upon individual party members has led to problematically classifying the British Labour party's selection process as "decentralised", thereby down-playing any centralising features found in other stages (Bille, 2001, pp. 365–367; Caul, 1999, pp. 85–95; Katz and Mair, 1992; Katz and Mair, 2002; Lundell, 2004, pp. 31–44; Norris and Lovenduski, 1995; Rahat, 2007, pp. 162–165; Scarrow, Webb, and Farrell, 2000). There is a case to re-examine the participants *and* rules at multiple stages and to re-classify the process.

Scholarly accounts of centralisation and the Labour party candidate selection process

This and the next chapter explore the relationship between the success of non-ideal aspirant candidate types (dependent variable) and the degree to which a party organisation's selection process is centralised (independent variable). Arguments concerning the relationship between descriptive representation and centralisation suggest more centralised selection processes result in higher rates of candidacy for women and other underrepresented groups, such as BAME and disabled people (Caul, 1999; Gallagher, 1988a, pp. 13–14; Rahat, 2007, p. 157). This positive rela-tionship finds support in the literature, with some arguing that party leaders and other national party agencies often positively respond to pressure for greater num-bers of women, BAME, and disabled people by engaging informal practices and implementing equality rules to counter a demonstrated lack of demand amongst local party selectors (Gallagher, 1988a, pp. 13–14; Caul, 1999, pp. 80–81; Mat-land and Studlar, 1996; Pruysers and Cross, 2016; Rahat, 2007, p. 158).

As shown, scholars examining aspirant candidate selection generally base their work on macro and meso level evaluations. In other words, they examine electoral systems or party systems to determine why some types of aspirant candidates are more often selected. In contrast, this study follows the work of others who sug-gest it is also useful to evaluate the fate of aspirant candidates by looking at micro level factors, as candidate selection is largely determined by central and local par-ticipants at various stages of the selection process (Norris, 1997a, pp. 1–2). Deci-sions taken by different participants at the different stages of selection ultimately reduce the aspirant candidate pool at each successive stage, thereby narrowing the aspirant candidate pools from which local party selectors, and ultimately the electorate, eventually choose. With the exception of the primary system used in the United States, most liberal democracies provide little in the way of state regu-lation regarding how parties choose candidates, leaving them relatively free to establish the procedures and rules regarding who selects candidates (central or local party agents) and how they are selected (equality rules that constrain their behaviour or no equality rules).[1]

The candidate selection process continues to be at the heart of all struggles between the central and local parties, as whoever controls selection controls the party (Ostrogorsksi, 1902). There are several perspectives on who controls the selection process. According to Ranney (1965), the most common pattern is selection by local parties under the supervision of the central party agencies (pp. 82–83). Epstein (1980) argues "oligarchical control over candidate selection is usual but is not always managed in the same way" (p. 225). In this sense scholars recognise how the central party wields at least some power over the process. As noted, centralisation, "the distribution of control over decision making within the party hierarchy" (Kittilson, 2010, p. 159), is normally assessed by determining if the main selector is a central or local party agent (Norris and Lovenduski, 1995, p. 4). Thus, party organisations where central party agencies play a key role are typically classified as centralised – with countries like Israel often viewed as having the most centralised party selection processes. Party organisations where constituency level agents dominate the selection process tend to be classified as decentralised – with the United States often cited as having one of the most decentralised candidate selection processes (Rahat, 2007; Norris and Lovenduski, 1995, p. 199). Party selection processes in most liberal democracies, however, fall between these two extremes and are not often easily identified as centralised or decentralised (see Gallagher, 1988a, p. 4; Ware, 1996, p. 262). In Britain, for example, scholars identify both central party agents and local party agents as playing important roles in party selection processes (Rahat, 2007, p. 162). As shown later, some of these scholars, confusingly, tend to describe this mixed-system as decentralised.

Recent efforts by parties to increase the number of party members and operatives in selection processes also emphasise the need to include the role played by formal *rules* in any assessment of selection process centralisation. According to the literature, a trend amongst many modern Western European parties is the adoption of more participatory selection processes, at least at the final stage of selection (Rahat, 2007, pp. 162–163). As noted, as parties move to allow more party members to vote in the final stage of the selection process they tend to add, paradoxically, more rules to constrain their local selectors' choices, as local and central party preferences are not always coterminous. For example, failing to implement constraints upon local party choices makes it challenging for the central party to achieve an electoral objective, where there is one, to increase the proportion of women aspirant candidates over local party objectives to select their "local son" (Rahat, 2007, p. 167). Thus extending the right to participate in the selection process to more or to all party members can create an *illusion of decentralisation* when in fact centralising features are present (Rahat, 2007, pp. 163–167; see also Pruysers and Cross, 2016).[2] In British parties, for example, historically selection processes were exclusive to only a handful of central and local party committees, with the role of individual party members relatively limited, almost non-existent. When the British Labour party opened up the selection process by allowing individual party members to vote in selection contests, it simultaneously centralised the process by implementing more equity rules (e.g., quotas for women and BAME aspirant candidates) to constrain local selector behaviour.

Although still somewhat controversial, quotas afford parties a "fast track" as opposed to an incremental approach to increase the representation of women and other groups (Dahlerup, 2013, p. 6; Hughes, Paxton, and Clayton, 2019). Quotas are increasingly accepted by parties as a pragmatic electoral strategy; competitively, centralisation affords party organisations a strategic incentive to capitalise upon the electoral voting gender gap whereby women voters support women candidates and the general electorate slightly prefer women candidates (Dahlerup, 2006; Russell, 2005, pp. 111–112; Ware, 1996, p. 9; Quota Project, 2019). In line with this reasoning, to varying extents parties are increasingly willing to consider and implement equality rules to bolster the number of women in their candidate pools in exchange for votes, even if this means placing constraints on local party agents. As it stands, over 51 countries now use voluntary party quotas for women – including the British Labour party – and over 30 countries use quotas for ethnic minorities; however, to date, few use quotas for disabled people (Dahlerup, 2013; IDEA, 2019; Bird, 2003, 2014).[3]

There is some unease within the academic community about classifying the Labour party selection process, even though most authors agree it is "decentralised". This nervousness often plays out in the decision to not incorporate the multistage nature of the selection process and rules used by the party to constrain the choices of local selectors. In influential early studies of the Labour party's selection process, Ostrogorski (1902) and McKenzie (1963) emphasise "who selects" aspirant candidates and "how aspirant candidates are selected" by exclusively focusing on the final stage of the selection process, where a final candidate is selected from a pre-determined slate of aspirant candidates. This approach sets the tone in most later British Labour party's selection process assessments, including Ranney (1965); Rush (1969); Holland (1986); Denver (1988); Bochel and Denver (1983); Marsh and Gallagher (1988); Norris and Lovenduski (1995); Rush and Cromwell (2000); and Russell (2005). It is critical to note that all of these studies classify the British Labour party selection process as largely "decentralised", meaning authors see local party members as being the dominant player in the entire selection process.

Despite the uniformity, various authors rightly feel uneasy about this classification. For example, in observing selections between 1951 and 1965, Ranney (1965) characterises the process as decentralised despite noting significant central party agent involvement throughout.[4] Ranney observes the central party, particularly the NEC, has considerable supervisory powers over selection insofar as it maintains and distributes lists with the names and details of aspirant candidates suitable for candidacy to the CLP and subjects their choices to "certain controls from the centre" (Ranney, 1965, pp. 129–133).[5] In assessing the British Labour party's selection process between 1964 and 1968, Rush describes it as decentralised for reasons similar to Ranney (1965). Rush too, however, recognises the central party organisation's de facto supervisory powers over the selection of parliamentary candidates and notes its control over selection includes constraints such as reserving the right to veto, and in extreme cases, disaffiliating organisations from the national federation.

Findings throughout the 1970s and 1980s are consistent with these early studies. In his study of selections for the 1979 General Election, Holland (1981) characterises the selection process as "predominantly local", yet identifies the NEC as one of the main bodies involved in the selection of aspirant candidates (pp. 30–31). Holland's findings are reinforced in Denver's (1988) study of selections for the 1983 British General Election. Although Denver (1988) finds the process as a whole decentralised, he too recognises the significant central party's powers over the process. He further raises the need for greater central party intervention at the shortlisting stage where, for example, he notes a strong potential for factional conflict between groups to "exclude aspirants even though they may have obtained a number of nominations" (Denver, 1988, pp. 33–34). Gallagher (1988b) also describes Labour's selection process as decentralised in his review of the 1980 election on grounds that local party agents make the final selection decision. At the same time, he stresses "the important role of the centre should not be overlooked . . . the 'clearing house' role of the centre . . . constitutes greater involvement than the centre has in many countries" (p. 240).

The most comprehensive assessment of the selection process to date is Norris and Lovenduski's (1995) analysis in the lead-up to the 1992 General Election. Norris and Lovenduski (1995) find the process as a whole as decentralised on the basis that the main decision is taken at the local constituency level. At the same time they recognise an increased involvement of the central party: "there has been a shift in selection powers in recent decades, away from the core activists in the constituency committees, simultaneously downward towards party members and upwards towards the national leadership" (Norris and Lovenduski, 1995, p. 53). Rush and Cromwell's (2000) assessment of selection processes between 1868 and 1999 is similar. Nonetheless, the authors highlight recent examples of the NEC's control over selections, including the subjection of local party shortlists to NEC approval and parachuting candidates into local constituencies (Rush and Cromwell, 2000, p. 467).

A more recent study of this topic is offered in Russell's (2005) analysis of Labour party selections from 1993 to 2005. Despite the presence of various central party rules that constrain selectors' choices, the party's process is classified as "highly decentralised", again on the basis that local party members make the final decision as to who becomes the party's candidate (p. 280). At the same time, Russell (2005) stresses recent reforms to the selection process have led to greater involvement of the central party relative to the CLPs. For example, and as discussed in greater detail later, although the adoption of one member one vote (OMOV) in 1993 extended the final selection vote to all eligible individual members and resulted in a more participatory process, the implementation of AWS seats in the same year and the NEC-monitored NPP in 1998 resulted in a more centralised process. At first OMOV appears to strengthen the decentralisation argument, but, as noted, it only made the process more inclusive rather than more decentralised for reasons that have already been discussed. Indeed, Russell

(2005) highlights the central party's increased role in selection in the post-1993 reform era: "As in the 1980s the balance of control tipped temporarily – this time to the leadership, that time to the activists" (p. 88). This discomfort within the scholarly community on the issue of centralisation suggests a need to re-examine how selection processes are classified.

Several recent British Labour party selections, in addition to the Ashfield case presented at the outset of this chapter, reveal the selection process is not as nearly decentralised as supposed. In addition to the NEC fully taking over the selection process in the lead-up to the 2017 (and 2019) snap election, which led to considerable fall out in seats such as Liverpool Walton, it also interfered in selections for the 2015, 2010, and 2005 General Elections. In 2010, for example, the NEC's Special Selections Panel (SSP) took over the local shortlisting responsibility despite local members' protestations.[6] Discontent emanating from the local party was also evident in Erdington, where the NEC allegedly arranged Deputy Leader's Harriet Harman's husband Jack Dromey's win. Local grumblings over central party interference were further voiced in Barrow, where, in a letter to the *Observer*, retired MP Colin Pickthall claimed party insider Jonathan Woodcock, backed by central party officials, held an unfair advantage over other aspirant candidates (Hinsliff, 2009).[7] Further, in the lead-up to the 2005 General Election, in Blaenau Gwent, which has since become the exemplar of the struggle between the Central and local parties for control over the selection process, Peter Law resigned from the Labour party in response to the constituency's designation as an AWS.[8] In the case of Normanton and Doncaster, local members expressed their frustration over the central party's decision to parachute in Ed Balls and Ed Miliband, respectively.[9] Moreover, leading up to the 2001 General Election, rumours abound in South Shields, where the central party secured former PM Tony Blair's star candidate David Miliband's selection only days before the writ dropped.[10]

Allegations of central party interference in what local parties perceive to be their jurisdiction are not entirely groundless. According to a Labour party official: "there are people, like, you know, the Ed Balls and Yvette Coopers, and the Milibands, sharp people, you know, that people would like to have as their MPs. They're top operators who get good seats. I think they're meant to".[11] At the same time, the local parties experienced *some* success in a few instances where they pushed back against the central party's interference. For example, in Newcastle Central's selection for the 2010 General Election, a complete outsider won over a Labour party staffer. Drawing again upon Liverpool Walton, as relayed in an interview with a local party official, the local party managed to get "their man" added to the NEC SSP shortlist.[12] Moreover, in Stoke Central the local party stood up to the NEC's SSP's imposed shortlists on grounds they were "engineered to secure the selection of one particular candidate" (Kenyon, 2010). Despite these small victories, local parties were not successful in altogether reducing the central party's creeping intrusion in the selection process. Such anecdotal evidence suggests it is time to reassess features of the party's selection process.

This evidence from the literature underpins the argument that any evaluation of candidate selection should be undertaken using a multistage approach by evaluating the role of various participants *and* constraining rules at all stages of the selection process. As Gallagher recognises, "devising a research strategy to pin down the exact point in the party where the decision is made is not straightforward", as "outcomes of the selection process often reflect the results of a complex set of interactions between many actors within the party, in which different actors have different degrees of influence but none has complete control" (1988a, p. 5).

The standard approach to identifying what is deemed to be the key participant in one stage of the selection process is not necessarily adequate to properly assess centralisation. Classifying a party organisation's selection process as "decentralised" solely on grounds that local party members vote in the final selection process stage does not take into account who makes key decisions in previous selection process stages nor does it account for the degree to which central party rules constrain choice. For example, in Norway, although the central party is not the key selector in the final selection process stage, equality rules in earlier stages, such as rigorously enforced gender guarantees, are "extremely important in deciding what kind of candidates will be selected" (Ware, 1996, p. 263). As discussed in more detail later, the presence of equity rules is a prime example of the central party's influence over the selection process, and, as such, parties with equality rules should be considered more centralised than those without such rules even if local party members are empowered in the final selection process stage. The next section presents a brief overview of the Labour party's organisational structure before presenting an overview of participants and rules at each selection stage.

Centralisation and the Labour party selection process

This next section provides an account of how the Labour party's candidate selection process developed, including an overview of the historically significant reforms to the candidate selection process. The reforms are briefly outlined and assessed along two criteria: 1) whether the reform further empowered central party agents and 2) whether the reform created rules to constrain local selector choice. The review suggests the overall effect of the reforms has centralised Labour's candidate selection process, which is at odds with how the process is currently characterised in some of the literature.

The roots of the British Labour party's candidate selection process can be traced to 27 February 1900, when 129 delegates gathered at the Memorial Hall in London to establish the Labour Representation Committee (LRC) and agreed to little more than "creating a Labour group in Parliament, who shall have their own whips and agree upon their own policy" (Pugh, 2010, p. 1).[13] The LRC, described as "a little cloud, no bigger than a man's hand" and as a party for a small minority of workers belonging to trade unions with "modest aspirations", went on to become one of Britain's "two leading parties of government even to the extent of regarding itself . . . as the natural party of government" (Pugh, 2010, p. 1).[14] Since 1900, the Labour party has formed government nine times, with six majority governments and three minority governments.[15]

The British Labour party's two founding principles may be understood in relationship to its candidate selection process: 1) its federal structure and 2) its commitment to representative democracy (Russell, 2005, p. 11). For example, as an extra-parliamentary party made up of trade unionists and socialist societies, Labour's original purpose was to gain representation for working people in parliament, thus explaining the dominant role trade unions have played in the selection of candidates (Russell, 2005, p. 11). Even despite its reform package in the 1990s, discussed later, and a watered down pledge to socialism, its 1995 revision of Clause IV outlining the party's commitment to representing workers was left untouched.[16] In this context, Labour's overall federal organisational structure reflects its origins in the labour movement and its early commitment to descriptive representation. Indeed the autonomous founding organisations included trade unions and socialist societies which had guaranteed seats at Annual Conference – responsible for defining the policy framework and rules. They also held seats on the CLP's Executive Committees (EC) and General Committees (GC) – responsible for selecting candidates (Norris and Lovenduski, 1995, p. 55; Russell, 2005, p. 11).

The Labour party did not have individual party members in its early years, and initially representation could only be gained through affiliated trade unions, cooperative societies, or socialist societies (Russell, 2005, p. 11). Delegates on local party committees were responsible for selecting candidates, and in this sense the selection process was relatively exclusive. In 1918, individuals for the first time were able to join the party, and local Labour parties gained formal representation (Russell, 2005, p. 11).[17] Then, as now, the party's NEC oversaw CLP activities. The principles of federalism and representative democracy transferred to the local level, with delegates from branches and affiliated organisations securing positions on bodies responsible for making local decisions. For example, up until 1987 the GC, comprised of elected local activists, made the final decision as to who would be the local party's candidate. However, the NEC could veto their choice and withhold endorsement, which is still required to become an official PPC.[18] The party's early organisational structure did not empower individual members in the selection process, as they were not given the right to vote at the nomination, shortlist, or final selection stages, and in this sense did not exercise much influence until 1993 when OMOV was passed at party conference.[19]

The Labour Party underwent a series of modernising reforms following its fourth consecutive loss to the Conservatives in the 1992 General Election, including candidate selection.[20] The most notable reforms include moving to OMOV and implementing AWS. OMOV decentralised the process by extending the right to participate to all individual members, thus reducing the power of unions and activists. On the other hand, AWS centralised the process by limiting local selection choice. According to Russell (2005), Labour felt it needed to increase the number of women candidates running for Labour to change its male dominated image to appeal to women voters (pp. 104–105). Indeed, these reforms are said to be "a symbolic step on the path to creating New Labour" (Russell, 2005, p. 34). The party went on to win the 1997 General Election with a 179-seat majority, which

Table 4.1 Key reforms to the Labour party candidate selection process[22]

Year	Reform	Effect
1980	Mandatory Reselection of Incumbent MPs	Decentralising
1989	Electoral College	Decentralising
1989	Women on Shortlists	Centralising
1993	One Member One Vote	Decentralising
1993	All Women Shortlists	Centralising
1996	Quotas for Women	Centralising
1998	Approval on the NPP	Centralising
2002	All Women Shortlists	Centralising
2009	Special Selections Panel (SPP)	Centralising
2010	Quotas for BAME Aspirant Candidates	Centralising
2011	Elimination of the NPP	Decentralising

Source: Labour Party Rule Books; Peter Kenyon, 2010; Norris and Lovenduski, 1995; Russell, 2005.

included a record 101 women MPs and marked the first of its historic three consecutive wins before losing in 2010 to the Conservative-Liberal Democrat coalition.

Indeed, an impetus behind many of Labour's key reforms to the selection process was to counter the preferences of local party members. These include the changes implemented in the 1990s as part of the modernising reform package (e.g., OMOV and AWS) as well those pushed as early as the 1970s through to the 1990s by the Campaign for Labour Party Democracy (CLPD) (e.g., mandatory reselection and the Electoral College) and by the Women's Action Committee (WAC) (e.g., one woman on a shortlist and AWS). Moreover, they include those adopted by the party in the late 1990s and early 2000s (e.g., early endorsement on the NPP and the NEC's SPP). Although many of the reforms originated with the CLPD and women's organisations (e.g., WAC) and had to pass a delegate vote at convention, it is clear from Russell's (2005) detailed review that central party agents, in particular leaders John Smith (1992–1994) and Tony Blair (1994–2007), and influential members of the PLP and the NEC, were key to their passage insofar that the proposals needed their support.[21]

Table 4.1 lists the key reforms and whether they had an overall centralising or decentralising effect on the party's selection process. Each reform is presented in the following, with an in-depth discussion of how they apply to each selection stage to follow in the next chapter.

1980 mandatory reselection

Mandatory reselection required all MPs to be reselected by their local parties' GCs. Prior to this, MPs were automatically reselected unless the GC passed a resolution asking them to retire. Nonetheless, the NEC could reverse the local party's decision. In 1991 it was modified: a triggering mechanism was added so that MPs only faced reselection if the local party members indicated this wish through a balloting process. More recently MPs are considered reselected if they receive a majority of the CLP's total nominations.[23] In terms of the key participant, mandatory reselection shifted power from the PLP and the local party GC to the local party members.

1980 Electoral College

The Electoral College reduced the local GC's power over selection by shifting to a weighted Electoral College where affiliated organisations (e.g., unions) received 40 percent of the college vote and individual members the rest. Until 1987, the final choice of the selection of candidates rested with the local parties' GCs, with eligible representatives of branches, affiliated trade unions, and socialist parties able to nominate one aspirant candidate from which the GCs chose the final candidate (Russell, 2005, p. 34). The Electoral College did not enhance the powers of the central party, rather, the power remained in the hands of the local party, nor did it include rules to constrain who the unions and members could select.

1989 women on shortlists

Women on shortlists required at least one woman to be automatically shortlisted by the GC shortlisting committee in cases where at least one woman was nominated. If a woman was nominated, but not shortlisted, the last man's name on the shortlist was dropped and a ballot was held to determine which woman's name would take his position. The rule can be considered centralising as it constrains local selector choice.

1993 One Member One Vote

OMOV resulted in dropping the weighted 1980 Electoral College and adopting the practice whereby individual members could choose their candidates at the final selection meeting on the basis of OMOV. OMOV reduced the powers of the GC and the unions by extending the final selection choice to individual members.[24] At the same time, OMOV reduced the role of the central party and served to decentralise the candidate selection process.

1993 all women shortlists

AWS seats were used in 38 of Labour's winnable seats for the 1997 General Election, with women winning in 35 of them (92 percent). Although the key selector remained the local party (e.g., GC's shortlisting committee at the shortlisting stage and individual members at the final selection stage), the GCs' choices were constrained by the NEC's equity rule as they had to choose a woman candidate for the AWS.[25] This new rule centralised the selection process.

1996 quotas for women

Quotas for women at the nomination and shortlisting stages were implemented in response to the ruling by the Leeds Industrial Tribunal against AWS on grounds that it violated the Sex Discrimination Act, 1975.[26] The key selector remained at the local level (e.g., nominating branches and unions and with the GC shortlisting committee); however, their choices as to who they nominated and shortlisted were constrained by this equity rule.

1998 approval on the National Parliamentary Panel

A panel of pre-approved candidates was first used in all parliamentary selections in the lead-up to the 2001 General Election and has been used in both the 2005 and 2010 General Elections.[27] Prior to this, the NEC retroactively endorsed candidates after they were selected. In essence the NPP is a vetting system designed to pre-approve aspirant candidates before they apply for seats to avoid situations where the CLPs select a candidate the NEC is unwilling to endorse. Aspirant candidates who do not receive early endorsement are excluded from the NPP and if selected must obtain retroactive endorsement from the NEC to stand as an official party candidate. Thus, early endorsement and the NPP have enhanced the NEC's selector role by requiring it to thoroughly vet *all* aspirant candidates who apply to the panel, which for each election year exceeds 1000, rather than just those who are selected. Early endorsement is not automatic: according to the author's interviews with party officials, the NEC rejects a fair number of applicants.[28] This is confirmed by the party data which show the NEC rejected 16 percent (724 of 4568) of all aspirant candidates who applied to the NPP between 2001 and 2010. Those who are rejected stand little chance of making it through the other selection stages.[29] Moreover, the NEC has retained its veto power over local party choices. As explored more in Chapters 6 and 7, aspirant candidates who were rejected from the NPP were told they lacked a clear understanding of the party's policies and lacked political and party experience.[30]

2002 all women shortlists

AWS were readopted for the selection of candidates for all elections since 2001. For the 2005 General Election, the party set aside 30 seats as AWS, with women winning in 25 (77 percent) of them. In the lead-up to the 2010 General Election, it set aside a record 63 seats as AWS, with women getting elected in only 29 (44 percent) of these. The key selector remained the local party's GC shortlisting committee at the shortlisting stage and individual party members at the final selection stage, but as with the 1993 AWS, the rule constrained the nominating bodies and shortlisting committees' choices to women aspirant candidates.

2009 special selections panel

The NEC SPP was set up to expedite selections in the lead-up to the 2010 General Election in the face of a record number of MPs retiring, as noted, due in large part to the election expenses scandal. To accommodate the late retirements and to ensure parties selected enough women to meet its target as well as credible candidates, the SSP was granted powers to bypass the local parties' nomination and shortlisting committees. In essence, the SSP made its own shortlists. The SPP increased the role of the NEC as a key selector by temporarily suspending the local GCs' shortlisting powers.

2010 quotas for BAME aspirant candidates

The Labour party first used quotas for BAME aspirant candidates at the nomination and shortlisting stages for the 2010 General Election. Party branches were obliged to nominate and shortlist BAME aspirant candidates in open and AWS seats where at least one BAME aspirant candidate had expressed an interest in the seat and where at least one BAME had been nominated to the seat. Thus, this rule placed additional constraints on the local parties' choices. More details on quotas for BAME aspirant candidates are provided in Chapter 5.

Post-2010 removal of the NPP

As noted, following the 2010 General Election the Party decided to do away with the NPP. Removing the NPP decentralises the process insofar that aspirants are no longer pre-screened and pre-approved by the NEC; rather they are all retroactively endorsed by the NEC as they were prior to the NPP's implementation. According to a party official, despite its problems, the NPP "still screened out a lot of people up front, so we didn't need to deal with them later", and "retroactive endorsement can lead to big problems because the NEC is reluctant to remove candidates or override local decisions after the fact, and when they do it leads to more politics". For example, "an aspirant who purposely and repeatedly hit her opponent's car – she wouldn't have made it onto the NPP; and another case is a person who said Gordon Brown was a terrible leader – so for 2015 he'd have been screened out, kept off the NPP".[31] While such immediate results of removing the NPP are felt by party officials, the longer term effects are less clear. However, there is a strong desire amongst several senior party officials to reinstate the NPP on the basis that it allows the party to more closely monitor diversity and hit its diversity targets in part by making the argument to local selectors that there is a list of qualified women from which to choose.[32]

Summary of reforms

Looking again to Table 4.1, the previous review of the key reforms to the selection process shows 7 of 11 have had an *overall* centralising effect upon the party's selection process insofar that the *key selectors* include more central party agents, and the central party's rules increasingly *constrain* the behaviour of local party selectors: 1989 Women on Shortlists; 1993 AWS; 1996 Quotas for Women; 1998 approval on the NPP; 2002 AWS; 2009 SSP; 2010 Quotas for BAME aspirant candidates.[33] Six of these reforms have directly influenced the British Labour party's selection process in the lead-up to selections for the election years of concern in this study: 1) OMOV; 2) approval on the NPP; 3) quotas for women; 4) AWS; 5) SSP, and; 6) quotas for BAMEs. As explained above, five of these six reforms have had a centralising effect upon the party's selection process: 1) AWS; 2) approval on the NPP; 3) quotas for women; 4) quotas for BAME aspirant candidates, and; 5) the SSP. The adoption of equality rules, in particular quotas for women and BAME aspirant candidates and AWS, demonstrates the increasing role of the central party and the potential connection between centralisation and selection outcomes.

Key participants and rules

In preparing for the analysis and hypotheses testing, this section describes key participants in the party's selection processes, including: the NEC, the CLP, local party members, and aspiring candidates. It then moves to explain the party's various equity rules. The role of these groups is outlined using information from the Labour party's constitution, rule books, and guidelines for parliamentary selections as well as by interviewing Labour party officials. The participants and rules specific to each stage of the selection process are more deeply discussed in the next chapter.

The NEC

The party's organisational structure, insofar as selection is concerned, has remained more or less stable. As the central party agency, the NEC continues to be the administrative authority of the party, although in practice it often takes its directives from the party leader, the General Secretary, other senior party staff, and the PLP.[34] The role of the NEC and the selection rules it implements are contained in the *Labour Party Rule Book* (1999–2010) and *NEC Guidelines for the Selection of Parliamentary Candidates* (2003, 2006, 2008). Overall, the NEC has the authority to modify the rules and procedures to achieve the party's objectives and principles. An example of this authority is evident in the lead-up to the 2010 General Election where, as noted, the NEC authorised its SSP to take over the CLPs' nominating and shortlisting responsibilities to expedite selections in constituencies with Labour MPs standing down only months before the general election (Helm, 2009).[35] Moreover, the NEC's powers of inclusion enable it to appoint candidates, whereas its powers of exclusion allow it to refuse an aspirant candidate endorsement and a spot on its NPP and to veto a local party's candidate choice (Gallagher, 1988b; Rahat, 2007).

The NEC's role in the selection process includes, but is not limited to, issuing the procedural rules and guidelines, and with the CLPs, implementing a timetable for the selection of candidates.[36] Additional activities include establishing the NPP, reviewing aspirant candidates' curricula vitae, interviewing aspirant candidates, endorsing or rejecting aspirant candidates, providing training events for aspirant candidates, determining positive action procedures and equality rules for selection, and positive action for seats with retiring MPs. Even beyond these activities the NEC is relatively active, yet its influence over the selection process is often, and mistakenly, downplayed in the literature (Norris, 1997b; Russell, 2005). As a party official notes, in the lead-up to the 2010 General Election, the

NEC screened out a considerable proportion of aspirant candidates seeking a place on the NPP:

> We need a filtering system. You have to remember that the people who have ambitions are sometimes zealous individuals who would create very big problems for the party . . . and that's why we have this kind of filtering system, and it's difficult because we want to get the best candidates, people who make good candidates and politicians. So, yeah, it's difficult.[37]

The CLP

A CLP is organised as a party unit comprised of the GC, Executive Committee (EC), Branch Labour Party (BLP), and organisations that affiliate to the BLP (e.g., trade unions and socialist societies), as well as the young labour group, ethnic minority's forum, and women's forum.[38] CLPs follow national government boundaries for the election to Westminster, whereas branches follow local government wards (local boundaries) for the election of councillors.[39] Each branch consists of individual party members within the particular CLP who either reside or who are registered as electors within it as well as trade unions and other affiliated organisations.[40] Branches, together with CLPs, maintain the machinery for elections within their area (Labour Party Rule Book, 2008, p. 37).

The CLP's role in the selection process is detailed in the 12-week model timetable shown in Table 4.2. The table shows the rules which the CLPs are required

Table 4.2 2010 General Election 12-week selection timetable[41]

Week	Activity
0	EC draws up timetable and approves membership list based on freeze date set by the NEC
0	GC shortlisting committee formed; list of party branches and CLPs set; percent of memberships and lists of other party units and affiliates set
1	Notice of procedures sent to party units, affiliates and interested aspirant candidates
2	Notices to members and postal vote applications sent
3	Closing date for aspiring candidates to declare their intentions
4–5	Aspiring candidates meet members
5	Membership appeals to NEC representative; EC considers detailed arrangements for ballot
6–7	Nomination procedure for party units
8	Postal vote applications closed; qualifying date for subscriptions being paid up to date; nominations from party units and affiliates close
8–9	Shortlist committee to conduct interviews and establish shortlist
10	Ballot papers issued to postal voters; notice of hustings meeting(s) sent to members
12	Hustings meeting(s)
12	Final selection count

Source: NEC Guidelines for the Selection of Parliamentary Candidates (2003, 2006, 2008).

to follow for candidate selections in the lead-up to elections.[42] The CLP EC along with the NEC establishes and publishes the 12-week timetable and agrees upon the freeze date for membership, which is the last day to sign up members to vote in the final selection contest. Amongst its duties, the CLP EC settles upon the list of units and branches responsible for nominating aspirant candidates and establishes a GC responsible for shortlisting. The CLP procedures secretary sends notices to interested aspirant candidates to acknowledge their applications as well as notices to party units/branches and members eligible to nominate. Although several local party agencies are responsible for carrying out the nomination, shortlisting, and selection of aspirant candidates, the NEC's monitoring role, together with its rules (e.g., procedures and equality quotas and guarantees) and equality and meeting guidelines, considerably constrain the local parties' choices.

The local party members

As noted, individual party members have the democratic rights of party membership, including the right to participate in the formal process of the party, stand for party office and elected office, and vote at party meetings.[43] The restrictions to party membership include age (minimum 15 years), citizenship and/or residency (UK), and annual subscription fee requirements (£36).[44] The NEC has the authority to rescind membership in cases where it finds a member neither resides in nor is on the electoral register or where a member is charged with a serious criminal office and/or serves a prison sentence of two years or more (Labour Party Rulebook, 2008, p. 19). Furthermore, the NEC is empowered to decide any disputes concerning party membership and refer it to the NEC's dispute panel whose decision on the matter is final. For example, a member may not belong to another political party or organisation deemed ineligible for affiliation by the NEC. Where applicable, an individual may only be a member of a trade union affiliated with the Trade Union Congress (TUC) or considered by the NEC to be a bona fide trade union and contribute to the political funds of that union. In addition to these restrictions, a member must accept and conform to the party's constitution, programme, principles, and policies, and is forbidden from engaging in conduct found to be prejudicial or "grossly detrimental to the party" (Labour Party Rulebook, 2008, p. 19).

In terms of participating in the selection of parliamentary candidates at the final selection stage, party members (i.e., eligible individual members and affiliated members) select aspirant candidates from the list of those shortlisted by their GCs. As noted, eligibility to select aspirant candidates requires individuals to be a member of a CLP for at least six continuous months and reside in the electoral area concerned by the freeze date laid down in the 12-week timetable (Labour Party Rulebook, 2008, p. 29). All exceptions to these conditions must be approved by the NEC.[45]

Aspirant candidates

Aspirant candidates are party members seeking parliamentary selection. To qualify, they must first fulfil the statutory requirements for national office, which stipulate they must be at least 18 years of age and possess British citizenship. Second, they must have 12 continuous months of membership and/or membership in a trade union (or affiliated to the Trades Union Congress [TUC] or a trade union considered by the NEC to be a bona fide trade union). Third, they must abide by the *Candidates' Code of Conduct*, which prohibits them from doing the following: producing and distributing promotional materials prior to the publication of the timetable and/or commencement of the selection process; canvassing members, units, and affiliates before the prescribed period; accessing the membership list without paying the £20 fee and/or in advance of the prescribed period; accessing a membership list used for a previous selection campaign; publicly disparaging other aspirant candidates; and interfering in postal ballots (Labour Party Rule Book, 2008, pp. 85–86). As stated in the *Labour Party Rule Book* and emphasised by several party officials, the penalty for breaking these rules includes rescinding party membership and forced withdrawal from the race. As a national party official notes:

> There are rules and regulations and a code of conduct for candidates which must be adhered to. And if it isn't you'll be disqualified. There's no two ways about that. We would disqualify you. And they're given a code of conduct and sign it. Local party gatekeepers must still abide by the code of conduct.[46]

Lastly, members disqualified as local government candidates are ineligible to seek parliamentary selection, and members of the EP, Scottish Parliament (SP), and National Assembly of Wales (NAW) may only seek selection with the permission of the NEC (Labour Party Rule Book, 2008, p. 30). Critically, as noted, selected aspirant candidates are only considered *official* candidates if they have received NEC endorsement and agreed to abide by the party's rules and standing orders (Labour Party Rule Book, 2008, p. 29). While this section identifies the key actors, the next section discusses the extent to which the central party's objective to increase the number of women aspirant candidates and members from other underrepresented aspirant groups, in particular BAME, permeates the process.

Equality rules

As noted, the party's equality strategies – equality rhetoric, equality promotion, and equality rules – potentially influence the demand for women and BAME aspirant candidates amongst party selectors – and to a much lesser degree disabled aspirant candidates. As stated in the NEC guidelines on the selection of parliamentary candidates:

> In pursuance of the party's objective of considerably increasing the number of women and candidates from BAME members and other groups currently underrepresented in Parliament, parties and affiliates should place particular emphasis on the need to positively encourage consideration of women,

BAME members, those with disabilities and those from clerical and manual backgrounds.

(Labour's Future, 2006)

The equality measures are discussed in the following in the order of the degree of constraint they place upon participant choice. The discussion begins by explaining *equality rhetoric and promotion strategies*, which place the least constraint on selectors, and concludes by describing *equality rules*, which place the most constraint on selectors.

Equality rhetoric and promotion strategies are designed to increase the supply of women aspirant candidates by encouraging women and aspirant candidates from other underrepresented groups to come forward and apply for seats. These rules also increase the demand for these groups by encouraging local parties to at least consider selecting them. Both equality rhetoric and promotion strategies were used in the lead-up to the 2001, 2005, 2010, and 2015 General Elections. Equality rhetoric strategies include public acceptance for representation through promotion in the party platform, discourse, campaign materials, and the party's website (see Lovenduski, 2005; Ashe et al, 2010). On the Labour Women's Network (LWN) website, for example, it is stated: "Women are not left behind the scenes or simply there to make the tea – Labour women can and do reach the top". Rhetoric is also present in media commentary, for example, in a *Guardian* article leading up to the 2010 General Election, Harriet Harman "complained that her party's election line-up is too male-dominated" (Stratton, 2010). Moreover, equality rhetoric is found in the party's speeches: at the 2009 Labour Conference, GS Ray Collins addressed anti-AWS sentiment amongst some of the party's grass roots activists: "What could be more undemocratic than a 21st century Parliament in which less than a fifth of its members are women – eighty years after they won the right to vote?" (2009). The Party's rhetoric may be further seen in its responses to the earlier discussed 2010 *Speaker's Conference* (SC) recommendations:

> The Labour party changed the law to permit political parties to use positive action to address the shameful underrepresentation of women in the House of Commons . . . whether the number of women MPs rises or falls, as long as women remain so shamefully underrepresented in the House, the need for all main parties to be assertive in their equality policies will remain pressing for a considerable time to come.
>
> (SC, Appendix 4, Labour Party's Responses, pp. 18–19)

Equality promotion strategies aim to encourage women and members from other underrepresented groups to enter politics by offering training and financial assistance and local selectors to choose them by setting targets for them to aspire. In the NEC procedures for the NPP, it is stated: "The NEC shall approve a thorough programme to promote the increased representation of women, BAME members, [and] disabled members" (Labour's Future, 2006, p. 11). Moreover, early in the selection process, CLPs are provided with handbooks outlining ways to recruit women and get them more involved in the party, and the LWN offers aspirant candidate women training, while Emily's List offers women financial support (Ashe et al, 2010, p. 470).

Straightaway, in the *Introduction* to the "NEC Guidelines for the Selection of Parliamentary Candidates" it is stated that the selection guidelines reflect three main principles: a transparent and straightforward process; maximum membership involvement; and quality and *diversity of candidates* (2006, p. 5). The last principle, *diversity of candidates*, is a key to the party's narrative, as seen in its next reference to "equality of outcome", which involves the NEC "actively encourage[ing] CLPs to consider equality and fair representation when selecting candidates" (NEC Guidelines to Parliamentary Selections, 2006, p. 5). It is made clear in the guidelines that the NEC's role in selection moves beyond equality rhetoric and promotion to equality guarantees:

> The NEC has determined that we should achieve at least equal numbers of men and women in the PLP with at least 40 percent of the PLP being women in the next general election [2010]. To achieve this all women shortlists will be required in selected constituencies where there is a retiring Labour MP or no sitting MP. The NEC will issue guidelines as to how decisions on which selected constituencies will operate all women shortlists will be made.
>
> (NEC Guidelines for the Selection of Parliamentary
> Candidates, 2006, p. 9)

Unlike equality rhetoric and promotion, quotas and equality guarantees are aimed at increasing demand for women and BAME aspirant candidates by making a particular social characteristic, for example, being a woman or a BAME, a required criterion for selection (see Ashe et al, 2010, p. 459; Childs et al, 2005; Lovenduski, 2005).[47] As the next chapter highlights, in all elections under study the party used quotas for women, but in 2010 and 2015 it used quotas for women *and* BAME aspirant candidates. Moreover, in 2005, 2010, and 2015 the party used equality guarantees for women in the form of AWS. Equality quotas and equality guarantees operate differently. Local parties are expected to meet NEC quotas for women and BAME aspirant candidates. However, they are not required to do so in cases where a woman or BAME aspirant candidate does not receive a nomination. They are, however, required to meet equality guarantees (i.e., AWS). While all British parties (Labour, Conservative, and Liberal Democrat) use some form of equality rhetoric and promotion strategies, to date only the British Labour party uses equality quotas for women and BAME aspirant candidates *and* equality guarantees in the form of AWS for women. However, equality guarantees for ethnic minorities (i.e., all black shortlists [ABS]), while endorsed by several prominent Labour MPs, such as Harriet Harman, and activist groups, such as Operation Black Vote (OBV), have yet to be implemented. Notably, no major British political parties use quotas or guarantees for disabled aspirant candidates.

As noted earlier and discussed in more detail in Chapter 5, the British Labour party's rhetoric and promotion efforts have become more robust, and its gender and BAME quotas and equality guarantees have become more ambitious from one election to the next (Childs et al, 2005; Ashe et al, 2010). This may be seen in its moving target for women MPs in its PLP. In 2010, the NEC's 2005 target for 35 percent women in its PLP increased by 5 percentage points to 40 percent, and in the lead-up to 2015, it increased by 10 percent to 50 percent. Thus, the quota requirements for women and BAMEs, the use of AWS seats, and the activities of the NEC SSP at the shortlisting stage have arguably increased the role of the NEC as a selector and increased the constraints placed upon the actions of local parties.

Conclusion

On the whole, the two main criteria of centralisation, the key participants and rules that constrain selectors' behaviour, ought to be assessed using a multistage approach whereby the key participants and the nature of rules are identified at each stage. The scholarship reveals that past assessments of the British Labour party's selection process often only take into consideration the activities of particIpants at the final selection stage and thus problematically classify the process as decentralised. Yet the multistage approach to assessing the party's selection process and the reforms to the process indicate the central party's role has increased as have the number of rules that constrain selectors' choices. This chapter lays the groundwork for the next, which explores the participants and rules at all selection stages of the party's process. This information is then used to assess the degree of centralisation at each stage and to test the centralisation hypotheses using Labour party data.

Notes

1 Liberal democratic countries with laws governing the selection process include the United States, Germany, New Zealand, Finland, and Norway (until 2002) (Rahat, 2007, p. 157).
2 According to Lundell (2004), "a more centralised process often implies a more exclusive candidate selection" (p. 30); only a few select central party agents play a key role in selection. On the other hand, decentralised organisations are thought to be more democratic with larger selectorates which include local party members. However, centralised systems may be inclusive just as decentralised organisations may be exclusive. For example, in centralised systems, party members may vote at the final selection meeting from aspirant candidate pools predetermined to varying degrees by central party agents. At the same time, in decentralised systems, a local notable alone or a local committee made up of a few delegates could strike a shortlist or choose a candidate with little if any input from a wider party membership (Rahat, 2007, p. 162).
3 Forty countries have introduced legislative or constitutional quotas in elections to national office by changing their electoral laws or amending their constitutions (Dahlerup, 2013, p. 1).
4 For example, the central party's NEC was responsible for: 1) authorising the CLP to select a candidate; 2) prescribing the CLPs with selection procedures; 3) setting the qualifications for candidatures; 4) regulating local financial arrangements; 5) endorsement; 6) suspension of normal procedure; and 7) special procedures for by-elections (Ranney, 1965, pp. 134–137).

5   At the time, there were two lists: the "A List" of union sponsored candidates and the "B List" of unsponsored candidates. By the late 1950s a growing number of party leaders argued a case for stronger central control over the "B List" (Ranney, 1965, p. 139). Soon after, the "B List" came to be regarded as the NEC endorsed list; inclusion on it offered aspirant candidates advantages. Inclusion on the "B List" did not guarantee endorsement nor did absence on it preclude endorsement (Ranney, 1965, p. 154). Thus the central party early on had placement objectives, which Ranney (1965) found to include a "roster [to make] the maximum possible contributions to the party's efforts to win a parliamentary majority, and to provide the party with the talents and backgrounds it need[ed] to conduct business in the House with the greatest effectiveness" (p. 141). To fulfil its objective, the central party pursued the right kinds of candidates and claimed to "place high value on achieving a truly representative national list – that is, one in which each major segment of the population [was] adequately represented" (Ranney, 1965, p. 141). In addition to its placement powers, the central party's NEC had considerable powers of exclusion relative to the powers of the CLPs, to include: exclusion from the "B List"; expulsion from the party; keeping names off the CLP shortlist; and withholding endorsement (Ranney, 1965, pp. 154–164). Further, the NEC could and did sack rebel MPs from the party, thereby disqualifying them for re-adoption (Ranney, 1965, p. 182).

6   The SSP was set up in the fall 2009 to expedite selections in the wake of a record number of Labour MPs retiring just months ahead of the 2010 General Election. To this end the SSP took over the local party GC's shortlisting responsibilities to ensure enough women were selected to meet the party's objectives.

7   Pickthall suggests Woodcock began his campaign ahead of the official timetable and had access to the membership list before his competitors. Pickthall goes on to claim that local members were told it was pointless to turn up to the nomination meeting as the candidate was already decided, and referred to a picture taken of Woodcock with former PM Gordon Brown outside a Barrow shipyard.

8   Law went on to stand as an independent and won the seat against the official party candidate Maggie Jones.

9   This enabled Ed Balls to run in the constituency neighboring his wife's, Yvette Cooper.

10   Allegedly, ex-cabinet minister David Clarke was tempted away from this safe seat with a peerage (ePolitix, 2010, 'Profile: David Miliband').

11   Interview with a Labour party official.

12   Interview with a party member at a Liverpool selection meeting.

13   The LRC adopted the name "Labour Party" on 15 February 1906.

14   For origins of the Labour party, see Pugh (2010, pp. 14–59).

15   The six-majority government were formed in 1945, 1950, 1974 (October), 1997, 2001, and 2005. The three-minority government were formed in 1923, 1929, and 1974 (February).

16   Clause 1V was revised at Conference in 1995 and reads: "The Labour Party is a democratic socialist party. It believes that by the strength of our common endeavor we achieve more than we achieve alone, so as to create for each of us the means to realize our true potential and for all of us a community in which power, wealth and opportunity are in the hands of many not the few; where the rights we enjoy reflect the duties we owe and where we live together freely, in a spirit of solidarity, tolerance and respect". Both the revised and old Clause 1V commits the party to social democracy. The old Clause 1V read: "To secure for the workers by hand or by brain the full fruits of their industry and the most equitable distribution thereof that may be possible upon the basis of the common ownership of the means of production, distribution and exchange, and the best obtainable system of popular administration and control of each industry or service".

17   CLPs are organised at the constituency level with seats corresponding to parliament and through smaller geographic branches or wards corresponding with the election of

councillors, with their activities overseen by the central party's NEC (Russell, 2005, pp. 11–12; see Ranney, 1965).

18 The number of delegates chosen depended on the size of the constituency.

19 Local party GCs were vulnerable to affiliates and trade unions (e.g., unions had 90 percent of votes at conference and controlled most seats on NEC), which had most of the formal power and provided most of the party funds and voting strength at conference respectively (Russell, 2005, p. 12). Moreover, the aspirant candidate types selected often resembled the delegates on the nominating and shortlisting committees who were overwhelmingly men.

20 See "New Labour, New Life for Britain" (1997), the party's manifesto setting out the "third way centre-left".

21 There is one exception to this: the 1988 "one woman on a shortlist" proposal, which passed without the NEC's support (Russell, 2005, p. 101). In terms of the leadership, John Smith (1983–1992) was much more comfortable with equality guarantees than Neil Kinnock and Tony Blair. Still, members on the NEC and PLP were able to negotiate their success. For a detailed review of the context under which these reforms took place, see Norris and Lovenduski (1995) and Russell (2005).

22 Two earlier reforms impacted the selection of parliamentary candidates, particularly around campaign finance: the 1933 Hastings Agreement, which placed limits on trade unions' contributions to sponsored MPs and constituency parties, and the 1957 Wilson Financial Reforms, which banned candidates from contributing to their own campaigns and limited candidate contributions to their constituency associations (see Norris and Lovenduski, 1995).

23 Mandatory reselection was first taken up in the early 70s by the CLPD initially to ensure accountability of MPs to the party's activists by increasing local party control over the process. The reform was pushed by those on the right in the party to address the automatic reselection of left-wing MPs and left-wing activists. At the 1979 conference, the NEC recommended the principle and passed it into party rules at the 1980 conference. This then led to worries from those on the right in the party that the left would use mandatory reselection to deselect moderate and right-wing MPs (Russell, 2005, p. 36).

24 The push for OMOV was taken up by the CLPD as early as the 1970s by those on the party's right to neutralise the potential effects of mandatory reselection that was being pushed by those on the left and subsequently adopted in 1980. One of the expected effects of OMOV was to reduce the influence of unions and increase the role of individual members who were thought to be more moderate and therefore less likely to select candidates that were too far to the party's left. Various forms of OMOV were raised and rejected again and again throughout the years (see Russell, 2005, pp. 34–61). For more detail on OMOV, see Russell's (2005) excellent overview (pp. 34–61).

25 AWS were first proposed as early as the 1980s when the party recognised that women candidates were popular with women voters. Thus the 1987 General Election results, which more than doubled the number of women in the PLP from 10 in 1983 to 21 in 1987, were worrisome to central party agencies as women still comprised less than 10 percent of the PLP. In 1993, women's representation in the PLP increased by only 4.5 percentage points to 13.7 percent, and the party's unexpected election loss led to considerable introspection. The central party recognised that its failure to appeal to women was critical to its loss with the electoral gender gap between it and the Conservatives costing them the election (Russell, 2005, p. 112). Thus women's selection and election became a top priority (Russell, 2005, p. 124). In June 1993, the NEC supported the use of AWS for selections in the lead-up to the 1997 General Election in 50 percent of the seats where a Labour incumbent retired and in 50 percent of the party's target seats (Russell, 2005, p. 112). The NEC did not tolerate local party dissent; for example, it imposed AWS in Slough in the face of the CLP's fierce opposition.

Moreover, when several CLPs organised to get rid of AWS at the 1994 conference, Tony Blair's push back proved crucial. The central party was again tested when two male party members who were denied access to run in constituencies designated as AWS argued the rule violated the Sex Discrimination Act, 1975. As earlier noted, in January 1996 the Leeds Industrial Tribunal agreed with them and ruled the constituencies indeed acted in a discriminatory way (Russell, 2005, pp. 114–115). By this point most of the selections for the 1997 General Election were complete, with scholars arguing the AWS already had the intended effect (Childs, 2004). Indeed, in 1997, a record 101 women MPs were elected (24 percent), a three-fold increase from 1993. Although AWS could not be used for the 2001 General Election, gender balanced shortlists were adopted requiring the GCs to select one woman and one man, but GCs were not required to select women. In the lead-up to the 2001 General Election only 1 in 5 new candidates were women (in safe seats 1 in 10), and on Election Day the number of Labour women elected decreased by six, from 101 in 1997 to 95. In January 2002, the Labour-led government introduced and passed the Sex Discrimination (Election Candidates) Bill into law to enable all parties if they so wished to use quotas to increase the representation of women (Russell, 2005, p. 120; see Childs, 2004). The NEC unanimously passed the renewed AWS proposal, and it was adopted at conference with little resistance.

26 This reform also included quotas for women on the party's executive committee.

27 Early endorsement and the NPP were first adopted in 1988 and applied to by-elections in which candidates underwent excessive scrutiny. It took the form of giving the NEC the power to draw up a shortlist of candidates from which the local members could select. Like other changes to the selection process, the idea of a pre-approved panel had been on the NEC's agenda for some time. For various reasons it was not adopted straightaway (e.g., some on the NEC felt that good local candidates might not apply for seats if they forgot to apply first to the NPP and the unions worried that the panel would interfere with their own processes for supporting candidates [Russell, 2005, p. 82]). By 1997 the idea of the NPP was part of the selection review process – the NEC's selection taskforce proposed an open panel whereby aspirant candidates were encouraged but not required to apply. If, however, they did not seek early endorsement and a place on the NPP, they would not carry the "mark of approval" and could be viewed as a risk to the CLP insofar that they might not receive retroactive endorsement if selected (Russell, 2005, p. 82).

28 Interview with a Labour party official.

29 Interview with a Labour party official.

30 Aspirant candidate responses from open-ended survey questions.

31 Interview with a Labour party official.

32 Interview with a Labour party official.

33 For more detail on the reforms that took place up to 1993, see Norris and Lovenduski, 1995, pp. 66–75, and for more detail on the reforms that took place up to 2005, see Russell, 2005, pp. 81–93.

34 The NEC is responsible for setting the party's objectives, overseeing the running of the party, and establishing the overall organisational structure of the party. The NEC is made up of representatives from each section of the party to include the government, MPs, MEPs, councillors, trade unions, and CLPs. Members vote for the CLP delegates in a ballot each year. Overall, it is composed of 24 elected members and the leader and deputy leader of the party, the leader of the European Parliamentary Labour party, the treasurer, three frontbench MPs, at least one of whom must be a woman, nominated by the cabinet or shadow cabinet in opposition, one youth member elected at Young Labour Conference who must be a woman at least every other term, one member elected by the Labour Party Black Socialist Society at its conference.

35 Toby Helm reported in *The Guardian* that by 9 August 2009, 63 Labour MPs had already informed then leader Gordon Brown they were retiring, and information passed on to party whips suggested this total would rise to some 93 by mid-October 2009. Moreover, one senior Labour figure said: "The total will go well over 100, probably to 120". In the end, a total of 100 Labour Party MPs (out of a total of 149 MPs) decided they would not seek re-election in 2010.

36 The CLPs and the appropriate regional director or other officer designated by the NEC must agree upon the procedures and timetable.

37 Interview with a Labour party official.

38 CLPs are managed by a GC, which is appointed by the Executive Committee (EC) and responsible for the carrying out of the day-to-day management of the CLP. The EC reports to the GC, the main decision making body of the CLP, which in turn is responsible for "conducting a ballot of all eligible individual members for the selection of parliamentary candidates" in accordance with the guidelines laid down by the NEC and subject to the party's national rules (Labour Party Rule Book, 2008, p. 40).

39 Branches are also referred to as wards.

40 Affiliated organisations include trade unions or other branches affiliated to the Trade Union Congress (TUC) or considered by the NEC to be a bona fide trade union affiliated to the party; co-operative societies; the Cooperative Party, other co-operative organisations; branches of socialist societies; and other organisations the NEC deems eligible for affiliation (Labour Party Rule Book, 2008, p. 36). Affiliated trade unions include the Associated Society of Locomotive Engineers; Broadcasting, Entertainment, Cinematograph and Theatre Union; Bakers, Food, and Allied Workers; Community, Communication Workers; Britain's General Union; Musicians Union, National Association of Colliery Overmen, Deputies, and Shotfirers; National Union of Mineworkers; Transport Salaried Staffs' Association; Union of Construction, Allied Trades, and Technicians; UNISON – the Public Service Union; UNITE – general workers in the public and private sectors; Unity; USDAW; and, GFTU. Affiliated organisations include the Co-operative Party; the Christian Socialist Movement; The Fabian Society; The Jewish Labour Movement; LGBT Labour; Labour Disabled members' group; Labour housing group; Labour Irish society; Labour Students; National Union of Labour and Socialist Clubs; Scientists for Labour' Socialist Educational Association; Socialist Environment and Resources Association; the Socialist Health Association; Society of Labour Lawyers; BAME Labour; and. the Labour Animal Welfare (see TULO, the Trade Union and Labour Party Liaison Organisation for an exhaustive list www.unionstogether.org.uk).

41 The timetable was suspended for the 2017 snap election and for late retirements in the lead-up to the 2010 General Election, but generally it varies little in the lead-up to selections for the General Elections.

42 Recently, some CLPs have merged the GC with the EC, while others have replaced the GC with all member meetings as a way to make decisions.

43 In 2001, the party had 272,000 individual members, in 2005, 198,000, and in 2010, 193,000 (McGuinness, 2012).

44 A member must be 15 years of age or older and be a subject or resident of the United Kingdom of Great Britain and Northern Ireland or citizen of Eire or resident in the United Kingdom of Great Britain and Northern Ireland for more than one year. Moreover, they must be a member of the CLP (where one exists) and be registered as an elector in that constituency (Labour Party Rule Book, 2008, p. 18). Each individual member of a party must pay an annual membership fee of £36, although certain categories of members pay less (i.e., unwaged persons, pensioners retired from work, members under age of 19, and students), while others pay more (i.e., MPs as well as MEPs, and MSPs and members of the Labour Group in the House of Lords must pay an annual subscription of £60) (Labour Party Rule Book, 2008, pp. 19–20). Members

may only participate in votes at party meetings if they are endorsed and have paid the annual subscription fee to the party's head office (disputes are resolved with regional director).

45 The NEC determines where a CLP shall be established. Only members who are fully paid up (they cannot be in arrears in part or in full) may participate in the selection of candidates at any level (Labour Party Rule Book, 2008, p. 20).

46 Interview with a Labour party official.

47 For a history of the legality and use of AWS seats in Britain, see Childs et al (2005) and Russell (2005).

5 Assessing centralisation in the British Labour party's selection process

The purpose of this chapter is to test hypotheses introduced in the previous chapter regarding how Labour party selection process outcomes are affected by the extent to which *key participants* control decision making and the extent to which selection process *rules* are centralised. Centralisation is thought to hold the key to understanding selection outcomes on grounds that centralised party agents counter local selectors' preferences for ideal candidates. Moreover, central party agents of the Labour party are "supposedly" committed to achieving "equality of outcome", suggesting they are less likely to disproportionately filter aspirant candidates from the process who do not fit the ideal aspirant candidate type (Labour's Future: A Guide to the Selection of Parliamentary Candidates, 2006, p. 9). More explicitly, data are used from all selection stages of the Labour party's selection process to test whether granting central party agents (as opposed to local party agents) the final decision making authority and/or the presence of equality rules (as opposed to unconstrained choice) results in fairer outcomes for women, BAME, and disabled aspirant candidates.

This chapter first reviews the multistage approach and then provides an in-depth look at the participants and rules at each selection stage. Next, it uses this information to classify the Labour party's selection process as centralised or decentralised. Lastly, it tests the centralisation hypotheses to determine whether the nature of Labour's selection process provides further insight into why some aspirant candidate types are selected over others. It is expected that centralised stages and processes reduce the likelihood that women, non-BAME, and disabled aspirant candidates will be disproportionately filtered out of the candidate selection process, while decentralised stages and processes increase the likelihood that non-ideal aspirant candidate types will be disproportionately filtered out of the process.

In total 48 tests were conducted in this chapter, of which 25 (52 percent) held. While this may seem to be a lukewarm confirmation of the centralisation theory, breaking this total into its component parts reveals an important finding. The centralisation theory holds in 10 of 14 (71 percent) tests conducted at centralised stages, but only in 15 of 34 (44 percent) tests conducted at decentralised stages. This result reveals that not all decentralised stages result in the unfair treatment of women, BAME, and disabled aspirant candidates. At the same time, it shows when central party agents become involved in the process, it almost always leads to fair or preferential treatment of women, BAME, and disabled aspirant candidates. Moreover, central party involvement always produced fair or preferential treatment for women (7 of 7 tests) and disabled aspirant candidates (2 of 2 tests), but only in 1 of 5 (20 percent) tests involving BAME aspirant candidates.

The multistage approach to understanding candidate selection processes

Candidate selection processes are generally assessed using data from only the final selection stage where local party selectors vote to choose a candidate. Focusing primarily upon the final selection stage of a multistage process is problematic for several reasons. As touched upon, during the Labour party's selection process, there are a range of selectors and rules at earlier stages that may affect aspirant candidate supply and demand in the final stage. In a multistage selection process, the same aspirant candidate faces many selectors, with filtering continuing throughout the entire process (Rahat and Hazen, 2001, p. 300). As noted by Norris and Lovenduski (1995), cross country studies attempting to summarise the main selection participants "often represent a considerable oversimplification: in practice many groups play a role at different stages of the recruitment process; a series of decisions, not one, produces the eventual outcome" (1995, p. 198). As shown in Chapter 3, the majority of filtering in the Labour party's selection process does not take place at the final selection stage. Moreover, it is possible that aspirant candidates who might otherwise stand a good chance with local party members at Stage 5) nomination and Stage 6) shortlisting of the selection process are rejected by central party screeners at earlier stages and eliminated from the process (Rahat and Hazan, 2001, p. 303).

The Labour party's selection process is complicated; multiple selectors and rules mean it is problematic to generalise whether the process is decentralised by examining a single stage. Such final-stage analyses tend to overemphasise the role of local party selectors and in turn understate the role of central party selectors and central party rules (Denver, 1988; Russell, 2005; Ranney, 1965, 1981). It is perhaps more useful to classify each stage as centralised or decentralised and calculate the number of stages that are centralised or decentralised to more precisely classify the selection process as a whole.

In terms of methodology, two initial measures are combined to determine whether a selection process stage is centralised or decentralised. The first measure, *key participant*, is represented using a binary score: "1" for centralised and "0" for decentralised. A value of "1" is assigned if the key participant is a central party agent, such as the British Labour party's NEC. A value of "0" is assigned if the key participant is a local party agent, such as party members. The second measure, *rules*, is also binary. A value of "1" is assigned if rules significantly restrict selector choice. A value of "0" is assigned if the party does not impose constraining rules such as quotas and/or AWS guarantees. If either the key participant score or the rules score is a "1" for a single selection process stage, then that stage is categorised as "centralised". If the key participant and the rule scores are both "0", then the stage is deemed "decentralised". This assessment is conducted for each of the seven selection process stages for each year.

The multistage Labour party candidate selection process: participants and rules

The purpose of this section is to provide an in-depth and updated review of the Labour party's selection stages using the multistage approach to identify the key selectors and rules at each stage. Party literature, interviews with party officials, and survey responses are used to identify and evaluate the key selectors and rules at each stage. Thus, this section identifies participants and rules in each of the Labour party's seven selection stages for the 2001, 2005, and 2010 General Elections: 1) party application, 2) NPP application, 3) NPP approval, 4) seat application, 5) nomination, 6) shortlisting, and 7) final selection. For 2015, Stages 2, 3, and 4 are eliminated, but the participants and rules at the reordered stages 2) nomination, 3) shortlisting, and 4) shortlisting are similar to those in 2001, 2005, and 2010. While the participants and rules are fairly consistent across these election periods, they are not identical. Subsections are included where variation requires further explanation. This information is needed to apply the multistage approach in order to identify which stages and election years are more or less centralised and to test whether women, BAME, and disabled aspirant candidates are less likely to be disproportionately filtered out at centralised stages and years and more likely to be filtered out at decentralised stages and years.

Table 5.1 presents a multistage summary of the key participants and rules. The entire selection process is highly institutionalised, a feature often associated with centralised party organisations. The formal rules for each stage are described in considerable detail in the party's rule books, guidelines, and constitution. Formalising and in turn standardising and professionalising the selection process have increased transparency and accessibility to non-ideal aspirant candidate types otherwise shut out of the process insofar that formal accounts of selection process rules are available to all rather than just a select few (Caul, 1999).

Stage one: party application

During *party application*, the participant pool includes aspirant candidates who indicate their willingness to pursue political office, which involves submitting a curriculum vitae and standard application to the central party's NEC. As earlier indicated, they must meet minimum statutory requirements for national office. In addition, they must be a member of the party for 12 continuous months and/ or a member of an affiliated trade union. If aspirant candidates do not meet these criteria, they are ineligible to seek selection.[2] As noted earlier and shown in Table 5.1, for all years this is a self-selection stage where central party participants and rules play only a minimal role in screening aspirants and constraining behaviour.

Table 5.1 Labour candidate selection process: key participants and rules[1]

	Stage 1: Apply to Party		
Key Participant	Aspirant Candidates		
Rules	No		
	Stage 2: NPP Application		
Key Participant	Aspirant Candidates		
Rules	No		
	Stage 3: NPP Approval		
Key Participant	NEC (Central)		
Rules	No		
	Stage 4: Seat Application		
Key Participant	Aspirant Candidates		
Rules	No		
	Stage 5: Nomination		
Key Participant	Constituency Labour Party Branches and Units		
Rules	Women/BAMEs Quotas and AWS	Women Quotas and AWS	Women Quotas
	Stage 6: Shortlisting		
Key Participant	CLP General Committee/NEC		
Rules	Women/BAME Quotas and AWS	Women Quotas and AWS	Women Quotas
	Stage 7: Candidate Selection Contest		
Key Participant	Individual members		
Rules	No		

Source: Labour Party rule books, various years.

Stage two: application to the National Parliamentary Panel

At the second stage of the process, aspirant candidates in the preceding pool choose or choose not to apply for position on the NPP. This is a route the party's NEC encourages because the names on the NPP are distributed to local parties for consideration, and aspirant candidates on the list are given information about upcoming seats and training programmes. As shown in Table 5.1, for all years this is a self-selection stage, although central party participants and rules strongly encourage aspirant candidates to apply. As noted, this stage does not apply for selections in the lead-up to elections held after the 2010 General Election for reasons given earlier.

Stage three: approval on the National Parliamentary Panel

The third stage of the selection process is approval on the NPP. With approval on the NPP comes early endorsement, which gives aspirant candidates the NEC's stamp of approval. To some extent early endorsement helps avoid situations where the CLPs select a candidate the NEC refuses to later retroactively endorse. Indeed one reason it was first adopted in 1998 for all selections was to avoid instances and in turn unwanted media and public attention in cases where the local parties chose candidates the NEC was unwilling to approve.[3] For example, in 1995 the NEC fielded complaints that CLP members selected an unsuitable candidate, Liz Davies. Davies' activities as a councillor in Islington, association with a hard left publication, and Trotskyite label led the NEC to refuse her endorsement despite Davies' and supporters' refutations, ruling "that on the basis of her stated views and track record, Liz Davies is not a suitable Labour candidate" (Russell, 2005, p. 82; The Guardian, 2001, 29 March).

Applying to the NPP is relatively straightforward. As described by a party official: "Aspirant candidates go to the website, download the application form, fill it in, send it to us here [party headquarters]. It would then get processed and we would arrange for an interview".[4] The application package provides a job description – listing the qualities the NEC seeks – for example, experience in the party, campaigning skills, and strategic thinking – and a standard application form. Initially aspirant candidates were vetted by a panel of up to three selectors (e.g., a member of the NEC, a member of the relevant regional executive, and an independent, experienced member of the party) who evaluated them on a wide range of criteria from meeting basic legal and party requirements such as age, citizenship, and length of party membership, to demonstrating knowledge of current party policies and political issues in a clear and communicative way. The aspirant candidates' application forms were marked blind by two of the panel evaluators, and if they achieved a minimum score, they were invited to a 20-minute interview and to write a short test. The application form, interview, and test scores were then added to determine whether the NEC would grant them early endorsement and a position on the NPP (Russell, 2005).

By 2010 the interview scoring system became somewhat more nuanced. As a party official noted:

> We used to use a point system, but we scrapped it. . . . It was openly recognised that the interview system is entirely subjective and depends on where you have your interview because they're held all over the country, with different members of the NEC and NEC appointed panels. They're not going to have the same standards. And using a grading system, it was very, very difficult to justify somebody putting down 'that was a bit mediocre I'll put down a 5'. So, on the actual forms they complete in the interview they have to give more information. It's not a lot of information they have to note down, just some more information to justify if people were particularity poor or weak on a subject . . . so there is now an explanation. So when you write back to people to say you haven't been accepted they want to know why and it's not enough to say 'because you're a 5 on this or a 4 on this'.[5]

A place on the NPP and early endorsement is not automatic, with a considerable number of aspirant candidates rejected. As a party official notes, screening:

> involves a set of questions upon which everyone is evaluated. You're normally evaluated, getting onto the panel, by the answers you give. Normally

you've met, partly met, or 'not met' the answers to the questions. Questions like: 'why do you want to represent the party?' or 'how much do you know about the issues?' We're looking to see how they'd handle themselves too.[6]

As another party official noted, "we don't just want anyone representing the party".[7] Party officials' reasons for rejecting aspirant candidates at this stage include coming across as "politically naïve", "not particularly good at communicating", "out of keeping with the party's policies", and "not having a clear idea of the role of a MP and the work that's involved".[8] Indeed, an aspirant candidate who was rejected at this stage felt that the selectors were "looking for any reason to decline [my] application", while another felt the NEC "didn't make very good choices".[9]

Essentially the NPP is a list of pre-approved aspirant candidates "who meet an agreed standard, regardless of their gender or ethnic background" that local constituencies are provided with and encouraged to consult on an advisory basis only (Labour's Future, 2008, p. 5).[10] As indicated, the panel is open; therefore aspirant candidates are not required to apply but are strongly encouraged by party officials to do so insofar that in addition to getting pre-approved, aspirant candidates on the NPP are alerted to seats when they become available and are invited to special training workshops. As a party official reveals, most who do not apply are under time pressures: "Some of them may have applied to the panel, but are waiting for an interview and while they're awaiting interview a seat becomes available and there's nothing else they can do so they self-nominate". Whereas others "want to stand in their own constituencies so they already have a lot of the links so they don't need NEC endorsement to provide any additional kudos".[11] However, the latter strategy has drawbacks. Local party members may wonder why an aspirant candidate's name was left off the list. As a party official suggests, "as a member I'd wonder why they didn't make it . . . there's reasons".[12] Or perhaps selectors will speculate that aspirant candidates who did not apply have something to hide. A party official suggested aspirant candidates who avoid early endorsement are "weaker at going to interviews with panels, so it might be a strategic thing".[13] In not knowing, local selectors may be reluctant to nominate, shortlist, or select aspirant candidates not on the NPP for fear the NEC will later refuse endorsement, thus putting the CLP at risk of unwanted publicity.

Aspirant candidates recommended by trade unions are automatically endorsed and included on the NPP. Their inclusion, however, is subject to an agreement that the latter "reache[d] the criteria for accreditation" (NEC Guidelines for the Selection of Parliamentary Candidates, 2006). As a party official notes: "As long as the trade union thinks they're good people then the trade union passes their details onto us, and provided they're Labour party members with required Labour party member requirements, they get incorporated onto the parliamentary panel".[14] Yet another party official indicates it is not all together automatic: "Unions will say to the Labour party 'we've got somebody who has passed the criteria and they wish to run as our candidate in a certain constituency', and we will give them our backing. Having said that, having done that, the Labour party will accept them to the NPP, but will still want to interview that candidate".[15] Each year the NPP is brought up to date as additional aspirant candidates come forward during the process. Aspirant candidates on the NPP for previous elections may remain on current panels if they submit a new application form. NEC appointed regional directors, however, may call such aspirants candidates for an interview with due reason.

At the approval to the NPP stage, the key participant for all years is the NEC insofar that it decides whether to endorse aspirant candidates and approve them for the NPP. There are no equality rules in place to directly constrain their choice; however, they undergo education to understand that targeted action is needed to "increase the representation of women, BAME members, disabled members, and those from manual and clerical backgrounds on the national panel" (Labour Party Rulebook, 2008, p. 30). The NEC endorsement stage is just one of several filtering stages and alone does not reveal all of the participants or their activities and the rules at the other stages. Indeed, as a party official notes: "you can't judge as much as you'd like on a panel in half an hour. So, the other filter is whether they get through all those other stages".[16] In light of this, the fourth stage, seat application, is next described. Again, this stage does not apply to selections for elections after 2010.

Stage four: seat application

Aspirant candidates may apply for seats during Week 4 according to the NEC's 12-week selection timetable. As explained by a party official, selection at this stage generally follows the following steps:

> In week zero, we send out details of the timetable, that's what we send out to people who've been approved on the NPP, and put it on the website and in the Tribune to let them know a selection is about to start, and members are informed and given details of postal applications. So . . . it's your responsibility after that to keep an eye out on the website and check your email to make sure that when a selection comes up and it's a seat you're interested in that you apply to that constituency.[17]

Aspirant candidates express their interest in a seat by submitting an application for a particular constituency on a standard application form provided by the NEC to the constituency's procedures secretary by the date agreed upon in the timetable, normally week three and one half. According to a party official, the procedures secretary "acknowledges all applications they receive. They read through them and there's a committee that meets that goes through the applications they received and then they write to people that they want to take part".[18] Only those who express an interest in a seat in this way are considered for nomination and shortlisting.

Following their expressions of interest, aspirant candidates are entitled to a list of the CLP's nominating bodies (e.g., party units and affiliated organisations), and for a £20 fee, a list of eligible members. The procedures secretary, as instructed by the NEC, sends copies of aspirant candidates' application forms to each branch affiliate entitled to nominate. As a party official notes: "Once they've applied and have copies of the membership lists they can actually start contacting members directly and gathering support".[19] This activity, as described in further detail in the next section, is crucial to shortlisting and final selection.

At this stage, for all years, neither the central nor local party participants play a key role in filtering aspirant candidates out of the process; rather aspirant candidates self-select by choosing or not choosing, for a variety of reasons, to apply for seats (e.g., "I didn't have enough time", "I changed jobs", "I moved", "I lost interest", "there were no open seats where I live").[20] If aspirant candidates choose not to apply to seats, they cannot progress any further in the process. In terms of 2015, as noted in Chapter 3, aspirants no longer need prior vetting by the NEC's NPP before applying to seats, and while they still directly apply to the local parties, the central party no longer tracks their seat applications.

Stage five: nomination

The NEC provides CLP procedures secretaries with a clear set of guidelines for nominating or longlisting aspirant candidates. Following the closing date for receipt of expressions of interest as set in the agreed timetable, aspirant candidates whose applications conform to the party's standard format are sent to the appropriate party unit secretaries.[21] The CLPs' procedures secretaries then ensure that any other organisations entitled to nominate are informed and that they are entitled to a copy of the set of aspirant candidates' applications (Labour Party Rule Book, 2008, p. 82). The CLPs are instructed to create as many opportunities as possible for aspirant candidates to meet with members from the eligible nominating bodies on a "fair and equal basis" prior to the nomination meeting, normally in week 4 to 5 of the 12-month timetable (Labour's Future, 2006, p. 15).[22] As with all hustings meetings, nomination meetings are subject to set guidelines, which are intended to create equal opportunities for women and aspirant candidates from other underrepresented groups. For example, questions on financial means of support, religion, or of a racist, sexist, homophobic, or anti-disabled nature are prohibited, as are questions about marital status or domestic circumstances (Labour's Future, 2006, pp. 28–29, p. 44).

The nomination meeting is a "special meeting"; before it commences memberships are checked and aspirant candidates' application forms and *Statement of Candidates' Qualities* are made available to members with the expectation that they will be given enough time to read them over.[23] Prior to the ballot, a 30-minute discussion may take place on aspirant candidates' qualities (Labour's Future, 2006, p. 38).[24] Eligible party branches and affiliated organisations must nominate from the list of aspirant candidates presented to them (Labour Party Rules, 2008, p. 82). The nomination is determined by an eliminating ballot on the basis of expressed preferences (Labour's Future, 2006, pp. 38–39).[25] There is a separate set of procedures for sitting MPs who wish to seek re-election.[26]

At the nomination stage, local party delegates agree upon a longlist of aspirant candidates who move to Stage 6 where they are considered for shortlisting. Aspirant candidates who fail to get nominated are no longer in the running for shortlisting or, in turn, selection. As a party official states: "Some of the blockage happens at nomination because you can get people making deals over the nomination process. . . . You can get people doing deals to keep people off. . . . That's the point where the GC is powerful. So the actual nomination point is quite important".[27] In light of this, a party official explains that the nomination rules in the lead-up to selections for each election year have become more rigorous with regard to equity rules. As a party official notes, one reason for this is to "make it fairer for women and BAMEs".[28] The nomination rules vary for selections in the lead-up to each general election; with this in mind, they are discussed separately in the following.

• Nomination Rules for the 2010 General Election

For selections in the lead-up to the 2010 General Election, where party branches made nominations in open seats (non-AWS seats), they were obliged to submit the names of up to three aspirant candidates, "with at least one being a woman and at least one being a BAME candidate in the event that at least one BAME aspirant candidate has expressed an interest in the seat at the deadline of expression of interest" (Labour's Future, 2006, p. 15). Moreover, "other party units and affiliated branches need[ed] to only ma[ke] one nomination, but [could] nominate up to three candidates with at least one being a woman and at least one being a BAME candidate if they so wish[ed]" (Labour's Future, 2006, p. 17). Nominating party units did not face gender or BAME restrictions if they chose to make only one nomination.[29] Additionally, aspirant candidates who received branch nominations representing more than 50 percent of the total membership were automatically nominated and in turn shortlisted (Labour's Future, 2006, p. 53).

In seats designated by the NEC or volunteered by CLPs as AWS, party branches that chose to nominate were obliged to "submit the names of up to two women with at least one being a BAME candidate in the event that at least one BAME candidate ha[d] expressed an interest in the seat". Other party units and affiliated branches, however, only needed to "make one nomination, but [could] nominate up to two women, with at least one being a BAME candidate in the event that at least one BAME candidate ha[d] expressed an interest in the seat" (Labour's Future, 2006, p. 15). Any nominations for men made by branches or party units in seats designated as AWS seats were ruled by the NEC invalid. The NEC appointed regional representative could waive the requirements in constituencies where too few expressions of interest were received (Labour's Future, 2006, p. 15). As elaborated upon later, the branch nomination quotas for women and BAME aspirant candidates were more robust in selections for the 2015 and 2010 General Elections than for selections in the lead-up to the 2005 and 2001 General Elections.

• Nomination Rules for the 2005 General Election

In 2005, for open seats (non-AWS), branches were required to nominate one man and one woman from the list (in 2010 they were required to submit three names, with one being a woman and one being a BAME).[30] In AWS seats, branches were obliged to make only one nomination with no obligation to nominate BAME aspirant candidates (in 2010 they were obliged to make two nominations) (Labour's Future, 2003).

• Nomination Rules for the 2001 General Election

In 2001, all seats were classified open (non-AWS). As noted, in 1996, AWS were ruled illegal by the Leeds Industrial Tribunal for violating the Sex Discrimination Act, 1975. In the face of this, party branches were obliged to nominate two aspirant candidates, one man and one woman, whereas party units and affiliated organisations could nominate one man and one woman if they wished (The National Rules of the Labour Party, 2001). Notably, there were no quotas for BAME aspirant candidates.

As shown in Table 5.1, for all years, the key participant at the nomination stage is the CLP, but its choices are constrained by quotas for women and BAME aspirant candidates and AWS for women. Thus, there are several dynamics operating at this stage. For all years the local party selectors' decisions are restricted by quotas for women. In 2010, they are restricted by quotas for BAME aspirant candidates. Moreover, in 2015, 2010, and 2005, their decisions are constrained by AWS. Although the rules are intended to reduce the obstacles women and BAME aspirant candidates are said to face, the potential for rule breaking (e.g., accessing memberships before the prescribed release date) and politicking (e.g., deal making amongst power brokers) still potentially makes it easier for the ideal aspirant candidate type to secure nominations. In light of this, several Labour party officials highlighted the party's increased efforts to address this behaviour with even more rules and central party monitoring at the shortlisting and final selection stages.[31]

• Nomination Rules for 2015 General Election

As in 2010, longlists for open seats in the 2015 General Election must include one woman where at least one woman applies and one BAME aspirant where at least one BAME aspirant applies, and in AWS, they must include one BAME aspirant where at least one BAME aspirant applies. According to a party official, the central party "does its best to enforce these rules, unless no women or BAME aspirants apply to the seat, which is rare. But the central party doesn't really have a follow-up mechanism".[32]

Stage six: shortlisting

Party literature and party officials indicate each CLP GC meet as a shortlisting committee normally in weeks 8 and 9 of the 12-week timetable to draw up a shortlist with "due regard to the nominations made by the party units and affiliates" at the preceding stage (Labour's Future, 2006, p. 15). Ahead of this it arranges a gathering for those aspirant candidates nominated to meet both informally and formally with the GC delegates on the committee.[33] At the gathering, if agreed in advance, the aspirant candidates address the shortlisting committee, who in turn may ask questions.

The final shortlist is decided by a single round preferential vote by GC shortlisting delegates.[34] Two to four tellers are elected to distribute and collect the ballot papers and four scrutineers elected to count the vote, overseen by the procedures secretary and a NEC representative. The approved shortlist it then forwarded to the appropriate regional director for validation (Labour Party Rule Book, 2008, p. 83).[35] The procedures secretary then issues shortlisted aspirant candidates a *Standardised Notice of Shortlisting by the CLP* notifying them of their success along with details of the final section meeting, including the length of time they have to speak and answer questions.[36] At this time their details (e.g., curricula vitae/application forms) are posted to eligible voting members along with the hustings and ballot details. As with the nomination stage, the shortlisting stage, perhaps even more so, is heavily prescribed with equality rules. According to a party official, this stage is also vulnerable to "deal making".[37] As with the nomination stage, the rules for the shortlisting stage vary for each election year.

• Shortlisting Rules for the 2010 General Election

In the lead-up to the 2010 election, aspirant candidates vying for open seats who were nominated by branches with a cumulative membership of over 50 percent of the CLP membership were automatically shortlisted. Moreover, in seats with no sitting MP and in cases where there were 6 nominees, 3 of whom were women, the minimum shortlist had to be 6, although a larger shortlist was allowed so long as 50 percent of those on it were women. In cases where shortlists of six were agreed, and where fewer than three women were nominated, they were automatically shortlisted.[38]

Further, where at least one BAME aspirant candidate applied, at least one BAME aspirant candidate had to be shortlisted. In all 63 AWS seats, a minimum of 6 women on the shortlist were required provided at least 6 were nominated. Where at least one BAME woman was nominated, at least one BAME woman had to be included on the shortlist. Sitting Labour MPs representing a constituency wholly or partially contained in the CLP were included on the shortlist if they chose to contest the seat and were nominated. As noted, the NEC SSP took the lead role in dozens of selections that took place after November 2009 and used its shortlisting powers to determine the aspirant candidates who moved forward to the final selection stage.[39]

• Shortlisting Rules for the 2005 General Election

For 2005, fewer nominees were required on a shortlist (four in 2005 and six in 2010), and there were no quotas for BAME aspirant candidates. In open (non-AWS) seats where no Labour MP contested the seat, an equal number of men and women were required on the shortlist, and if four or more aspirant candidates were nominated, there had to be a minimum of four on the shortlist (two women and two men). In the 30 seats where AWS were in operation, there had to be a minimum of 4 women on the shortlist provided 4 women were nominated.

- Shortlisting Rules for the 2001 General Election

For 2001, the rules were similar to 2005 with the exception of AWS seats – all seats were open – and there were no quotas for BAME aspirant candidates. In light of this, where no sitting Labour MP contested the seat, an equal number of men and women were required on the shortlist. If four or more were nominated, there had to be a minimum of four on the shortlist, for example, two men and two women. At the shortlisting stage, the key participant for all years is the CLP GC, and in 2010 also includes the NEC SSP. CLP GCs' decisions are constrained by AWS in 2010 and 2005, by gender *and* BAME quotas in 2010, and by gender quotas in 2005 and 2001.

- Shortlisting Rules for the 2015 General Election

There were no formal changes to the shortlisting rules for the 2015 General Election, with the 50 percent of target and safe seats appointed as AWS seats still in place. However, from interviews with Labour party officials, in 2015, key feminist activists within the party pushed beyond this formal rule to appoint more than half of its seats AWS. This decision does not reflect a formal rule change; rather it reflects the will of then leader Ed Miliband and MPs such as Harriet Harman and others committed to gender parity in the PLP. Additionally, a party official noted, women were selected to more open and safe seats than ever before (58 of 106 open target seats).[40]

Stage seven: candidate selection

In week 10 of the 12-week timetable, the CLP procedures secretary sends a *Hustings Meeting Notice* to all members eligible to vote in the final selection (hustings) meeting along with the names of the shortlisted aspirant candidates and their statements (Labour's Future, 2006).[41] Normally the final selection meeting takes place in the last week of the 12-week timetable; members unable to attend may be eligible to vote by post.[42] The procedural arrangements for the final hustings meeting are agreed upon by the EC in advance (e.g., maximum time limits for statements and questions, order of appearance, appointment of scrutineers, door stewarding arrangements, chairing of hustings, etc.) (Labour Party Rule Book, 2008, p. 83).

All aspects of the meeting are highly regulated.[43] For example, members must arrive before the first aspirant candidate speaks, present their credentials and membership cards, and remain in the room for the duration of the meeting in order to be eligible to cast ballots (*NEC Guidelines for the Selection of Parliamentary Candidates*, 2006, p. 79).[44] Once the door stewards report the number of eligible members present, the first aspirant candidate speaks with each aspirant candidate in turn, addressing the members and answering questions within the pre-agreed upon time limits.[45] Aspiring candidates leave the meeting room after the question and answer period, at which time scrutineers pass members' ballot papers.[46] Members drop their ballot papers into the box upon exiting the room.[47]

In terms of the voting procedure, the ballot is conducted on the basis of OMOV by eliminating ballot on the basis of members' expressed preferences with no aspirant candidate selected until a majority of the valid votes cast in a particular round is received (Labour Party Rule Book, 2008, p. 84).[48] Under the supervision of a NEC representative, the ballot box is opened at the GC meeting, where scrutineers proceed to count the ballots cast at the final hustings meeting along with the valid postal votes (Labour's Future, 2006, pp. 13–14).[49] Any disputed votes are decided by the NEC representative, whose decision is final.[50] The count is normally held in the last week of the timetable, and the results are announced by the GC at a meeting to which all shortlisted aspirant candidates are invited to attend.[51] The selection of candidates is not considered complete until NEC endorsement is granted.[52]

At the final selection stage, for all years the key participants are the CLPs' members, whose decisions are not directly constrained by equality rules. However, they select from shortlists drawn up at the preceding nomination and shortlisting stages by selectors whose choices are constrained by equality quotas for women in 2001, 2005, and 2010 and for women *and* BAMEs in 2010, and equality guarantees for women (AWS) in 2005 and 2010. The only notable rule change for the 2015 General Election is all selected aspirants were required to seek retroactive endorsement from the NEC.

Summary of the British Labour party's selection stages

The multistage review of the selection process indicates key participants and rules vary from one stage to the next and often from one year to the next. In terms of rules, in 2015, all demand-side stages are influenced by quotas for women and BAME aspirants, as is the case for 2010, except for approval to the NPP. Moreover, in 2015, all stages are influenced by equality quotas (AWS), as is the case for 2010, but again with the exception of approval to the NPP. In 2005, all stages but approval to the NPP are influenced by quotas for women (but not for BAME aspirant candidates), and all stages but approval to the NPP are influenced by guarantees for women. In 2001, on the other hand, all stages but two, approval to the NPP and selection, have quotas for women (but not for BAMEs), while no stages have equality guarantees for any other group. Of note, there are no equality rules in place at any stage in any year for disabled aspirant candidates. On the whole, this multistage and multiyear review of the Labour party's selection process reveals the central party participants have become more involved in the process and the equality rules have become more forceful with each election year for women and BAME aspirant candidates, but not for disabled aspirant candidates. At the same time, the impact of the elimination of the NPP upon the central party's role in the selection process is still uncertain and warrants ongoing attention.

Applying the multistage approach to the British Labour party

This section applies the multistage approach to the British Labour party by using the details on the key participants and rules to classify its stages and processes as a whole as centralised or decentralised. In terms of key participant, a value of a "1" is assigned if the final decision in any stage is made by the party leader, NEC, senior party staffer or official, or PLP. A value of "0" is assigned if local branches, units, affiliates, committees, delegates, or members make the final decision. In terms of rules, a value of "1" is assigned if the selection process stage includes quotas or AWS. A value of "0" is assigned if no rules constrain behaviour. If either the key participant or rule score is "1" for a particular stage, then the stage is categorised as "centralised". If both measures are "0", then the stage is categorised as "decentralised". The multistage assessment is presented below for women, BAME, and disabled aspirant candidates for each year, with a separate discussion provided for the 2015 General Election.

Women aspirant candidates

Table 5.2 shows key participant and rule values as well as final scores for each Labour party candidate selection process stage as they apply to women. The first column for each year shows binary key participant scores. The second column shows rule scores, while the third column for each year shows the final score used as the independent variable value to test hypotheses later in the chapter. Scores are generated for each stage for each year.

Starting with 2001, Stage 1 of the selection process is a self-selecting stage where aspirant candidates submit their curricula vitae to the NEC for consideration.

Table 5.2 Multistage assessment of the Labour party selection process (women)

Stage	2010			2005			2001		
	Key Participant	Rules	Final Score	Key Participant	Rules	Final Score	Key Participant	Rules	Final Score
1	0	0	*0*	0	0	*0*	0	0	*0*
2	0	0	*0*	0	0	*0*	0	0	*0*
3	1	0	*1*	1	0	*1*	1	0	*1*
4	0	0	*0*	0	0	*0*	0	0	*0*
5	0	1	*1*	0	1	*1*	0	0	*0*
6	0	1	*1*	0	1	*1*	0	0	*0*
7	0	0	*0*	0	0	*0*	0	0	*0*

Note: Key: 1 = Centralised, 0= Decentralised.

As it is not controlled by a central party agent, the key participant score is "0". In terms of rules, while the central party uses rhetoric and promotion to encourage women, BAME, and disabled aspirant candidates to apply for candidacy, there are no rules restricting selector choice. As such, the rule score is also "0". As this stage in the 2001 process is fully decentralised, the final score for Stage 1 of the Labour party's selection process is "0". As this is also the case for 2005 and 2010, Stage 1 final scores in these years are also "0". Given this assessment, it is expected women will be disadvantaged as they seek to enter Stage 1 of the selection process in all years.

Key participant and rule scores for Stage 2 in 2001 are assigned a value of "0" as the final score. During Stage 2, aspirant candidates decide whether or not to apply to the NPP – so the final decision to apply is left to non-central party agents. While the NEC encourages all aspirants to apply, it does not set aside reserved positions for women or guarantee they will later receive NEC endorsement. The same assessment holds for 2005 and 2010. As this stage is fully decentralised, it is expected that the percentage of women aspirant candidates entering Stage 3 will be lower than those participating in Stage 2.

Looking next to Stage 3 – acceptance on the NPP and NEC endorsement – the key selector for all years – 2001, 2005, and 2010 – is the central party's NEC. Thus, this stage receives a key participant value of "1" for centralised. In terms of rules, the central party did not constrain NEC choice in any of the years under review, earning a score of "0". However, as one of the underlying centralisation measures was present, the stage is seen as centralised, and it is expected that a percentage of women, BAME, and disabled aspirant candidates will be the same or higher as the preceding stage.

Stage 4, seat application, is another self-selecting stage for aspirant candidates. Therefore a key participant of "0" is assigned. Moving to rule scores, there were no equality rules in place constraining who could or could not apply to seats, and therefore a value of "0" for decentralised is given in 2001. However, in 2005 and 2010, AWS were used, and thus a value of "1" is given. Therefore the final score for 2001 is "0", but is "1" for 2005 and 2010. Given this, it is expected that women will not be disproportionately filtered out at this stage in 2005 and 2010 but will be disproportionately filtered out in 2001.

In terms of Stages 5) nomination and 6) shortlisting, local party agents (nominating branches, GCs, and members) are the key participants for 2001, 2005, and 2010. Thus, both stages are given a score of "0" on this attribute. Moving to rules, in 2001 no quotas for women or AWS were in place to constrain local party agent choice, and therefore this factor is given a score of "0". However, in 2005 and 2010 quotas for women were implemented for open seats (non-AWS) at the nomination and shortlisting stages as were AWS seats. Therefore Stages 5 and 6 are given scores of "1" for being centralised. Thus, it is anticipated that women aspirant candidates will be disproportionately filtered out in 2001, but not in 2005 and 2010.

Moving to Stage 7) selection, for all years the key participant, rule, and final score is "0" for decentralised. Local party members choose their candidates, and their choices are not directly constrained by central party participants or rules. It is therefore expected that women aspirant candidates will be disproportionately filtered out at this final selection stage.

Overall, the selection process as it applies to women has considerably evolved since 2001 and may be described as much more centralised. In 2001, central party agents made the final decision over selection in only one of seven stages, and no rules were in place to constrain the behaviour of local party agents. However, new rules used in 2005 and 2010 caused the process to become much more centralised by constraining local agent choice. If centralisation matters, the percentage of women aspirant candidates will remain the same or increase at the affected selection process stages.

In terms of 2015, the selection stages 1) application, 2) nomination, 3) shortlisting, and 4) selection mirror the results for 2010 – with the participants and rules at Stage 1) application classified as "0" for decentralised and the rules at Stages 2) nomination and 3) shortlisting classified as "1" for centralised. Thus, two of the four stages, nomination and shortlisting, have final scores of "1", and these centralised stages are expected to have the same or a higher proportion of women aspirants than in 2010.

BAME aspirant candidates

Turning to BAME aspirant candidates, Table 5.3 shows the evolution of the Labour party's selection process for this group is similar to that of women. However, we can see an extremely decentralised process in 2001 and 2005, followed by a sudden move to centralisation in 2010, as is the case for the 2015 General Election. These developments are further discussed following the table.

Beginning with 2001, looking to Stages 1 through 7, only Stage 3 (NPP approval) is centralised – thus it is expected that the percentage of BAME aspirant candidates will be the same or higher at this stage than at the preceding stage. All other stages are decentralised; therefore it is expected that BAME aspirant

Table 5.3 Multistage assessment of the Labour party selection process (BAME)

Stage	2010			2005			2001		
	Key Participant	Rules	Final Score	Key Participant	Rules	Final Score	Key Participant	Rules	Final Score
1	0	0	0	0	0	0	0	0	0
2	0	0	0	0	0	0	0	0	0
3	1	0	1	1	0	1	1	0	1
4	0	0	0	0	0	0	0	0	0
5	0	1	1	0	0	0	0	0	0
6	0	1	1	0	0	0	0	0	0
7	0	0	0	0	0	0	0	0	0

Note: Key: 1 = Centralised, 0 = Decentralised.

Table 5.4 Multistage assessment of the Labour party selection process (disabled)

Stage	2010			2005			2001		
	Key Participant	Rules	Final Score	Key Participant	Rules	Final Score	Key Participant	Rules	Final Score
1	0	0	*0*	0	0	*0*	0	0	*0*
2	0	0	*0*	0	0	*0*	0	0	*0*
3	1	0	*1*	1	0	*1*	1	0	*1*
4	0	0	*0*	0	0	*0*	0	0	*0*
5	0	0	*0*	0	0	*0*	0	0	*0*
6	0	0	*0*	0	0	*0*	0	0	*0*
7	0	0	*0*	0	0	*0*	0	0	*0*

candidates will be disproportionately filtered out at all stages but Stage 3. Looking to 2005, the final scores and thus expected relationships are the same as for 2001. In 2010, however, given the use of quotas for BAME aspirant candidates at Stages 5) nomination and 6) shortlisting, it is expected that the percentage of BAME aspirant candidates will be the same or higher at these stages and in this year than at the preceding stages and year.

Looking to BAME aspirants for the 2015 General Election, the participants and rules at Stage 1) application are classified as "0" for decentralised, and the rules at Stages 2) nomination and 3) shortlisting are classified as "1" for centralised. Thus, the nomination and shortlisting stages have final scores of "1", and it is expected that the percentage of BAME aspirants will be the same or higher at these centralised stages in 2015 than in 2010.

Disabled aspirant candidates

This section concludes by examining centralisation as is applies to people with disabilities. Table 5.4 demonstrates an extremely decentralised selection process structure in 2001, 2005, and 2010. This is very different than how the process evolved for women or even BAME aspirant candidates. Whereas the party began to use rules to constrain local selection choice for women in 2005, and for BAME aspirant candidates in 2010, no such rules exist for disabled aspirant candidates. As this is the case, participants with disabilities can be expected to be disadvantaged in all stages of the process with the exception of Stage 3 (NPP approval). As nothing has changed since 2010, the results are expected to be the same for 2015, with all four of its selection stages classified as "0" for decentralised.

How centralisation impacts participant success

This section draws upon the census data in Chapter 3 and the earlier centralisation/ decentralisation classifications to conduct 48 tests as to how centralisation affects participant success for women, BAME, and disabled aspirant candidates. As a reminder, the dependent variable for these tests is the extent to which the percentage of women, BAME, and disabled aspirant candidates increases or decreases as participants pass from one selection process stage to the next. The percentage of women, BAME, and disabled aspirant candidates is expected to be the same or higher than the percentage in the preceding stage if centralising features are present and lower if the stage is decentralised. The main independent variable, centralisation, is measured by whether the final selection decision is made by a central party agent and/or whether central party equality rules are in place. In total, 17 tests are conducted for women and BAME aspirant candidates in 2001, 2005, and 2010. However, due to unavailable data, it is possible to conduct only 14 tests for disabled aspirant candidates seeking candidacies in 2005 and 2010. Results for the 2015 General Election are discussed separately.

Women aspirant candidates

Table 5.5 presents the results of tests for women as they move through the Labour party's selection process. The first column indicates the selection stage. The second column (H) shows the hypothesis for the particular year and whether the stage is classified as decentralised ("D") or centralised ("C"). In 2010, Stage 1 is decentralised ("D"), indicating the percentage of women aspirant candidates is expected to be lower at Stage 1) party application than the previous stage (Pop %). If Stage 1 was classified as centralised ("C"), the percentage of women aspirant candidates would be expected to be the same or higher than at the previous stage. The next column (%) indicates a group's percentage of the total participants at each selection stage. For example, women made up 51 percent of the population and 29 percent of all Stage 1 aspirant candidates in 2010. The fourth column (+/-) indicates if the percentage of a group has increased, decreased, or stayed the same in relation to the preceding stage. The last column for each year indicates if the hypothesis is confirmed "Y" or disconfirmed "N".

As shown in Table 5.5, 12 of 17 (71 percent) hypotheses are confirmed. Moreover, all 7 (100 percent) tests conducted at centralised stages confirm the

Table 5.5 The effect of centralisation on women

Stage	2010				2005				2001			
	H	%	+/-	T	H	%	+/-	T	H	%	+/-	T
Population %		51%	-	-		51%	-	-		51%	-	-
1. Party application	D	29%	-22%	Y	D	30%	-21%	Y	D	26%	-25%	Y
2. NPP application	D	29%	0%	N	D	30%	0%	N	D	26%	0%	N
3. NPP approval	C	30%	+1%	Y	C	30%	0%	Y	C	27%	1%	Y
4. Seat application	D	31%	0%	N	D	32%	+2%	N	D	n/a	n/a	-
5. Nomination	C	32%	+1%	Y	C	34%	+2%	Y	D	n/a	n/a	-
6. Shortlisting	C	32%	0%	Y	C	34%	0%	Y	D	n/a	n/a	-
7. Selection	D	31%	-1%	Y	D	27%	-7%	Y	C	23%	n/a	-

centralisation hypothesis. In other words, women were not disproportionately filtered out at centralised stages in 2010, 2005, or 2001. At the same time, women aspirant candidates were disproportionately filtered out at 5 of 10 (50 percent) decentralised stages. The tests confirm that women are less likely to get disproportionately filtered out of the process at centralised than decentralised selection process stages. It must be noted that for all years, Stage 1) party application is decentralised, and the supply of women is much lower than the supply of men. However, once women apply to the NPP, their success rate is quite good until they lose ground at Stage 7) selection, which is decentralised. As a reminder, this is the stage where the central party has the least control over local party members.

From these results, there is prima facie evidence that quotas and AWS directed at increasing the demand for women amongst local party selectors are working and should at the very least remain in place and even become more robust to offset Stage 7 (selection) filtering. The 4-percentage point increase in women aspirant candidates in Stage 7 (selection) from 2005 to 2010 is likely due to the NEC's SSP activities in late 2009 and early 2010. In many cases, the SSP took over the nomination and shortlisting role of local parties to ensure enough women were selected so as to meet the party's target. Thus, 2010 was more centralised than 2005, and as predicted, the percentage of women in the final PPC pool is higher, reaffirming that women are more successful at centralised stages and in more centralised years. Although data for 2001 is incomplete, it is likely that fewer women were selected than in 2005 and 2010 because of the absence of quotas and AWS.

In terms of selections for the 2015 General Election, the centralisation hypotheses hold for Stage 2) nomination and Stage 3) shortlisting, where the percentage of women aspirants increased by 4 percentage points and 2 percentage points respectively. Moreover, the decentralisation hypothesis holds for Stage 4) selection, where the percentage of women decreased by 4 percentage points, which is 3 percentage points lower than in 2010. As with the 2010 General Election, the case again could be made for stronger sex quotas going forward as well as for a return to the NPP to allow the central party fuller monitoring capacity.

BAME aspirant candidates

In terms of BAME aspirant candidates, looking to Table 5.6, only 6 of 17 (35 percent) hypotheses are confirmed: 2 in 2010 and 4 in 2005. Moreover only 1 of 5 (20 percent) tests on centralised stages hold: Stage 6) shortlisting in 2010. At the same time, only 5 of 12 (42 percent) tests on decentralised stages hold. It would seem BAME aspirant candidates do not perform better at centralised stages than at decentralised stages. There is no undersupply of BAME aspirant candidates at Stage 1) apply to party. Instead there is a 4-percentage point surplus. There is inter-year variation between 2010 and 2005 at Stages 5) nomination and 6) shortlisting. In 2010, these stages are classified as centralised on the grounds that the central party implemented quotas for BAME aspirant candidates, whereas in 2005 these stages are classified as decentralised in light of the absence of quotas for BAME aspirant candidates.

Table 5.6 The effect of centralisation on BAME

Stage	2010				2005				2001			
	H	%	+/-	T	H	%	+/-	T	H	%	+/-	T
Population %		*12%*	-			*12%*	-			*8%*		
1. Party application	*D*	*16%*	*+4%*	N	*D*	*14%*	*+2%*	N	*D*	*12%*	*+4%*	N
2. NPP application	*D*	*16%*	*0%*	N	*D*	*14%*	*0%*	N	*D*	*12%*	*0%*	N
3. NPP approval	*C*	*15%*	*-1%*	N	*C*	*12%*	*-2%*	N	*C*	*9%*	*-3%*	N
4. Seat application	*D*	*16%*	*+1%*	N	*D*	*10%*	*-2%*	**Y**		*n/a*	*n/a*	
5. Nomination	*C*	*15%*	*-1%*	N	*D*	*8%*	*-2%*	**Y**		*n/a*	*n/a*	
6. Shortlisting	*C*	*15%*	*0%*	**Y**	*D*	*7%*	*0%*	**Y**		*n/a*	*n/a*	
7. Selection	*D*	*8%*	*-7%*	**Y**	*D*	*5%*	*-2%*	**Y**		*4%*	*n/a*	

In terms of the key findings, with the exception of Stage 6) shortlisting in 2010, as noted, BAME aspirant candidates do not do any better at centralised stages than at decentralised stages or years as predicted. At the same time, however, in 2010 the Stage 6) shortlisting hypothesis holds. This is due to the implementation of quotas for BAME aspirant candidates at this stage as well as the preceding nomination stage. The results for BAME aspirant candidates illustrate they face a considerable demand-side problem throughout the process amongst local selectors and, contrary to the centralisation theory, amongst central party agents. An increase in BAME aspirant candidates requires greater central party involvement and much more robust policy measures, such as all-black shortlists (ABS), to address the lack of demand amongst local party selectors.

Looking to selections for the 2015 General Election, all hypotheses hold, with BAME aspirants doing proportionally better at centralised Stages 2) nomination (+3 percentage points) and 3) shortlisting (+6 percentage points), and proportionally worse at decentralised Stage 4) selection (-8 percentage points). As earlier, there is a strong case for the implementation of ABS to counter this result.

Disabled aspirant candidates

Table 5.7 shows hypotheses testing for disabled people. Only 7 of 17 (41 percent) hypotheses are confirmed. A closer look at the results reveal 2 of 2 (100 percent) tests on centralisation stages hold. Thus, as hypothesised, disabled aspirant candidates are not disproportionately screened out at centralised stages. At the same time, 5 of 12 (42 percent) tests on decentralised stages are confirmed, revealing that disabled aspirant candidates are disproportionately filtered out in almost half of all decentralised stages. Looking to Stage 1 results, there is an undersupply of disabled aspirant candidates for both years. Disabled aspirant candidates are not disproportionately filtered out of the process as they move between Stages 2) NPP application and 6) shortlisting. However, at Stage 7) selection, they are disproportionately filtered out by local party members. As a reminder, there were no equality rules in place at any stage or year for disabled aspirant candidates,

Table 5.7 The effect of centralisation on disabled aspirants

Stage	2010				2005			
	H	*%*	*+/-*	*T*	*H*	*%*	*+/-*	*T*
Population %		*10%*	-			*10%*	-	
1. Party application	*D*	*4%*	*-6%*	**Y**	*D*	*3%*	*-7%*	**Y**
2. NPP application	*D*	*4%*	*0%*	N	*D*	*2%*	*-1%*	**Y**
3. NPP approval	*C*	*4%*	*0%*	**Y**	*C*	*2%*	*0%*	**Y**
4. Seat application	*D*	*4%*	*0%*	N	*D*	*2%*	*0%*	N
5. Nomination	*D*	*4%*	*0%*	N	*D*	*2%*	*0%*	N
6. Shortlisting	*D*	*4%*	*0%*	N	*D*	*2%*	*0%*	N
7. Selection	*D*	*2%*	*-2%*	**Y**	*D*	*1%*	*-1%*	**Y**

suggesting the deficit at Stage 7) selection could be corrected by stronger central party involvement.

Lastly, selections for the 2015 General Election reveal support for the centralisation hypotheses, with a proportionally higher percentage of aspirants with disabilities at the centralised Stage 2) nomination and with no change at the centralised Stage 3) shortlisting. The decentralised hypothesis also holds at Stage 4) selection, where aspirants with disabilities are disproportionly filtered (-2 percentage points). These findings support the call for stronger measures to increase the number of aspirants with disabilities on the party's candidate slate.

Conclusion

This chapter first offers a fresh and updated account of the key participants and rules at the party's selection stages for the 2001, 2005, 2010, and 2015 General Elections. It then uses this information to perform multistage classification assessments to determine the extent to which the stages and processes are centralised or decentralised. Centralisation is measured by the extent to which central or local party agents participate at a particular stage and the extent to which equality rules constrain participant behaviour. The multistage assessment reveals the party's selection processes are not as decentralised as characterised in the literature and that centralisation is associated with variations in aspirant candidate success. For example, some stages – nomination and shortlisting – are centralised for some groups but not others. The degree to which the process is centralised also varies over time. For example, 2015 and 2010 are more centralised than 2005 and 2010, and 2005 is more centralised than 2001.

The centralisation/decentralisation classifications were used to perform 48 tests concerning the effect centralisation has on the success of women, BAME, and disabled aspirant candidates. Testing confirmed 25 of 48 (52 percent) hypotheses. In terms of centralised stages, 10 of 14 (71 percent) hypotheses hold. Women and disabled aspirant candidates perform better at all centralised stages, whereas BAME aspirant candidates perform better at only 1 of 5 (20 percent) centralised stages. In terms of decentralised stages, 15 of 34 (44 percent) hypotheses hold, with 5 of 10 (50 percent) holding for women aspirant candidates, 5 of 12 (42 percent) holding for BAME aspirant candidates, and 5 of 12 (42 percent) holding for disabled aspirant candidates. Overall, these results support the idea that non-standard, non-ideal aspirant candidate types, in this case women and disabled aspirant candidates, are more successful when selection stages and processes are centralised. However, the results also show centralisation does not benefit all groups equally.

In terms of women aspirant candidates, for all years, they are disproportionally filtered out of the process at the final selection stage, which is also the most decentralised stage. There is some year to year variation. The filtering is worse for women aspirants in 2005 than it is in 2010, which is a slightly more centralised year due to the increased role of the NEC's SSP at the nomination and shortlisting stages. However, the filtering is harshest for women aspirants in 2015, perhaps due to the elimination of the centrally monitored NPP. For all years, BAME aspirant candidates appear to be disproportionately filtered out at almost all stages, in particular the final selection stage. This is even more so in 2015 and 2010 than in 2005, despite quotas in place for BAME aspirant candidates. Disabled aspirant candidates appear to be disproportionately filtered out of the process only at the final selection stage.

Given the results, there is a strong case to be made that AWS should remain in place if not strengthened. An equally strong case is made here for an increased role of central party participants in the selection process, for example, a return of the NPP, and for more robust quotas and guarantees for women and BAME aspirant candidates at the nomination and shortlisting stages, and for ABS. It appears that a systematic analysis of a party's entire selection process reveals equality quotas and guarantees are indeed the most effective way to bring about equality in party candidate pools. Chapters 6 and 7 further explore selector demand for the ideal aspirant candidate type at multiple stages of the party's selection process. In addition to sex, race, and physical ability, the relationship between aspirant candidate success and up to 41 other variables is tested using survey data.

Notes

1 As noted, these stages are reordered for the 2015 General Election as 1) application, 2) nomination, 3) shortlisting, and 4) selection.
2 In 2001 and 2005, aspirant candidates were required to be a member for 24 and 12 months respectively, unless waived by the NEC.
3 The NPP was first adopted in 1988 for by-elections.
4 Interview with a Labour party official.
5 Interview with a Labour Party official.
6 Interview with a Labour party official.
7 Interview with a Labour party official.
8 Interviews with Labour party officials.
9 Aspirant candidates' survey comments.
10 Aspirant candidates recommended by affiliated organisations (e.g., trade unions) are automatically endorsed and included on the panel (NEC Guidelines for the Selection of Parliamentary Candidates, 2006). The panel is brought up to date as additional aspirant candidates come forward during the process.

11 Interview with a Labour party official.

12 Interview with a Labour party official.

13 Interview with a Labour party official.

14 Interview with a Labour party official. Another Labour party official observed, the "trade union screening process is often tougher than our own", still, the "NEC may still want to interview that candidate".

15 Interview with a Labour party official.

16 Interview with a Labour party official.

17 *The Tribune* is the Labour party's weekly magazine. Interview with a Labour party official.

18 Interview with a Labour party official. The procedures secretary's acknowledgment of receipt of an aspirant candidate's interest is in the form of a standardised letter based on a template provided in the parliamentary selection pack titled *Acknowledgement of Declaration of Interest*. In the letter, the procedures secretary confirms the aspirant candidate is eligible to receive nominations for selection in a particular CLP. Enclosed with the letter is the Candidates' Code of Conduct, which the aspirant candidate is reminded to strictly adhere to. Additionally, a copy of the timetable and a list of secretaries of affiliated bodies to the CLP branch to which the aspirant candidate should forward copies of their application forms is enclosed.

19 Interview with a Labour party official.

20 Aspirant candidates' open-ended survey responses.

21 In cases where the list is inaccurate, the CLP procedures secretary or NEC representatives are contacted, and it is brought up to date. Members' participation in branch nominations is restricted to those who joined the CLP at least six months prior to the agreed freeze date (this is normally the Executive Committee timetable meeting to commence the selection process) and who are up to date with their subscription (Labour's Future, 2006, p. 37).

22 Meetings may be informal or formal; either way aspirant candidates must be notified of the format at least one week prior to the meeting. Where the aspirant candidates address the members, they draw lots to determine the order of appearance, and they may not be present at each other's interview. A maximum time for each aspirant candidate to address the meeting and to answer questions must be agreed upon in advance. Appropriate arrangements are made for aspirant candidates to meet with members, which, depending on geography and local party structure, may be a single branch, several branches, or on a constituency wide basis.

23 The Statement of Candidates' qualities lays out the job description of MP (e.g., responsibilities such as representing the constituency, making decisions in areas of parliament, competency, working with MEP, MPs, councillors) and "person specification" (e.g., knowledge, skills, experiences, and demonstrable abilities such as Labour party experience, other life experience, knowledge, and campaigning skills) (Labour's Future, 2006, pp. 30–33). The Statement of Candidates' Qualities is a standardised form to assist aspirant candidates with describing how their experience and qualities match up with the party's job description of MP. Aspirant candidates are reassured in the instructions that the "PLP is keen for candidates to draw on a wide range of knowledge, skills and experiences and backgrounds, and also demonstrate the relevance of these abilities to Parliament" (Labour's Future, 2006, p. 31). To this end, aspirant candidates are encouraged to complete each corresponding section in the application form, which includes Labour party experience, other life experience including work, family, or caring experience, policy knowledge, communication skills, campaigning skills, and problem solving skills (Labour's Future, 2006, p. 31).

24 With no member speaking more than once or for longer than three minutes.

25 Aspirant candidates' names must be moved and seconded in order to be included on the ballot. The ballot count is performed by two to four elected tellers and witnessed by a member designated by the CLP.

26 As in constituencies without a sitting MP, the NEC is responsible for setting a timetable for nomination from eligible party branches and affiliates as to whether they wish to select their sitting MP without triggering a full selection via a trigger ballot. If by the decided date a majority of party units and affiliated branches indicate their preference not to proceed with a full selection, the MP is selected as the PPC for the constituency subject to NEC endorsement (NEC Guidelines for the Selection of Parliamentary Candidates, 2006). If, on the other hand, a majority of party units and branches decide to open the ballot, then a full selection is held (NEC Guidelines for the Selection of Parliamentary Candidates, 2006). In cases where sitting MPs have constituency boundary changes, the General Secretary asks sitting MPs which constituency they wish to pursue (they must have a territorial interest in the seat, e.g., 40 percent or more of registered electors of the parliamentary constituency prior to the freeze date transferring to the new constituency).

27 Interview with a Labour Party official.

28 Interview with a Labour Party official.

29 The nominating bodies are required to follow the step-by-step procedure guidelines produced by the NEC.

30 Unless waived by the NEC appointed regional representative due to local circumstances.

31 Interview with a Labour party official, 2016.

32 Interview with a Labour party official, 2017.

33 The *Guidelines for Meeting with Nominated Candidates* applies; all aspirant candidates are supposed to be treated equally and given equal access to delegates. Moreover, there should be a separate waiting room where they can be "received by CLP officers prior the start" (Labour's Future, 2006, p. 53). The reason given for this is the "event allows all candidates to make an impression on a key section of the membership which may affect the final selection" (Labour's Future, 2006, p. 53; Labour Party Rule Book, 2008, p. 82). Furthermore, CLP officers are encouraged to circulate during the gathering and "seek to ensure that all candidates have the opportunity to meet all GC members" (Labour's Future, 2006, p. 53).

34 In terms of the counting procedure, the ballot is eliminated from the bottom until the required number of nominees are elected to the shortlist (Labour's Future, 2006, p. 51). Detailed regulations for the counts are issued in advance by the NEC. Full details of the counting procedure, along with example ballots, are outlined in the NEC guidelines and Labour Party Rule Book (Labour's Future, 2006, pp. 51–52).

35 In cases where an insufficient number of nominations are secured, the timetable may be extended in consultation with a designated representative and regional director to allow for further nominations to be considered (Labour Party Rule Book, 2008, p. 83).

36 The speaking order is determined by lots drawn before the meeting commences (Labour's Future, 2006, p. 74).

37 Interview with a Labour party official.

38 The ballot includes those nominees who were not automatically shortlisted (Labour's Future, 2006, p. 51).

39 See Peter Kenyon (2010).

40 Interviews with a Labour party official, 2016.

41 Members are given at least seven days in advance of the meeting. Listed alongside the shortlisted aspirant candidates is the name of the branch or affiliated organisation that nominated them.

42 At this point, the procedures secretary issues ballot papers to postal voters. To receive a postal vote ballot, members must fill out a standardised *Postal vote application form* and submit it to the procedures secretary by the date agreed in the timetable, normally week eight. Postal votes are normally issued to those who cannot attend the husting meeting due to medical reasons, impossible travel arrangements, holidays, work/caring responsibilities, or any other reason agreed upon by the NEC representative (Labour

Party Rule Book, 2008, p. 84). In the application form, they are asked to indicate the reason they are unable to attend the hustings; postal votes are not granted to those who "choose not to attend" (Labour Party Rule Book, 2008, p. 84; Labour's Future, 2006, p. 24). Members may apply for an emergency postal vote if they only discover they cannot attend the hustings after the closing date for postal votes has passed. They do this by directly sending the *Emergency postal vote application* form to the designated NEC representative, whose decision is final (Labour Party Rule Book, 2008, p. 84).

43 As in the preceding stages, the guidelines outlined in the *Conduct of a Hustings Meetings* and *Equal Opportunities Guidelines* are followed to encourage an atmosphere of equality and fairness. Thus questions of financial means or support, religion, or of a racist, sexist, homophobic, or anti-disabled nature are prohibited (Labour Party Rule Book, 2008, p. 83; Labour's Future, 2006, pp. 28–29, pp. 32–33).

44 On arriving at the meeting, members present their credentials to the stewards; in cases where these are challenged, the designated representative may ask for further proof of identity (e.g., residency) (Labour Party Rule Book, 2008, p. 83).

45 Normally, the same questions are posed to all aspirant candidates. These are agreed upon by the shortlisting committee ahead of the meeting (Labour Party Rule Book, 2008, p. 83).

46 The shortlisting committee appoints up to 12 members of the GC as scrutineers in addition to the procedures secretary: at least half of whom must be women. In addition, other eligible GC delegates may be present for the count, and each aspirant candidate may appoint a representative who is a member of the CLP to observe the count (Labour Party Rule Book, 2008, p. 84).

47 In some cases, the designated NEC representative may feel it necessary to use a roll call to prompt members to come forward to collect their ballot papers and/or to locate the ballot box in a separate polling room (Labour Party Rule Book, 2008, p. 84). The final count includes the postal vote ballots. The ballot box remains in the possession of the designated representative until the final count, normally held within the same week.

48 A ballot paper template is provided to CLP procedures secretaries in the NEC Guidelines for the Selection of Parliamentary candidates (Labour's Future, 2006, p. 81).

49 There are specific rules for postal votes: postal votes must be accompanied by a declaration of identity, which is then verified against the list of agreed upon postal voters. Moreover, the signature on the postal vote application form and declaration of identity must match (Labour Party Rule Book, 2008, p. 84).

50 The CLP procedures secretary may be consulted.

51 A record of the count is retained by the procedures secretary and the NEC representative. The CLP chair, procedures secretary, and candidates must complete and sign a form to accept financial responsibility of the election campaign (Labour Party Rule Book, 2008, p. 84). The candidate, additionally, must sign forms agreeing to the party's code of conduct as well as complete a register of interest (Labour Party Rule Book, 2008, p. 84).

52 The criteria for endorsement is approved and carried out by the NEC selection's board. Cases where any disputes arising out of the selection procedures cannot be resolved between the complainant(s) and designated representative are referred to a NEC approved independent Selection Monitor for further investigation. The Selection Monitor reports back to the NEC, whose decision on its final report is final and binding (Labour Party Rule Book, 2008, p. 85).

6 Assessing early stage selector preference for "ideal" candidates

While past chapters looked at 3 variables – sex, race, and physical ability – this chapter expands to 38 variables to test the ideal aspirant candidate theory. Data are collected from 566 original surveys completed by British Labour party aspirant candidates for the 2005 and 2010 General Elections to better understand why some and not other types of aspirant candidates survive the first 6 stages of the party's selection process. As explained, selections for the 2015 General Election and the 2017 and 2019 snap elections are not included in the analysis in this chapter or the next due to a lack of comparable data. After using initial statistical tests to further combine the 6 stages into 2 groups, the chapter uses 2 main logistic regression models to explore how 38 independent variables affect aspirant candidate success at Stage 3) approval on NPP and Stage 6) shortlisting of the selection process. It is expected successful aspirant candidates will tend to resemble the "ideal candidate" type and therefore be men, non-BAME, non-disabled, heterosexual, speak English as a first language, hold a university degree, have higher incomes, be employed in an instrumental occupation, identify as middle class, own their own home, have no dependents, and/or have a partner. Moreover, it is expected they will have considerable party experience, political experience, political networks, and political support and hold the appropriate political attitudes and be politically ambitious.

Surprisingly, none of the 38 variables are found to be significant during Stage 3 when central party officials decide which aspirant candidates are listed on the NPP, greatly undermining the idea that central party selectors in any way prefer particular types of aspirant candidates. Only three variables aid in explaining variance in the dependent variable during Stage 6 of the selection process, when local selectors shortlist those aspirant candidates applying for seats. Local selectors prefer aspirant candidates who live in the local constituency, who are not disabled people, and who are less wealthy. These findings suggest that local selectors do prefer certain types of candidates and support the ideal candidate theory when it comes to where aspirants live and physical ability, but undermines this ideal candidate theory when it comes to income. Using further regression testing to explore subsamples of Stage 6 data reinforces the importance of living locally to becoming shortlisted by local members but also reinforces the importance of how rules imposed by the central party act to shape Stage 6 outcomes, especially when it comes to improving the fortunes of women aspirant candidates.

Testing selector preferences for "ideal candidates"

This chapter starts with the idea that selectors prefer aspirant candidates with so-called ideal candidate traits and, as such, will choose these types of candidates when serving as gatekeepers during various stages of the candidate selection process. Thus, while the bivariate dependent variable measure used in this chapter will vary according to the selection process stage, it is always "selected" or "not selected". The independent variables capture various ideal aspirant candidate traits and generally reflect the qualities of previous candidates and MPs. In other words, the political norm, synonymous with the ideal aspirant candidate type, emerges from "what has come before" (Murray, 2013, p. 304; Prewitt, 1970). MPs, candidates, and, as argued in this study, aspirant candidates who do not reflect the ideal model are seen by party selectors as political outsiders. Indeed, Nirmal Puwar (2004) argues, "the white male body is taken to be the somatic norm within positions of leadership and the imagination of authority, and therefore women and 'black' MPs are space invaders" (p. 67). Beyond gender and ethnicity, it is posited aspirant candidates who do not resemble the political norm in terms of ability, qualifications, experiences, networks, political attitudes, and/ or levels of ambition are more likely to be screened out of the selection process. In this light, the political norm excludes all aspirant candidates who are "other", not just in terms of gender and ethnicity, but in terms of several other characteristics.

As shown in Table 6.1, the 38 independent variables used in this chapter depict many ideal aspirant candidate traits and are grouped into seven categories: social background, party experience, political experience, political network, personal support, political attitudes, and political ambition. Many of these variables have not been tested within the low information context of party selections in the UK or within the British Labour party since Norris and Lovenduski (1995) did so almost 20 years ago. As such, little is known about their effect upon party selector demand in the context of candidate selection processes. Moreover, relatively little is known about party selector preferences at multiple stages of selection or the degree to which demand for certain aspirant candidate types play a role in their evaluations. Problematically, much of the literature assessing these variables tested here do so within the context of election campaigns rather than candidate selection contests. This literature is further limited insofar that it tends to focus upon a few well-established core variables, such as sex and to a lesser degree race, and on data from the US (Campbell and Cowley, 2013, p. 1). Further, research in the UK also tends to solely focus on sex and race (Campbell and Cowley, 2013; Durose et al, 2013; Norris et al, 1990; Saggar, 2013).[1]

As explained, ideal candidate traits are likely not static but subject to change. This suggests constant evaluations of selection process fairness may be required. For example, many authors suggest a new professionalised pathway to parliament has replaced the older, traditional pathway (Durose et al, 2013, p. 259; Cairney,

Table 6.1 Independent variables and associated categories

Category	Associated Variables					
Social Background	Gender	Ethnicity	Ability	Age	Sexual Orientation	
	Language	Religion	Education	Occupation	Income	Employment
	Housing	Class	Children	Adult Dependents		Partner
Party Experience	Years in Party		Hours Worked		Employment	Volunteer
Political Experience	Councillor	Prior Elections		Interest Group	Union	
Political Networks	Recruited	Central Party		Local Party	Councillor	Union
	Interest Group		Local Resident			
Personal Support	Family or Friends		Employer			
Political Attitudes	Speak Out	Left/Right		Old/New Labour		
Political Ambition	Score					

2007; Allen, 2012). The traditional pathway involved being active in a trade union and the local party, standing for local council, and only then standing for MP. It also involved having a "brokerage" career conducive to a political career such as in law, medicine, or education (Norris and Lovenduski, 1995). The new pathway to parliament is said to involve going to university, joining a party, then working for a party, political organisation, interest group, or local council, and, finally, standing for MP. As such, new pathway aspirant candidates are expected to have careers or be involved in activities that are more directly instrumental to supporting a political career (Durose et al, 2013, p. 259; Cairney, 2007).

The next sections provide details for each of the 38 variables tested in this chapter, grouped by the categories shown in Table 6.1. Subsequent sections provide descriptive statistics for each variable and statistically test the relationship to the independent variable using Chi-square, Spearman's Rho, and, ultimately, logistic regression. Methodological and measurement details are provided in footnotes throughout the rest of this chapter.[2]

Social background variables

Beginning with *sex*, it is the most explored variable in party selection processes, with men hypothesised to be preferred to women by local party members due to highly gendered selection processes (Kenny and Verge, 2016; Lovenduski, 2005, 2016).[3] Still, it is somewhat unclear the extent to which women's underrepresentation in party aspirant candidate pools results from party selector preference for men over women. In this sense it is worthwhile to revisit this within the context of the British Labour party's selection process, and even more so in light of the party's considerable efforts during the last 30 years to address women's underrepresentation.

As noted in earlier chapters, women's underrepresentation is thought to result from party selector discrimination and prejudice and their use of stereotypes, with party selectors presuming women will lose votes and/or perceive women to lack the skills and resources needed for political success (Norris and Lovenduski, 1995, p. 115). Thus, parties are less likely to recruit women (Fox and Lawless, 2010), support women (Niven, 2006), and select women (Norris and Lovenduski, 1995). As noted by survey participants for this study, women aspirant candidates were often met with gender-based hostility from local selectors:

> When I first became involved with my local CLP, for the first two months I was not known by my name but was called "Little Miss" by the males (bar none) and elderly members. I took it as affectionate, but I doubt it was, not to begin with at least. Had it not been for the elderly female member, who directly encouraged me and first suggested that I stand, I probably would have left. This experience is not uncommon.

> . . . I was told explicitly and persistently by local party members that they weren't prepared to look at the CVs of or vote for any women – this was borne out in the selection results, whereby the three female candidates (who

were more experienced than the male candidates) got less than 20 votes (out of 270) between them.[4]

Race is included in this study as the literature suggests party selectors are biased against BAME aspirants as they assume such candidates will lose votes in the general election (Black, 2017; Campbell, 2011; Tolley, 2019).[5] Yet less is known about why BAME aspirant candidates are more underrepresented than women within the context of party selection processes. As with women, this study hypothesises that BAME aspirant candidates are not viewed as ideal candidates by the party's selectors. However, public attitudes toward race have changed, with new generations indicating lower levels of prejudice than the last (Campbell, 2011, pp. 206–207).[6] Still the underrepresentation of BAME aspirant candidates is thought to result from party selector prejudice (Saggar, 2013, p. 89; Norris and Lovenduski, 1995, p. 118; Norris et al, 1990; Bochel and Denver, 1983).[7] Indeed, studies in the US, the UK, and Canada have found electors use racial stereotypes to evaluate candidates, but it is unclear if these play out in selection processes (McDermott, 1998; Campbell and Cowley, 2013; Black, 2017). Although the central party has implemented quotas at the nomination and shortlisting stages, some BAME aspirant candidates feel this is not enough to counter an overall lack of demand amongst local party selectors:

> My experience was that as an ethnic minority woman, I often got shortlisted as rules said the shortlist should have one woman and one BAME candidate. This was only done to fit the rules, not that there was any chance of getting selected.[8]

At the same time, Saggar (2013) explained the modest increase in the proportion of BAME MPs in the British Parliament as a result of the "acceptably different" argument discussed earlier insofar that BAME aspirant candidates are accepted if they "tick off" other boxes associated with the ideal candidate type, such as having an instrumental occupation and/or being local (see Durose et al, 2013, p. 258).[9]

Even less is known about *ability* and the fortunes of disabled aspirant candidates during the selection process insofar that it is challenging to get absolute numbers (Durose et al, 2013, p. 248; Gould, 2011).[10] It has been argued that the prejudice and stigma experienced by disabled people may lead party selectors to perceive disabled aspirant candidates as "vote losers" and/or they might decide not to support disabled aspirant candidates on the premise that they will need extra support (Gould, 2011).[11] A survey participant relays: "I was asked whether I would be able to do the job as a disabled person".[12]

It has been established that legislatures are disproportionately comprised of middle-aged legislators, but little is known about the *age* preference for middle-aged over younger or older aspirant candidates during the selection process.[13] Younger aspirant candidates may be perceived as inexperienced, and older aspirant candidates may be perceived as over-the-hill. Middle-aged aspirant candidates, however, are more likely perceived by party selectors as "ideal", as they possess seemingly desirable attributes: they are energetic and committed with the right level of maturity and experience (Norris and Lovenduski, 1995, p. 120).

Systematic studies on *sexual orientation* and selection success are rare; however, scholars suspect party selectors are prejudiced against LGBTQ aspirant candidates insofar that they do not reflect the political norm and are likely underrepresented in legislatures (Everitt and Camp, 2014; Wagner, 2019).[14] In line with this, an aspirant candidate revealed, "I was bullied incessantly by a handful of sexist and homophobic men. . . . I was forced to leave the Labour party because of this behaviour".[15] However, there has been a shift in the attitudes toward gay rights particularly within the Labour party (Campbell, 2011, pp. 197–198).[16] Given this, aspirant candidate's sexual orientation is a timely variable to include in the analysis, with non-LGBTQ aspirant candidates hypothesised as being ideal to selectors.

Looking to *first language*, although the majority of MPs speak English as a first language, little is known about whether party selectors prefer aspirant candidates whose first language is English.[17] However, speaking English may be preferred by party selectors insofar that it is perceived as a sign of "Britishness" and as belonging to the in-group (Campbell, 2011). In terms of *religion*, it may be that party selectors prefer Christian over non-Christian aspirant candidates on the grounds that the former reflects the political norm and therefore the ideal aspirant candidate type.[18] Whether this is the case within the context of party selections is of interest given the shift in attitudes toward religion. For example, the percentage of the public identifying as Christian has decreased, while the percentage identifying as having no religion has increased.[19]

Legislatures are disproportionally comprised of members with higher than average *educational* levels; at the same time, there is little recent research on whether party selectors prefer aspirant candidates with university or polytechnic degrees over those with no degrees (Norris and Lovenduski, 1995, p. 386).[20] Further grounds to assess education is rooted in the argument that education is a measure of the "quality" of candidates (Campbell and Cowley, 2013, pp. 3–4). In this spirit, party selectors may prefer aspirant candidates with degrees on the basis that they perceive them as possessing the skills necessary for political office, such as being articulate and being well equipped to debate policy (Norris and Lovenduski, 1995, p. 113). Indeed, a party official noted aspirant candidates who are not approved fail to demonstrate sound political knowledge and "that [they] can put a case across".[21] Moreover, some argue that party selectors are more likely to choose their "betters", which, in the context of education, include aspirant candidates with post-secondary degrees (Norris and Lovenduski, 1995, p. 113).

In terms of *occupation*, there has been a good deal of attention paid to the professionalisation of politics in the UK and elsewhere, finding legislators are increasingly drawn from a narrowing range of political and occupational experiences (Campbell and Cowley, 2013, pp. 1–3).[22] However, less is known about the way in which party selectors react to aspirant candidates' occupations. As noted, past research reveals party selectors preferred those with brokerage occupations, for example, barristers and teachers, which are complementary to politics (Norris and Lovenduski, 1995, pp. 110–113, pp. 120–121). However, more recent research suggests instrumental careers, such as journalism, public relations, trade union official party worker, parliamentary staff, think tank staff, and local government councillor provide "apprenticeship for higher elected office" (Cairney, 2007, p. 3). The logic here is occupations such as journalism and public relations provide training in the "arts of persuasion or publicity", whereas trade union official, interest group representative, and local councillor have "obvious links to existing decision makers (party worker, MP assistant, think tank)" (Cairney, 2007, p. 3). Instrumental occupations do not include brokerage occupations "because these professions involve significant barriers to entry (such as extensive training and professional commitments) and a much less direct link with politics" (Cairney, 2007, p. 3). Allen (2012) adds the type of experience that is identified as instrumental to political careers can be both paid and unpaid and both full-time and experiential, additionally, it can be pursued in tangent with non-political full-time work. Moreover, instrumental experience can be partisan or nonpartisan and located at Westminster or elsewhere. In other words, it can involve working or volunteering for a non-partisan interest group (p. 23; Durose et al, 2013, p. 259).

The premise here is that party selectors prefer aspirant candidates who have demonstrable connections to government acquired by being "policy and public relations advisors to MPs, former and current officials at Millbank, researchers in Labour-linked think tanks . . . members of the new public relations consultancies that have sprung up over the last decade or so" (Cairney, 2007, p. 7). Moreover, party selectors look for traits, such as "good communicators and 'ambassadors' for the government", that tend to develop with occupational occupations and experiences (Cairney, 2007, p. 7).[23] An aspirant candidate reflects the odds are against those who do not fit this profile:

> You are up against a number of usually younger prospective candidates who often work for MPs or in Westminster and are in the know long before anything is made public and have advanced and unfair access to membership lists, unlimited time off work with pay unaffected and no other life or family to consider, in at least one case with a sponsoring organisation buying them a new car and paying hotel bills etc. to stay locally while they canvassed.

Relatedly, little research since Norris and Lovenduski (1995) has been done assessing the influence of aspirant candidate *income, employment status, housing tenure,* and *class* upon selection success.[24] However, legislatures are still disproportionally comprised of MPs who, prior to being elected, drew high incomes from full-time work and owned their own homes. In other words, they are more likely middle to upper class than working class. It has been argued that the middle class is increasingly the political class (Hector, 2012). Reflecting on the resources needed to secure a position on a shortlist and eventually a seat, an aspirant candidate notes the selection process is "not an equal opportunity, people with more money and resources to print glossy newsletters have the edge".[25] At the same time, a Labour party official suggests party members do not necessarily seek aspirant candidates who appear to have too much money:

> somebody who can be quite unassuming tends to impress people in the Labour party because people in the Labour party don't really like show-offs. . . . They really don't want somebody driving in a Bentley to their meeting with some Savile Row suit on talking about their three houses in a villa in Spain. . . . Those sorts of things are not ever going to appeal.[26]

It is expected aspirant candidates with no *children* or no *adult dependents* in their care are more likely shortlisted than aspirant candidates with dependents in their care insofar that the former will have much more free time to pursue a position on a shortlist and be seen by selectors as in a "better position to pursue a seat".[27] A survey participant notes: "I was asked how I thought I would manage at Westminster with two young children back at home – the fact that my husband would be looking after them did not seem to impress!"[28]

Beyond the imagining of legislators with the requisite supportive *partner*, little research has been done on assessing the relationship between having a partner and political success.[29] A recent study in Canada, however, found local party selectors are much more likely to select aspirant candidates with a partner than those without a partner (Ashe and Stewart, 2012). Arguably, party selectors perceive aspirant candidates with partners as more likeable and trustworthy and as a resource insofar that the constituency gets two campaigners for the price of one. An aspirant candidate recalls: "I was asked about marital status and told that married candidates were best". Another aspirant candidate still was told by a local party selector to "get a husband!"[30]

Party experience

This category of variables is viewed by many authors as well as party officials as an essential component of any political career (Allen, 2012; Cairney, 2007; Durose et al, 2013). Party experience includes the *years* the aspirant has been in the party, *hours worked* for the party, whether the aspirant has been *employed* by the party, and if they have *volunteered* for the party.[31] During interviews with Labour party officials, it was disclosed that party selectors look for aspirant candidates with significant party experience:

> "They need to demonstrate some campaigning skills, demonstrate knowledge of party policy and demonstrate interpersonal teamwork and liaison skills, things like that".

> "They need to show [their] experience in carrying out voluntary activities in the Labour party or trade union movement. Supporting it not as a professional but supporting it as an activist. [The] types of things [they] have done to advance the Labour movement . . . that would be something that would definitely be expected".

"They need to show commitment to the party, for example, by selling raffle tickets".[32]

Moreover, when asked what kind of people are shortlisted and selected in Labour's most winnable seats, a Labour party official replied: "They're advisors to ministers and doing government and party work".[33] Further, some authors suggest aspirant candidates wishing to succeed must demonstrate their commitment to the party, as it is a show of their willingness to put in the amount of time required to succeed (Norris and Lovenduski, 1995, p. 156).[34] Speaking to this, an aspirant candidate surmises: "It appears the reason I was not successful was because of a 'lack of commitment' to the party. This translated as not canvassing, etc.".[35] Yet the extent to which party selectors still prefer aspirant candidates who have been long-time party members and who spend considerable time on party related activities and/or have been employed by the party is unclear. Indeed, party officials present a case for selecting fresh faces, in other words, aspirant candidates with less history in the party may be at an advantage:

> if you've been a member of a party for a decade, a couple of decades, before you go for a seat, I'll guarantee you'll have something in your past that if the wrong person is going up against you they'll know. Although our code of conduct says you can't disparage people quite a few of these things get out and these things are known and in that instance . . . in any sort of group, if you're actually a strong individual with strong enough views you're . . . quite likely to be the kind of person who'll have ended up making quite strong friends, but also quite strong enemies. If you've got a local party it's not necessarily always an advantage to be the local candidate.[36]

Political experience

Other than dedication to the party, political experience is also often linked with political success.[37] The new pathway to parliament may indeed place even greater emphasis on political experience, such as being elected as a *councillor*. In this study, *prior election* attempts as well as holding office in an *interest group* or *trade union* are treated as ideal candidate traits. Arguably, party selectors prefer aspirant candidates who have a record of experience, skills, knowledge, and networks necessary to securing a seat (Norris and Lovenduski, 1995, p. 159; Allen, 2012). A Labour party official revealed successful aspirant candidates "need quite a strong party background, evidence of activity at the local level, or national level, maybe they've been a councillor".[38]

Political networks

Political networks supposedly provide aspirant candidates with access to key central and local party decision makers. Indeed, according to a party official, networks are all important, without them, "inexperienced candidates fall down".[39] According to another party official, "networks can't be overestimated enough . . . you don't get that from any sort of formal training. . . . You do get people who read the handbook on the selection guidelines and if you're just going to follow those . . . you've lost already".[40] Moreover, another party official suggests networks:

> introduce you to people, they could give you an opportunity to speak, they could let you know when the dinners were, when the events were, who else to speak to, who not to speak to, who was supporting other people. If you've got somebody who actually knows what's going on who could tell you who the other people's main supporters are so you don't sort of go down blind alleys with people and you don't give away information to other people you wouldn't want necessarily to share otherwise.[41]

Building on the work of Fox and Lawless (2010), aspirant candidates who are *recruited* and who receive central party, local party, trade union, and interest group support and encouragement throughout the selection process are potentially more likely to seek and receive nominations and positions on shortlists.[42] Starting with *residing locally*, recent research in the UK finds elections are increasingly localised insofar that the local candidate effect is of growing importance (Campbell and Cowley, 2013; Evans, 2012). Further, the idea of local candidates seen as best able to represent local constituent interests is increasingly important to party electoral strategies, as evident in their amplified efforts to address the lack of diversity in their candidate and legislator pools (Campbell and Cowley, 2013, p. 1). In addition, aspirant candidates with *central party*, *local party*, *union*, and/ or *interest group* support are likely to have stronger networks than those who do not have such support and, as such, may be considered ideal candidates (Norris and Lovenduski, 1995, p. 162).[43]

Of all the political network measures, being a *local resident* emerges as the most discussed amongst party officials and aspirant candidates.[44] A party official notes, "the only way you can go about [selection] is you can't be a stranger to the CLP. You'd have an advantage as a local candidate – you'd have a stronger network".[45] Moreover, an aspirant candidate suggests: "Currently the process means that branches are faced with a pile of 50 plus CVs with very little information on how to choose between candidates. Naturally they will pick faces they already know locally".[46] Another aspirant candidates muses:

> There is a bias towards local candidates, especially local councillors, possibly because of name recognition or having a good local network to win a selection. It is very difficult to break into a local CLP unless the CLP is forced to consider external candidates by the NEC excluding them.

Additionally, several aspirant candidates indicate those with *local networks* are more likely to get the membership list in advance of other aspirant candidates.

Thus, local networks are assessed insofar that it is a variable that is present in much of the recent literature as well as party official and survey participant comments, but, as with the other variables tested in this study, it is understudied in the context of selection process outcomes (Campbell and Cowley, 2013; Childs and Cowley, 2011; Evans, 2012).

Political attitudes

By loosely drawing upon *May's Law of Curvilinear Disparity*, it is argued here that political attitudes potentially influence aspirant candidates' selection success. According to May, there is an ideological disparity between the three party strata: 1) the party elite comprised of MPs, selected candidates, and central party officials (e.g., the NEC); 2) the middle elite comprised of local office holders, party members, party voters, and as proposed here, aspirant candidates, and 3) the non-elite comprised of non-members who may sometimes support the party (May, 1973). More precisely, it is suggested that the middle elite (e.g., aspirant candidates, party members, and local party office holders) is much more ideologically radical and emotional than the party elite and the non-elite (May, 1973). This theory suggests the party elite, that is, central party selectors, are more likely to grant approval to aspirant candidates who do not speak out against the central party, who are more right than left, and who identify more as new Labour than old Labour. On the other hand, local party selectors responsible for nominating, shortlisting, and selecting are more likely to choose aspirant candidates who speak out against the central party, who are more left than right, and who identify more as "old Labour" than "new Labour".[47] Indeed, a Labour party official provides comment on the role political attitudes potentially play in the selection process:

> what a process that's basically fair doesn't recognise is that different constituencies are quite different – the politics of one constituency might be quite different from the politics of another, so some of the constituencies, you'd walk into a meeting there and think 'well they're quite new Labour' whereas most other constituencies you'd walk into and they're much more left of the party. So although the process is fair you're never going to get beyond the fact that politics is about opinion. You can be the brightest person in the world, but if you say stuff on an issue that a large proportion of the membership felt strongly about then you've lost. That doesn't mean you need to go in and say things you don't believe in.[48]

Although there are challengers to May's theory, it is useful for understanding, if it is at all the case, whether aspirant candidates who speak out, and/or are more left than right, and/or more old Labour than new Labour are more or less likely approved to the NPP, nominated, shortlisted, and/or selected as candidates (Holland, 1987; Norris, 1997b; Seyd and Whiteley, 1992).

Political ambition

Studies of political ambition tend to focus on potential aspirant candidates rather than actual aspirant candidates. However, the often reported finding that men are more likely to foster political ambitions and/or pursue careers in politics than women is frequently used to explain why some aspirant candidates succeed over others (Fox and Lawless, 2004, 2010; Lawless and Fox, 2005). Political ambition is associated with selection success insofar that ambitious aspirant candidates more likely possess the political drive needed to get nominated, shortlisted, and later selected.[49] Moreover, they are more likely to develop the political networks, experience, and resources than less ambitious aspirant candidates (Norris and Lovenduski, 1995, p. 174). Further to this, party selectors may perceive ambitious aspirant candidates as go-getters and more willing to do what it takes to win a seat.

Sample choices and statistical methods

The remainder of this chapter uses logistic regression analysis to examine the relationship between aspirant candidate success during two key demand stages of the candidate selection process: 1) Stage 3, when central party selectors either choose to include aspirants on, or reject them from, the NPP and 2) Stage 6, when GCs decide whether or not to shortlist aspirant candidates for Stage 7 selection contests. The remainder of this section explains why Stage 7 is left for the next chapter and why surveys from Stages 1 to 3 (apply to the party, apply to the NPP, and approval on the NPP) are grouped together in the first regression and surveys from Stages 4 to 6 (apply for seats, nomination, and shortlisting) are grouped together for the second regression. The section concludes with a brief discussion of related methods.

Table 6.2 presents a stage-by-stage count of surveys collected from aspirant candidates participating in the 2005 and 2010 British Labour party selection processes. "D" indicates stages where aspirant candidate pools are shaped by party selectors: Stage 3) screening is conducted by *central party selectors*, Stages 5 and 6 by *local party delegates*, and Stage 7 by *local party members*. "S" indicates stages where aspirants filter themselves out, including Stages 1, 2, and 4, where aspirant candidates formally apply or do not apply to the party, NPP, and seats. For comparative purposes, the final row of Table 3.1 shows similar stage-by-stage assessments using the 2005 and 2010 census data discussed in Chapter 3.

Table 6.2 shows 566 aspirant candidates responded to the survey, a full 18.5 percent of the 3,064 aspirants who applied to the party to become candidates in 2005 and 2010. The table shows 566 survey respondents began the process, with 527 of those entrants reaching Stage 2, 487 reaching Stage 3, and so on, with 208 of those completing surveys indicating they were ultimately selected as candidates in Stage 7. The percentage of reduction in surveys is also included, with the overall pool reduced by 7 percent by Stage 2, 14 percent by Stage 3, and so on, with 63 percent of the pool being reduced by Stage 7. For the most part, these percentage reductions in surveys are very similar to actual percentage reductions

Table 6.2 Survey data from aspirant candidates (2005 and 2010 selection processes)

Stage	1		2		3		4		5		6		7	
(Filter)	*(S)*		*(S)*		*(D)*		*(S)*		*(D)*		*(D)*		*(D)*	
	All Aspirant Candidates	%	Apply NPP	%	Approved NPP	%	Apply to Seat	%	Nomination	%	Shortlisted	%	PPC	%
Survey	566	0	527	7	487	14	430	24	358	37	334	41	208	63
Census	3064	0	3010	2	2635	14	2250	27	1917	37	1759	43	1269	59

Note: (Filter): S = Supply-Side Filter, D = Demand-Side Filter.

revealed through the Chapter 3 examination of census data from 2005 and 2010, lending additional confidence of the representativeness of the survey data.

As stated earlier, this Chapter examines two demand-focused stages: Stages 3 and 6; leaving the Stage 7 analysis for Chapter 7. It is thought appropriate to separate Stages 1 through 6 from Stage 7 as aspirant candidates must first be short-listed in order to be selected in Stage 7; thus, it would be problematic to compare *all* aspirant candidates (Stage 1) with *all* selected candidates and non-selected aspirant candidates at the final selection stage (Stage 7). Doing so could potentially skew the results, as the analysis would include aspirant candidates who do not apply for seats and in turn do not get nominated or shortlisted.

The choice to group Stages 1 and 3 for one analysis and Stages 4, 5, and 6 for another is made for logical and statistical reasons. First, earlier chapters show demand is more of a hindrance to particular groups progressing through the selection process than supply, suggesting it is more important to understand what happens during Stages 3, 5, and 6 than Stages 2 and 4. Looking again to Table 6.2, that the first demand-side filter occurs at Stage 3 suggests a "natural" break and a good reason to group Stages 1, 2 and 3.[50]

While it initially might seem prudent to perform separate statistical tests on all stages of the selection process, this is not possible. As shown in Table 6.2, the percentage reduction of aspirant candidates between any two adjacent stages is too small to yield statistically significant relationships – described in the literature as "rare events" (King and Zeng, 2001, pp. 137–163). For example, the 7 percent reduction in aspirants between Stages 1 and 2 also shows 93 percent remain in the process. Using such lopsided ratios for comparative purposes within a relatively small sample almost guarantees no independent variables will prove related in a statistically significant way. The remedy, to group surveys to create a more balanced ratio of those who are successful and not successful, perhaps reveals the first disadvantage of this micro-approach to assessing fairness during the candidate selection process.

To recap, regression analysis is used to build an initial model to predict what types of aspirant candidates who begin the process in Stage 1 have a better chance of being approved for the NPP in Stage 3. It then presents a second model to predict, of all those who apply for seats in Stage 4, what types of candidates have better odds of being shortlisted to stand for seats by local party selectors in Stage 6. Each model is built using a series of similar steps. First, frequency tables are presented to describe the composition of each sample in relation to the 38 independent variables. Second, Chi-square and Spearman's Rho tests are used to test which of the 38 variables are shown to have an initial statistical relationship with the dependent variable.[51] Finally, those variables found to be significant through Chi-square and Spearman's Rho tests are further examined using logistic regression. The results of these models are then looped back to discuss the idea of the ideal aspirant candidate and whether selectors tend to favour certain types of candidates. In terms of hypotheses, it is expected party selectors are more likely to favour aspirant candidates who reflect the ideal aspirant candidate type. It is also worth noting that this study also creates an "idealness score" for each sample to get a sense of the overall quality of the pool. The idealness score is calculated for each sample by determining whether 50 percent or more of a particular variable is from the ideal category and assigning the variable a score of "1" for 50 percent or more ideal and "0" if under 50 percent. These binary scores for each of the 38 individual variables are then summed and calculated as a percentage for an overall idealness score out of 100 percent.[52]

Model 1: approval on the National Parliamentary Panel

Approval to the NPP is the first demand-side filter where central party selectors make known their preferences for aspirant candidate types through whom they do and do not choose to the NPP. As discussed in Chapters 4 and 5, one of the original intentions of the NPP was to pre-endorse aspirant candidates before they moved further through the selection process. As a central party official notes:

> We want to get the best candidates, people who will make good candidates and politicians. . . [this individual . . . pointing to a man's name] is somebody who is never going to get selected. . . . Because he's a poor candidate . . . he's been on for, this is his third time I think, he doesn't ever get anywhere.[53]

Thus, the NPP is seen as a critical juncture in the process insofar that lack of central party approval comes with a stigma.[54] For example, local party selectors refer to the NPP for centrally approved aspirant candidates and are wary of those whose names do not appear on it. As a party official describes, "the fact that they have not been approved by NEC is a part of their record so it'd be unlikely that they'd be selected anyway".[55] In terms of criteria, interviews with party officials reveal they are looking for aspirant candidates who are presentable and articulate, and who "have the politics and political ability in terms of networks and things like that".[56] Reasons for rejecting aspirant candidates at this stage include:

> sometimes it's just that they are politically naïve, sometimes it's that it's a language barrier issue, somebody's not particularly good at communicating, or their politics are out of keeping with the party and that would be a concern if we were to endorse them and they go on to seek selection. So, a variety of things. They might not understand the role of an MP, and the work that's involved.[57]

Frequencies

Table 6.3 shows the frequencies for each variable as well as Chi-square and Spearman's Rho relationship test results.[58] The frequencies describe all surveyed aspirant candidates who applied to the party to stand as candidates in Stage 1 during the selection processes for the 2005 and 2010 General Elections, with the relationship tests determining the statistical relationship between variables. Each variable is described according to the raw number and percentage of predictor

Table 6.3 NPP approval: variables, descriptive statistics, and relationship tests

		n	Predictor	#	%	Comparator	#	%	Median
Dependent Variables	On NPP	566	Yes	487	86%	No	79	14%	-
Social Background	Sex	566	Man	400	71%	Woman	166	29%	-
	Race*	566	Non-BAME	474	84%	BAME	92	16%	-
	Ability	566	Non-Disabled	528	93%	Disabled	38	7%	-
	Age	487	-	-	-	-	-	-	44 yrs
	Sex Orient.	418	Heterosexual	384	92%	LGBTQ	34	8%	-
	Language	440	English	412	94%	Other	28	6%	-
	Religion	373	Christian	166	45%	Other	207	55%	-
	Education	482	Degree	398	83%	No	84	17%	-
	Occupation	438	Instrumental	242	55%	No	196	45%	-
	Income	433	-	-	-	-	-	-	£40–50k
	Employment	415	Full-time	340	82%	No	75	18%	-
	Class*	394	Middle	213	54%	No	181	46%	-
	Housing	374	Owner	300	80%	No	74	20%	-
	Children	384	No	259	67%	Yes	125	33%	-
	Adults	393	No	352	90%	Yes	41	10%	-
	Partner	404	Yes	287	71%	No	181	29%	-
Party Experience	Membership*	560	-	-	-	-	-	-	14 yrs
	Hours	417	-	-	-	-	-	-	7 hrs
	Employee	491	Yes	60	12%	No	431	88%	-
	Volunteer	487	Yes	437	90%	No	50	10%	-
Political Experience	Councillor	534	Yes	236	44%	No	298	56%	-
	Prior Election*	534	Yes	408	76%	No	126	24%	-
	Interest Group	483	Yes	345	71%	No	138	29%	-
	Union*	482	Yes	208	43%	No	274	57%	-

(Continued)

Table 6.3 (Continued)

		n	Predictor	#	%	Comparator	#	%	Median
Political Networks	Recruited*	458	Yes	163	36%	No	295	64%	-
	Local Res.	411	Yes	153	37%	No	258	63%	-
	Central Party*	449	Yes	313	70%	No	136	30%	-
	Local Party*	448	Yes	393	88%	No	55	12%	-
	Councillor	376	Yes	182	48%	No	194	52%	-
	Union*	452	Yes	264	58%	No	188	42%	-
	Interest Group	449	Yes	289	64%	No	160	36%	-
Personal Support	Fam/Friends*	442	Yes	370	84%	No	72	16%	-
	Employer	426	Yes	169	40%	No	257	60%	-
Political Attitudes	Speak Out	406	Yes	193	48%	No	213	52%	-
	Left/Right	414	-	-	-	-	-	-	Left (3)
	Old/New	400	Old	142	36%	New	258	64%	-
Ambition	Score	427	-	-	-	-	-	-	Fairly (7)

Note: * = Chi-square or Spearman's Rho test statistically significant at <.05.

and comparator categories. For bivariate independent variables, predictor traits are associated with those hypothesised as being "ideal" and thus preferred by party selectors. The median value is shown for independent variables with scale measures.

Starting with the dependent variable, the table shows 487 respondents (86 percent) indicated they were approved to the NPP (predictor) and 79 (14 percent) stating they were not approved to the NPP (comparator value). Turning to the *independent variables*, this initial sample generates an idealness score of 68, in other words, ideal aspirant candidate types make up a majority of those who apply in 26 of the 38 assessed variables.[59] This score of 68 shows a somewhat ideal pool of aspirants who seek party candidacies, although it also reflects the fact that 12 categories (32 percent) are dominated by non-ideal type aspirant candidates.

Moving to individual variables, in terms of sex, race, and physical ability, the survey data broadly reflect the census data collected from the Labour party. Moreover, the survey data reflect the general population in terms of ethnicity, first language, housing tenure, and religion. However, there are striking differences between Labour's initial aspirant candidate pool and the general population. For example, the pool contains a lower proportion of women and the educational attainment level of Labour party aspirants is much higher than the general population. Indeed, 47 percent of those surveyed hold a post-graduate degree and 35 percent a university or polytechnic degree. Labour's aspirant candidate pool is also disproportionately middle class with high household incomes. Notably, however, not a single aspirant candidate identified as upper class. Further, their annual household incomes range from £5000 to £200,000, with 2 aspirant candidates reporting incomes less than £5000 and 9 reporting incomes over £200,000. Moreover, a majority are employed in professional, instrumental occupations. Additionally, in terms of political resources, the initial aspirant candidate pool has extraordinarily high levels of party and political experience, political activism, and political networks.

• Social Background Variables

"Idealness scores" are also calculated for each category, with ideal aspirant candidates making up a majority in 93 percent (15 of the 16) of the social background variables.[60] Thus, the aspirant candidates who began the process overwhelmingly possess social background characteristics commonly associated with the ideal aspirant candidate type. The only ideal variable in which they do not make up a majority is "Christian", with 45 percent of the aspirant candidates (166 of 373) identifying as Christian and 55 percent (207 of 373) identifying as "other".[61] To note, that over half of the aspirant candidates are employed in instrumental occupations reflects the argument that many political hopefuls are embarking upon the new pathway to parliament discussed earlier. Indeed, in terms of their occupations, the most to least frequently cited include: policy advisors/directors/consultants/researchers; trade unionists; councillors; parliamentary assistants; party employees; civil servants; lawyers; lecturers/teachers; CEOs/directors/managers;

academic staff; communication officers; local government officers; journalists; doctors; accountants; charity/social/community workers; IT consultants/computer programmers; engineers; economists; housing/estate managers; postal workers; call centre workers; and, retail/sales.

• Party Experience Variables

The "idealness score" for political experience variables is 2 of 4, thus ideal aspirant candidates who begin the process make up just half of the aspirant candidates in 50 percent of the variables.[62] Not surprisingly, aspirant candidates spend a considerable number of hours per week on party activities, and almost all volunteer for the party in some capacity. This reflects the emphasis party officials place upon the ability to demonstrate a high degree of commitment to the party. To consider, aspirant candidates frequently comment that too many party staffers are seeking selection and winning; thus the percentage of party employees in the pool is at first glance lower than expected.

• Political Experience Variables

As with party experience, the idealness score for political experience is two of four. As noted, a strikingly high percentage of aspirant candidates who begin the process attempted to secure political office in the past and have held office in an interest group. In terms of the latter, this too reflects aspirant candidates' willingness to follow the new pathway to parliament. Moreover, a much higher percentage of aspirant candidates have experience in interest groups than in trade unions. This finding further bolsters the new pathway idea but challenges the archetypal image of the "union" Labour party candidate. That almost half of the aspirant candidates have been councillors is also remarkable and reflects the idea that many who seek higher political office have first served as local councillors – an instrumental occupation from which national parties commonly draw (Allen, 2012; Cairney, 2007).

• Political Network Variables

The idealness score for the political network variables is four of seven, in other words, ideal aspirant candidate types make up a majority in 57 percent of the variables. That a considerably high percentage of aspirant candidates received support from the central and local parties speaks to the influential roles they play in the selection process. Given a higher percentage of aspirant candidates are drawn from interest groups than from trade unions, this is not altogether surprising. Again, the new professionalised pathway idea intimates that the skills developed while working with an interest group are directly instrumental to politics. At the same time, it challenges the idea that trade unions determine the party's candidate pool. Indeed, as discussed in Chapter 4, central party reforms have, over time, reduced the influence of trade unions upon the selection process. At the same time, however, that over half of all aspirant candidates still draw support from trade unions indicates unions still wield considerable influence.

In terms of recruitment, that 36 percent of aspirant candidates were recruited – although less than half – supports the idea that central party as well as local party encouragement is linked with political success (Fox and Lawless, 2010). To consider, the most frequently mentioned recruiters include: "10 Downing Street", regional directors, MPs, and party staff. This was followed by local party recruiters, such as branch chairs/secretaries and treasurers. Aspirant candidates also indicated they were recruited by councillors as well as national and local trade unionists.

- Personal Support

Only one of two variables included in this category leans toward the ideal. That more aspirant candidates have support from family and friends is expected, while the low level of support from their employers is surprising. The lack of employer support may be caused by employers worried about lower employee productivity during the selection process and/or disdain for the Labour party. Nonetheless, it is noteworthy that aspirant candidates are still willing to seek candidacies even without support from their employers who could very well reprimand or even dismiss them.

- Political Attitudes

The idealness score for political attitudes is one of three.[63] The political attitudes of the aspirant candidates are surprising. For example, almost half of all aspirant candidates have spoken publicly against the party's policies. Qualitative survey data show aspirants most frequently spoke out against the party's position on Iraq, Trident, and ID cards. This is somewhat disconcerting for the party given the screening process is in part intended to screen out potentially problematic candidates, in other words, those who do not share its policies. At the same time, a solid majority of aspirant candidates identify as new Labour as opposed to old Labour, reflecting the overall shift toward the latter as was discussed in Chapter 4. Moreover, the median score on the left-right political continuum – with one being extremely left and seven being extremely right – is three, slightly left of centre. To some degree this suggests those coming forward still have ties with the party's democratic socialist roots.

- Political Ambition

With a median score of seven, the political ambition score favours the ideal.[64] It is not altogether surprising that aspirant candidates who seek candidacies have relatively high levels of political ambition, otherwise they would not aspire to higher political office. Notably, there is no difference between women's and men's stated level of political ambition. This finding builds on Fox and Lawless (2010) insofar that the level of political ambition between women and men does not necessarily differ once they have committed to running for office. Nor are there any differences between non-BAME and BAME or disabled and non-disabled aspirant candidates' stated levels of political ambition.

Statistical tests

As shown in Table 6.3, initial Chi-square and Spearman's Rho tests reveal 10 of the 38 variables are related to the dependent variable in a statistically significant way. These include race, class, membership length, prior election experience, holding union office, recruitment, central party support, local party support, union support, and family/friends support.[65] The relationship between approval on the NPP and these variables is further tested using binary logistic regression.[66]

Logistic regression tests reveal none of the earlier identified independent variables to be statistically related to the dependent variable. Thus, none of the earlier hypotheses about ideal aspirant candidate types hold. Given this, central party selector demand for aspirant candidates does not appear to reflect a preference for the ideal aspirant candidate type. This is a critical finding, as it reveals the first demand stage of the Labour party's selection process to be neutral in that the central party selectors demonstrate no preference for any particular type of aspirant candidate.[67] Moreover, although the NPP provides an opportunity for central party selectors to do more to bolster the representation of non-ideal aspirant candidates by *favouring* underrepresented groups, the finding in Table 3.3 illustrates party officials are not taking advantage of this opportunity. These findings are discussed further in the concluding section.

Model 2: shortlisting

This section presents the second demand-side regression model, this time testing local selector demand at Stage 6 when those aspirant candidates who apply for seats in Stage 4 are shortlisted.[68] The dependent variable is "1" shortlisted and "0" not shortlisted, and the 38 independent variables are the same as in the preceding section. Also consistent with the proceeding section, it is hypothesised that local party selectors are more likely to shortlist aspirant candidates who resemble the ideal type. This section reviews frequencies, relationship tests, and logistical regression results.

Frequencies

Table 6.4 presents the frequencies for all variables and the initial relationship tests. In terms of the dependent variable, shortlisting, 334 (78 percent) of 430 aspirant candidates who apply for seats in Stage 4 are shortlisted compared to 96 (22 percent) who are not shortlisted. Looking to the independent variable frequencies, overall it appears aspirant candidates in this pool almost exactly resemble those aspirant candidates who began the process in Stage 1. Indeed, comparing

Table 6.4 Shortlisting: variables, descriptive statistics, and relationship tests

Dependent	Shortlisted	n	Predictor	#	%	Comparator	#	%	Median
		430	Yes	334	78%	No	96	22%	
Social Background	Sex	430	Man	293	68%	Woman	137	32%	-
	Race*	430	Non-BAME	366	85%	BAME	64	15%	-
	Ability*	430	Non-Disabled	400	93%	Disabled	38	7%	-
	Age*	385	-	-	-	-	-	-	43 yrs
	Sex Orient.	334	Heterosexual	307	92%	LGBTQ	27	8%	-
	Language	368	English	350	95%	Other	18	5%	-
	Religion	301	Christian	138	46%	Other	163	54%	-
	Education	388	Degree	324	84%	No	64	16%	-
	Occupation	362	Instrumental	205	57%	No	157	43%	-
	Income*	344	-	-	-	-	-	-	£40–50k
	Employment	345	Full-time	287	83%	No	58	17%	-
	Class	322	Middle	182	57%	No	140	43%	-
	Housing	304	Owner	240	79%	No	64	21%	-
	Children	320	No	217	68%	Yes	103	32%	-
	Adults	326	No	290	89%	Yes	36	11%	-
	Partner	335	Yes	239	71%	No	96	29%	-
Party Experience	Membership	429	-	-	-	-	-	-	14 yrs
	Hours*	337	-	-	-	-	-	-	7 hrs
	Employee	406	Yes	50	12%	No	356	88%	-
	Volunteer	402	Yes	361	90%	No	41	10%	-
Political Experience	Councillor	423	Yes	190	45%	No	233	55%	-
	Prior Election*	423	Yes	331	78%	No	92	22%	-
	Interest Group*	404	Yes	287	71%	No	117	29%	-
	Union	403	Yes	168	42%	No	235	58%	-

(Continued)

Table 6.4 (Continued)

Dependent		n	Predictor Yes	#	%	Comparator No	#	%	Median
	Shortlisted	430	Yes	334	78%	No	96	22%	
Political Networks	Recruited	375	Yes	145	39%	No	230	61%	-
	Local Res.*	399	Yes	146	37%	No	253	63%	-
	Central Party*	370	Yes	280	76%	No	90	24%	-
	Local Party*	368	Yes	337	92%	No	31	8%	-
	Councillor*	349	Yes	173	50%	No	176	50%	-
	Union	371	Yes	222	60%	No	149	40%	-
	Interest Group	368	Yes	368	67%	No	121	33%	-
Personal Support	Fam/Friends	362	Yes	317	88%	No	45	12%	-
	Employer	352	Yes	149	42%	No	203	58%	-
Political Attitudes	Speak Out	332	Yes	160	48%	No	172	52%	-
	Left/Right*	339	-	-	-	-	-	-	Left (3)
	Old/New	327	Old	113	35%	New	214	65%	-
Ambition	Score	349	-	-	-	-	-	-	Fairly (7)

Note: * = Chi-square or Spearman's Rho test statistically significant at <.05.

Table 6.4 with the baseline produced in the first sample in Table 6.3 reveals the total idealness score for this second sample is 26 of 38. In other words, ideal aspirant candidate types make up a majority in 68 percent of the variables. The "idealness scores" for each category are the same with one exception, political networks. Within this category, those aspirant candidates who receive support from local councillors move from 48 percent of the sample used in Model 1 to 50 percent in Model 2 – shifting the score for this individual variable from "0" to "1". This similarity in samples is somewhat surprising, as it is reasonable to expect the aspirant candidates who apply for seats to be more ideal than the pool of all aspirant candidates.

In terms of social background variables, there are some instances where the aspirant candidates are more ideal in this sample than in the baseline sample insofar that the percentages of variables in the predictor column are higher. For example, a higher percentage have instrumental jobs (2 percentage points) and identify as middle class (3 percentage points). Turning next to the political experience variables, there are slightly more aspirant candidates with prior election experience (2 percentage points).

In terms of political networks, a higher percentage of aspirant candidates who apply for seats are recruited (3 percentage points) than in the larger all aspirant sample. Notably, more receive central and local party support (6 percentage points and 4 percentage points respectively), as well as support from local councillors, unions, and interest groups (2 percentage points, 2 percentage points, and 3 percentage points respectively). Lastly, aspirant candidates in the "apply for seats" sample have more personal and employer support – although employer support is still well below 50 percent. Whether any of the 38 variables are associated with shortlisting is determined in the next section.

Statistical tests

As shown in Table 6.4, Chi-square and Spearman's Rho testing reveals 11 statistically significant variables. These are race, ability, age, income, hours spent on party activities, prior election experience, holding office in an interest group, local residency, central party support, local party support, and placement on the left/right political continuum. As with the last modelling exercise, these statistically significant variables form the basis of the logistical regression model.

Table 6.5 Model 2 logistic regression predicting likelihood of being shortlisted

Variable Predictor	B	Std Error	Exp (B)
Ability (Non-disabled)	1.233	.542	3.430
Local Resident (Yes)	.939	.410	2.558
Income	-.115	.041	.892
Constant	.347	1.369	1.415

Notes: Nagelkerke Pseudo R2 = .163; p value <.05; N = 258.

As seen in Table 6.5, logistic regression is used to assess the likelihood that certain types of aspirant candidates get shortlisted by local party selectors.[69] In total, 258 cases are included in the model, which contains the 11 independent variables found to be significant through previous Chi-square and Spearman's Rho testing. In terms of model strength, the Nagelkerke Pseudo R-Square score shows the model as a whole explains 16.3 percent of the variance in the dependent variable (getting shortlisted). The model also correctly classifies 82 percent of cases as either shortlisted or not shortlisted.

Only 3 of the 11 independent variables included in this model are statistically significant at the .05 level (p value): ability, local resident, and income.[70] The strongest predictor of getting shortlisted is ability, recording an odds ratio of 3.430. This ratio indicates the odds of an aspirant candidate who is not disabled getting shortlisted are 3.430 times higher than those of an aspirant candidate who is disabled, controlling for all other factors in the model.[71] The next strongest predictor is living in the constituency. With an odds ratio of 2.558, the odds of an aspirant candidate who lives in the constituency getting shortlisted are over two times higher than the odds of an aspirant candidate who does not live in the constituency. Lastly, the income odds ratio of .892 indicates the odds of getting shortlisted *decrease* by 11 percent for every additional £10,000 of annual household income. These results show two ideal aspirant candidate hypotheses hold in this model. Local selectors prefer non-disabled aspirant candidates to disabled aspirant candidates and those who have a local address over those who do not live locally. The finding that aspirant candidates with lower incomes are preferred to those with higher incomes is contrary to the ideal aspirant candidate theory.

The preference for non-disabled aspirant candidates is not entirely surprising given the absence of equality quotas and guarantees for disabled aspirant candidates at the nomination and shortlisting stages such as those in place for women and BAME aspirant candidates. Nor is it surprising that local selectors prefer aspirant candidates with local addresses insofar that the literature and interviews for this study frequently mention living locally as critical in terms of establishing all-important local networks with the key political actors in the constituency. In terms of income, again, although the literature suggests party selectors prefer those with higher incomes, as indicated, party selectors have a disdain for those who are too well off. At the same time, aspirant candidates' incomes may be less important to selectors at this stage compared to the final selection stage, where they need to demonstrate they have the resources to win the seat to which they are selected.

Additional statistical tests using refined samples

Model 2 findings concerning shortlisting suggest it is worth conducting additional statistical testing to better understand local selector preferences at Stage 6 – especially when it comes to shortlisting in the different types of seats. For example, the sample used for Model 2 includes all shortlisted seat types: those that are *open* to all contestants and those that are open only to women due to Labour's AWS rules, and those that are *winnable* and *unwinnable*.[72] Additional modelling may add details as to why some and not other types of aspirant candidates do or do not become shortlisted, as the motivations of selectors and aspirant candidates may vary between these different types of seats.

This section explores two additional samples. Model 3 tests demand in open seats by excluding surveys from aspirant candidates who applied for AWS seats. Model 3 includes the same dependent and independent variables as Model 2. Again, it is expected that local party selectors are more likely to shortlist ideal aspirant candidate types in open seats than non-ideal types. Model 4 testing narrows the sample further by eliminating surveys from those applying for AWS seats and surveys from those applying to unwinnable seats. Using the same dependent and independent variables as Models 2 and 3, Model 4 examines why some and not other types of aspirant candidates are selected in open and winnable seats only. The chapter concludes by tying together findings from all models.

Model 3: shortlisting in open seats

Model 3 includes surveys from 344 aspirant candidates who applied for open (non-AWS) seats. Of these 344 applicants, 285 (83 percent) were shortlisted compared to 59 (17 percent) who were not shortlisted. These statistics indicate a smaller proportion of those who applied to non-AWS seats were eliminated (17 percent) in these contests than in the larger Model 2, which contains AWS and non-AWS seats (22 percent).

Looking to Table 6.6, the overall idealness score for aspirant candidates who apply for seats in open (non-AWS) seats is 27 out of 38, or 71 percent – 3 points higher than the idealness score baseline of 68 produced by the variables contained in Model 1. A closer look at the frequencies reveal some notable differences between the two groups of aspirant candidates. To begin, there is a sharp 14 percentage point drop in the percentage of women aspirant candidates who apply for open seats – from 29 percent in Model 1 to 15 percent in Model 3. The obvious explanation for this is the removal of AWS from the sample. This important and later discussed finding suggests women are disproportionately clustered into AWS.

At the same time the aspirant candidates are slightly more ideal across some of the individual variables. In terms of their social backgrounds, a higher percentage are employed full-time (4 percentage points) and identify as middle class (5 percentage points). Looking to political networks, those surveyed have a slightly higher score than the baseline frequency for the "all aspirant" sample (e.g., a majority receive support from councillors). Further to this, a higher percentage receive support from the central party (5 percentage points) and the local party (3 percentage points). The frequencies further reveal that the aspirant candidates are slightly less ideal across three individual variables. For example, a lower percentage identify as heterosexual. As well, and contrary to what was expected, a lower percentage volunteer and have union experience (2 percentage points and 3 percentage points, respectively). Lastly, a lower percentage identify as old Labour

Table 6.6 Shortlisting: descriptive statistics and relationship tests for open seats

Dependent	Shortlisted	n	Predictor	#	%	Comparator	#	%	Median
		344	Yes	285	83%	No	59	17%	
Social Background	Sex	344	Man	293	85%	Woman	51	15%	-
	Race*	344	Non-BAME	291	85%	BAME	53	15%	-
	Ability	344	Non-Disabled	319	93%	Disabled	25	7%	-
	Age*	306	-	-	-	-	-	-	42 yrs
	Sex Orient.	265	Heterosexual	238	90%	LGBTQ	27	8%	-
	Language	294	English	278	95%	Other	16	5%	-
	Religion	240	Christian	115	48%	Other	125	52%	-
	Education	307	Degree	259	84%	No	48	16%	-
	Occupation	289	Instrumental	158	55%	No	131	45%	-
	Income*	271	-	-	-	-	-	-	£40–50k
	Employment	275	Full-time	236	86%	No	39	14%	-
	Class	258	Middle	151	59%	No	107	41%	-
	Housing	242	Owner	186	77%	No	56	23%	-
	Children	255	No	170	67%	Yes	85	33%	-
	Adults	260	No	232	89%	Yes	28	11%	-
	Partner	268	Yes	190	71%	No	78	29%	-
Party Experience	Membership	344	-	-	-	-	-	-	14 yrs
	Hours	275	-	-	-	-	-	-	7 hrs
	Employee	327	Yes	35	11%	No	292	89%	-
	Volunteer	323	Yes	284	88%	No	39	12%	-
Political Experience	Councillor	339	Yes	145	43%	No	194	57%	-
	Prior Election	339	Yes	262	77%	No	77	23%	-
	Interest Group*	325	Yes	226	70%	No	99	30%	-
	Union	324	Yes	128	40%	No	196	60%	-

Political Networks									
Political Networks	Recruited	303	Yes	108	36%	No	195	64%	-
	Local Res.*	316	Yes	124	39%	No	192	61%	-
	Central Party	299	Yes	223	75%	No	76	25%	-
	Local Party*	298	Yes	272	91%	No	26	9%	-
	Councillor	280	Yes	139	51%	No	141	50%	-
	Union	300	Yes	172	57%	No	128	43%	-
	Interest Group	299	Yes	189	63%	No	110	37%	-
Personal Support	Fam/Friends	293	Yes	253	86%	No	40	14%	-
	Employer	283	Yes	120	42%	No	163	58%	-
Political Attitudes	Speak Out	266	Yes	129	49%	No	137	51%	-
	Left/Right	273	-	-	-	-	-	-	Left (3)
	Old/New	263	Old	88	34%	New	175	66%	-
Ambition	Score	281	-	-	-	-	-	-	Fairly (7)

Note: * = Chi-square or Spearman's Rho test statistically significant at <.05.

Table 6.7 Model 3 logistic regression results for shortlisting in open seats

Variable Predictor	B	Std Error	Exp (B)
Local (Yes)	1.151	.406	3.161
Constant	2.153	1.071	8.612

Notes: Nagelkerke Pseudo R2 = .139; p values <.05; N = 226.

(2 percentage points). The next section discusses the statistical significance of the variables.

As shown in Table 6.7, 226 cases are included in the model, which contains 6 independent variables found to be statistically significant through previous Chi-square and Spearman's Rho: race, age, income, holding office in an interest group, residency, and local party support. In terms of model strength, the Nagelkerke Pseudo R-Square score of .139 shows the model explains approximately 14 percent of the variance in the dependent variable (shortlisted). The model also correctly classifies 79 percent of cases as either shortlisted or not shortlisted.

Only one of the six independent variables included in the model is statistically significant at the .05 level (p value): local resident. With an odds ratio of 3.161, the odds of an aspirant candidate who lives in the constituency getting shortlisted are over three times higher than the odds of an aspirant candidate who does not live in the constituency, controlling for all other factors in the model. These results indicate only one hypothesis holds: local selectors prefer aspirant candidates who live in the constituency. This finding reinforces the importance of this variable to political success.

Model 4: shortlisting in open and winnable seats

Model 4 tests local party selector demand at the shortlisting stage in seats that are open (non-AWS) and winnable (as opposed to unwinnable). Arguably the most competitive selection processes will occur in winnable seats, and in this light, local party selector preference for the ideal aspirant candidate type is expected to be at its strongest. The dependent and independent variables and hypotheses are the same as in Models 2 and 3.

The overall idealness score of 29 out of 38 (76 percent) is 8 percent percentage points higher than the baseline score of 68 and indeed higher than all previous models' idealness scores calculated thus far. Thus, aspirant candidates who apply for winnable seats are, as expected, "more" ideal than aspirant candidates who begin the process and who apply for less desirable seats.[73] A closer look at the frequencies in Table 6.8 reveal aspirant candidates are more ideal across all social background variables except race, with a slightly higher percentage of BAME aspirant candidates (1 percentage point) competing for open and winnable seats than in the "all aspirant" sample. In terms of sex – almost the entire sample – 89 percent – is comprised of men aspirant candidates. The implications of this for women aspirant candidates are discussed more later. Also of note, a

Table 6.8 Descriptive statistics and relationship tests for open and winnable seats

		n	Predictor	#	%	Comparator	#	%	Median
Dependent	Shortlisted	132	Yes	78	59%	No	54	41%	-
Social	Sex*	132	Man	117	89%	Woman	15	11%	-
Background	Race	132	Non-BAME	109	83%	BAME	23	17%	-
	Ability	132	Non-Disabled	126	96%	Disabled	6	4%	-
	Age	122	-	-	-	-	-	-	45 yrs
	Sex Orient.	103	Heterosexual	96	93%	LGBTQ	7	7%	-
	Language	110	English	106	96%	Other	4	4%	-
	Religion	93	Christian	48	52%	Other	45	48%	-
	Education	119	Degree	106	89%	No	13	11%	-
	Occupation	113	Instrumental	65	58%	No	48	42%	-
	Income	109	-	-	-	-	-	-	£50–60k
	Employment	107	Full-time	93	87%	No	14	13%	-
	Class	103	Middle	62	60%	No	41	40%	-
	Housing	96	Owner	80	83%	No	16	17%	-
	Children	102	No	64	63%	Yes	38	37%	-
	Adults	102	No	87	85%	Yes	15	15%	-
	Partner	106	Yes	79	75%	No	27	25%	-
Party	Membership*	132	-	-	-	-	-	-	16 yrs
Experience	Hours*	111	-	-	-	-	-	-	8 hrs
	Employee	123	Yes	18	15%	No	105	85%	-
	Volunteer	123	Yes	112	91%	No	11	9%	-
Political	Councillor*	130	Yes	70	54%	No	60	46%	-
Experience	Prior Election	130	Yes	103	79%	No	27	21%	-
	Interest Group*	124	Yes	88	71%	No	36	29%	-
	Union	123	Yes	45	37%	No	78	63%	-

(Continued)

Table 6.8 (Continued)

		n	Predictor	#	%	Comparator	#	%	Median
Political Networks	Recruited	122	Yes	45	37%	No	77	63%	-
	Local Res.*	129	Yes	39	30%	No	90	70%	-
	Central Party	121	Yes	89	74%	No	32	26%	-
	Local Party	120	Yes	109	91%	No	11	9%	-
	Councillor	115	Yes	63	55%	No	52	45%	-
	Union*	121	Yes	73	60%	No	48	40%	-
	Interest Group	120	Yes	87	73%	No	33	27%	-
Personal Support	Fam/Friends	118	Yes	104	88%	No	14	12%	-
	Employer	115	Yes	49	43%	No	66	57%	-
Political Attitudes	Speak Out	105	Yes	45	43%	No	60	57%	-
	Left/Right*	108	-	-	-	-	-	-	Left (3)
	Old/New	102	Old	36	35%	New	66	65%	-
Ambition	Score	111	-	-	-	-	-	-	Fairly (7)

Note: * = Chi-square or Spearman's Rho test statistically significant at <.05.

higher percentage of the aspirant candidates are Christian (7 percentage points); indeed, this is the first instance where the majority of aspirant candidates identify as such. As well, a much higher percentage hold university/polytechnic degrees (6 percentage points) and identify as middle class (6 percentage points). In line with this, aspirant candidates' annual household incomes increase by £10–20,000.

Continuing with party experience, the length of party membership is two years more than the baseline model and the number of hours devoted per week to party activities increases by one hour. This suggests those competing for winnable seats bring with them greater demonstrable party experience. As well, a slightly higher percentage are party employees (3 percentage points). Thus, there may be something to the idea that party employees are turning up in higher numbers, at least in winnable constituencies.

Looking next to political experience, a much higher percentage (10 percentage points) of aspirant candidates have been councillors, again, this reflects the idea that such a career path is the key stepping stone to national office (Allen, 2012; Cairney, 2007). Furthermore, the aspirant candidates competing for a spot on a shortlist in winnable seats have stronger networks. Notably, a much higher percentage (9 percentage points) have received support from interest groups. Again, this potentially reflects the increasing influence interest groups have in shaping the party's candidate pool relative to other organisations, in particular, trade unions. In terms of political attitudes, a somewhat lower percentage speak out against the party when seeking a shortlist in a winnable seat, suggesting aspirant candidates may not be as willing to risk alienating the central party or local officials/members or attracting unwanted media attention with rogue comments.

As touched upon earlier, the percentage of women in open (non-AWS) and winnable seats plummets to 11 percent, an 18 percentage point drop. This is assuredly the result of removing AWS from the sample. This finding reinforces the idea that women are being ghettoised into AWS – perhaps for fear of losing in open and winnable seats. This should be a red flag to those in the Labour party who seek to increase the number of women candidates: crowding over half of all women aspirant candidates into approximately 10 percent of all constituencies for which the party is fielding candidates means even if more women come forward, their chances of getting selected will not increase. All 38 variables are tested for statistical significance in the next section.

In terms of initial relationship testing, there is a statistically significant relationship between eight of the 38 variables. These include: sex, party membership, hours spent on party activities, holding local office as a councillor, holding office in an interest group, local residence, union support, and left/right on the political continuum. Thus, these variables are entered into the regression analysis, with the results presented in the following table.

As seen in Table 6.9, logistic regression assesses the impact of the included variables on the likelihood aspirant candidates will get shortlisted in open *and* winnable seats. In total, 100 cases are included in the model, which contains the independent variables found to be statistically significant through previous Chi-square and Spearman's Rho testing. In terms of model strength, the Nagelkerke

Table 6.9 Model 4 logistic regression results, shortlisted (open and winnable seats)

Variable Predictor	B	Std Error	Exp (B)
Sex (Man)	-2.100	.929	.122
Year Joined LP	.083	.041	1.087
Councillor (Yes)	2.306	.615	10.038
Local Resident (Yes)	1.472	.649	4.357
Left/Right (Left)	-.889	.377	.411
Constant	2.116	1.619	8.299

Notes: Nagelkerke Pseudo R2 = .503; p value <.05; N = 100.

Pseudo R-Square score shows the model explains approximately half of the variance in the dependent variable (getting shortlisted).

Five of the independent variables made a statistically significant contribution to the model at the .05 level (p value): sex, membership length, councillor, local resident, and position on the left/right political continuum. The strongest predictor is holding office as a councillor. The odds ratio of 10.038 indicates the odds of an aspirant candidate with experience as a councillor getting shortlisted in open and winnable seats are over ten times higher than those of an aspirant candidate without experience as a councillor, when controlling for all other factors in the model. The next strongest predictor for shortlisting in open and winnable seats is living in the constituency. The odds ratio of 4.357 indicates the odds of an aspirant candidate who lives in the constituency getting shortlisted are over four times higher than the odds of an aspirant candidate who does not live in the constituency. Next, the odds ratio of 1.087 for length of Labour party membership indicates the odds of getting shortlisted are 10 percent more for every additional year of membership. Turning to those predictors going against the ideal candidate hypotheses, the left/right odds ratio of .411 indicates the odds of getting shortlisted are 59 percent less for every one step left on the 7 seven point left/right scale (with 1 being left, 4 being centrist, and 7 being right). Most surprisingly, with an odds ratio of .122, the odds of an aspirant candidate who is a man getting shortlisted is 78 percent less than the odds of an aspirant candidate who is a woman – perhaps compensation for the large drop in the overall pool of women standing in this selection process stage.

Conclusion

This chapter performs statistical testing on data collected from original surveys completed by Labour party aspirant candidates for the 2005 and 2010 General Elections to determine why some and not other aspirant candidate types are approved on the NPP and shortlisted. Beginning with the premise that ideal aspirant candidate types are more likely to be approved and shortlisted, this chapter uses various samples and four regression models to test the statistical significance of 38 independent variables. This testing reveals a number of important findings.

First, from a methodological perspective, it is important to note with 18.5 percent of the total pool of actual aspirant candidates completing surveys, the survey sample closely reflects the census data presented in Chapter 3. Similar percentages of the total number of aspirant candidates were filtered out through the various selection stages, with these similarities between sample and census holding along various other variables including sex, race, and physical ability. Moreover, not only do the survey data broadly reflect the census data collected from the Labour party, data collected in the survey also reveal the pool of those applying to stand for the party in Stage 1 and reflect the general population in terms of race, first language, housing tenure, and religion. However, as noted, there are also strong differences between Labour's aspirant candidate pool and the general population.

Table 6.10 summarises results for all four regression models. Overall, frequencies reveal central and local party selectors enjoy a choice between ideal and non-ideal aspirant candidate types throughout the selection process. At first glance, the finding that ideal candidate scores increase as seats become more competitive and winnable is intriguing, as it suggests removing unwinnable and AWS seats *increases* the overall idealness of the aspirant pool. However, the higher idealness score is an effect of removing unwinnable seats from the sample rather than AWS, as is explored further in the next chapter. Comparing frequencies between models also shows the percentage of women aspirant candidates plummets once AWS are removed from the sample. Indeed, that more than half of all women aspirant candidates apply to AWS would seem a critical finding, as it indicates over half of the party's women aspirant candidates chase approximately a mere 10 percent of seats. This means women

Table 6.10 Regression model summary

Model	1	2	3	4
Stage	3	6	6	6
N	566	258	226	100
Idealness Score	68	68	71	76
Pseudo R2	n/a	.163	.139	.503
Sample	All Aspirants	All Seat Applicants	Open Seat Applicants	Open and Winnable Seat Applicants
Selector	Central Officials	Local Officials	Local Officials	Local Officials
Dependent Variable	On NPP (1) Not on NPP (0)	Shortlisted (1) Not Shortlisted (0)	Shortlisted (1) Not Shortlisted (0)	Shortlisted (1) Not Shortlisted (0)
Significant Independent Variables	- - - - -	Local Resident* Ability* Income	Local Resident*	Local Resident* Years Member* Councillor* Gender Left

Note: * = supports ideal candidate hypothesis.

aspirant candidates are bypassing open and winnable seats and clustering into AWS seats – perhaps for fear of losing. Given this finding, even if supply were to increase and if more women applied for seats, there is little reason to believe more women will be shortlisted or selected in higher numbers, as they are drawn to AWS and away from open (non-AWS).

That none of the 38 variables are statistically significant in Model 1 suggests central party officials do not exhibit a preference for or against any aspirant candidate type. This is not entirely surprising given the findings presented in Chapters 3 and 5 that show central party selectors are less likely than local party selectors to disproportionately filter out non-ideal aspirant candidate types. Thus, Model 1 results suggest whatever past advantage or disadvantage may have existed, Stages 1–3 of the process are now neutral, with this largely attributable to the efforts of central party agents to ensure fairness. At the same time, this finding also suggests the central party is doing little to bolster the representation of underrepresented, non-ideal aspirant candidates. While aspirant candidates on the NPP receive training and advanced notice of seat availability, central party agents are not using the NPP to increase the percentage of underrepresented candidate groups, including women, BAME, and disabled aspirant candidates. This is a missed opportunity as the central party could, for example, implement an equity balanced NPP to boost the pool of women, BAME, and disabled aspirants moving from Stage 3 to Stage 4.

While Model 2 results show very few of the 38 included independent variables are related to shortlisting success, testing supports the ideal candidate hypothesis in two cases: local party selectors are over three times more likely to shortlist aspirant candidates who are non-disabled and over two times more likely to shortlist aspirant candidates who are local residents. In terms of ability, this finding is not surprising. There are central party rules in place designed to increase the number of women and BAME aspirant candidates, but there are no such rules in place for disabled aspirant candidates.

In terms of being a local resident, this finding is consistent with party officials and aspirant candidate observations that local aspirant candidates have a real advantage in the process insofar as they can develop the networks seen as invaluable to shortlisting success. Moreover, this finding is consistent with the recent literature that suggests fielding local candidates who can represent and further local interests are increasingly important to the local election campaign (Campbell and Cowley, 2013; Evans, 2012). Indeed, that this relationship is supported in all seat conditions indicates that being a local resident consistently trumps most other characteristics, including sex, race, and physical ability. Aspirant candidates who are local residents, but who are otherwise non-ideal, for example, in terms of being a woman, BAME, or disabled person, may be shortlisted insofar that they are seen as "acceptably different" (Durose et al, 2013). That is, they check off what is likely the single most important factor to success during the first six selection stages: being local. Lastly, in terms of preferring aspirant candidates with slightly lower annual incomes, this could reflect local party disdain for "show offs", or it could reflect their acknowledgement that less money is required to secure a position on a shortlist than is required to get selected or even elected.

In Model 3, AWS surveys are removed from the sample of those who apply for seats. Regression test results reveal local selectors are over three times more likely to shortlist aspirant candidates who are local residents. No other relationships hold. These results reinforce the importance of living in the constituency during the shortlisting process. Also notable is the fact that local selectors are *not* more likely to shortlist men over women in open (non-AWS) seats, as increasingly proposed in the literature (Murray, 2014).

Model 4 excludes AWS and unwinnable seats from the sample on the premise that local party selectors are even more likely to shortlist ideal candidates as they are looking for candidates who will not only win the selection, but get elected to the legislature. This model has the highest explanatory value (Pseudo $R^2 = .503$). Further, regression tests portray greater local party demand for ideal aspirant candidates: local party selectors are over ten times more likely to shortlist local councillors; four times more likely to shortlist local residents, and slightly more likely to shortlist longer-term party members. As with the other demand-side tests, these findings reaffirm the importance of local connections. Moreover, they support the current literature, which proposes the new pathway to parliament includes occupations that are directly instrumental to politics, such as being a councillor. At the same time, local party selectors are slightly less likely to shortlist aspirant candidates who are left of centre; a further challenge to May's Law of Curvilinear Disparity and the ideal candidate theory. However, given this preference is only in open and winnable seats suggests the local selectors are thinking ahead to the general election and may be inclined to shortlist more centrist candidates on the grounds they will have a wider appeal amongst the general electorate.

Unexpectedly, local party selectors in Model 4 are slightly less likely to shortlist men over women even in non-AWS and winnable seats. As noted, this bias toward women can largely be attributed to the success of the central party's long term efforts to circumvent local party selector bias against women aspirant candidates at this stage. However, it is unclear whether this will hold in the final selection stage where candidates are ultimately selected. Indeed, as an aspirant candidate notes: "As a woman I found it very easy to get shortlisted as they needed to fill the women's quota. But locals get picked in the end".[74] However, this bias is still not strong enough to boost the fortunes of the initial pool of women entering the candidate selection process to the point where the proportion of women shortlisted is equal to the proportion of men who are shortlisted. Significantly, as noted earlier, considerably more supply- and demand-side efforts are needed to achieve gender proportionality through the first six stages of Labour's candidate selection process. If Labour is to reach its target of 50 percent women in its parliamentary party, Labour will have to entice hundreds more women aspirants to come forward to increase supply or implement many more AWS to stimulate demand.

Overall, it is confirmed that demand plays a strong role in who is and who is not shortlisted for candidacy. At the same time, that so few variables determine who is and is not shortlisted indicates most of the factors thought to be associated with selection success may not at all matter. Moreover, central party officials do not appear biased toward or against any particular aspirant candidate type when listing aspirants on the NPP. At the same time, perhaps being neutral is not something the central party should necessarily aspire to, given the pool of women, BAME, and disabled aspirant candidates is not proportional to their presence in the population. Lastly, that local selectors are more likely to shortlist women in non-AWS and winnable seats at first is a challenging finding insofar that it counters current thinking. At the same time, it suggests central party policy success with quotas for women in non-AWS. Whether local party members responsible for selecting shortlisted aspirant candidates have the same preferences as the selectors assessed in this chapter is tested next.

Notes

1 In terms of research on candidate sex, as in the US, there is little evidence that the UK electorate discriminates against women candidates (Campbell and Cowley, 2013). At the same time, research reveals the US electorate relies on stereotypes when evaluating candidates, with a growing body of research finding the same in the UK (McDermott, 1998; Sanbonmatsu, 2002; Campbell and Cowley, 2013). However, there are grounds to separately evaluate the UK insofar that its selectorate appears less progressive than the US electorate (Campbell and Cowley, 2013, pp. 1–2; see Norris and Lovenduski, 1995; Shepherd-Robinson and Lovenduski, 2002).

2 Many of the survey questions used in this study are drawn from those asked in the British Representation Study (1992, 1997, 2001, and 2005), with others drawn from interviews with Labour party officials and candidates.

3 Surveyed aspirant candidates were asked to indicate whether they are a male or female, with males coded as "1" and females coded as "0".

4 Open-ended survey response from a Labour party aspirant candidate who participated in this study.

5 Aspirant candidates were asked to indicate whether they considered themselves to be an ethnic minority. Non-ethnic minorities (non-BAMEs) are coded as "1", whereas ethnic minorities (BAMEs) are coded as "0".

6 Recently there has been an increase in concerns about immigration, which may well affect this reversal of attitudes (Campbell, 2011, p. 207). At the time of writing, new right parties in the UK and France ran on anti-immigration platforms and secured seats in the European Elections (for example, see European Parliament Results, 2014; McDonald and Lichfield, 2014).

7 Saggar (2013) argues, compared to non-BAME people, BAME people "acquire weaker educational qualifications, attend less successful schools, live in more deprived neighbourhoods", and "crucially, [they] lack appropriate contacts and networks that can act as bridges into public life and political careers. These added together amount to a very significant set of barriers to progression" (p. 89).

8 All quotes are from open-ended survey responses from Labour party aspirant candidates surveyed for this study.

9 By 2010, the number of ethnic minority MPs increased by nearly three-quarters to 26, or 4 percent of the total House of Commons. All ethnic minority MPs are either Labour (15) or Conservative (11) (Keep, 2010).

10 The survey question asked aspirant candidates "do you have a physical disability?" with yes coded as "0" and no coded as "1". Survey participants were not asked to identify their disability. The Office for Disability Issues (2014) uses the language disabled and non-disabled people to describe people living with and without disabilities.

11 A substantially higher proportion of disabled people in the UK live in poverty, lack educational qualifications, and live in "non-decent accommodation". Moreover, a higher percentage of disabled people are unemployed and treated unfairly at work. Further, disabled people are less likely to participate in cultural and leisure activities and to engage in formal volunteering and have access to the internet (The Office for Disability Issues, 2014; see also *BBC*. (2013) 'Why Aren't More Disabled People Becoming Politicians?')

12 Open-ended survey response from a Labour party aspirant candidate who participated in this study.

13 Aspirant candidates were asked to indicate the year in which they were born. Middle-aged is defined here as 40 through to 55. For the last 30 years, the average age of MPs in the British Parliament has remained stable at about 50 years old (Keep, 2010, pp. 10–11).

14 Aspirant candidates were asked to indicate if they were heterosexual, gay, bisexual or transgendered. The responses were recoded with heterosexual as "1" and non-heterosexual as "0". The percentage of aspirant candidates indicating they are LGBTQ is close to this group's overall proportion of the general population (1.5 percent) (UK Office of National Statistics).

15 Open-ended survey response from a Labour party aspirant candidate who participated in this study.

16 As well as women and younger people (Campbell, 2011).

17 Survey participants were asked "is English your first language?", with yes coded as "1" and no coded as "0". These data reflect the census 2011 data in which 92 percent of England's and Wales' population indicated their first language is English (UK Office of National Statistics).

18 Religion is measured by asking aspirant candidates "what is your religion?". Responses were collapsed into Christian and non-Christian. Non-Christian responses include Muslim, Hindu, Jewish, Sikh, Buddhist, and none. These data somewhat reflect the 2011 census data, which reveal 59 percent of people in England and Wales identify as Christian. The second most common choice amongst the survey sample, "no religion", reflects the trend in the 2011 census data; however, a lower percentage (25 percent) of England's and Wales' populations chose "no religion".

19 According to the UK Office for National Statistics' 2011 Census, 59 percent of the population in England and Wales identify as Christian, 25 percent identify as having no religion, 5 percent identify as Muslim, and 4 percent identify as "other". Moreover, according to the 2008 British Social Attitudes Survey, just over half of the British public believe religious diversity has been good for Britain (Campbell, 2011, p. 207).

20 To assess this variable, aspirant candidates were asked to record their highest educational achievement, which was then collapsed into "1" for degree (university/polytechnic degree and post-graduate qualification) or "0" for no degree (secondary or other). In contrast, 12 percent of the aspirant candidates attended a post-secondary or other institution, but did not earn a degree, while 6 percent of the aspirant candidates' highest educational achievement is secondary school. The 2011 census data for England and Wales reveal 27 percent of the population has bachelor degrees, with no information for post-graduate degrees. This suggests that the survey sample has a considerably higher level of educational attainment than the general population.

21 Interview with a Labour party official.

22 Aspirant candidates were asked to indicate the type of work they were doing immediately prior to their selection attempts, with responses coded and collapsed into "1"

for "instrumental" and "0" for "non-instrumental". Instrumental occupations include journalists, public relations experts, trade union officials, interest group representatives, full-time councillors, members of a devolved office or European Parliament, party workers, parliamentary staff, and think tank staff. Non-instrumental jobs include lawyers, teachers, education, service providers, small business owners, and manual labour (Allen, 2012, p. 4; Cairney, 2007, pp. 3–5; Durose et al, 2013).

23 Norris and Lovenduski (1995) note the underrepresentation of women and BAME candidates may "work through" occupation insofar that they are less likely employed in occupations that do not directly facilitate a political career (p. 111).

24 In terms of income, survey participants were asked to indicate their household's annual income in pounds sterling around the time of the election for which they sought selection. In terms of employment, aspirant candidates were asked what they were doing prior to their selection attempt. Their responses were collapsed into "1" for full-time employment (30+ hours per week) or "0" for non-full-time employment (part-time employment (10–29 hours per week), looking after the home, unemployed, retired, or other). In terms of class, aspirant candidates were asked if they think of themselves as belonging to the working class, middle class, or upper class. Responses were collapsed into "1" for middle class and '0' for other (working class and upper class).

25 Open-ended survey response from a Labour party aspirant candidate.

26 Interview with a Labour party official.

27 In terms of dependent children, aspirant candidates were asked how many children they had in their care under 5 years of age and how many children they had in their care between 5–15 years of age. The answers were collapsed and recoded with "1" indicating no children in care and "0" indicating children in care. As for dependent adults, aspirant candidates were asked if they had adult dependents in their care with "1" indicating they do not and "0" indicating they do.

28 Open-ended survey response from a Labour party aspirant candidate.

29 Aspirant candidates were asked to identify their relationship status, with those in a relationship (married or cohabitating with their partner) coded as "1" and those not in a relationship coded as "0" (single, divorced, and widowed).

30 Open-ended survey responses from a Labour party aspirant candidate.

31 Aspirant candidates were asked "in what year did you join the British Labour party?" and "how many hours a week do you work on party related activities?" to develop scale variables. They were also asked "have you ever been employed by the party?" Party volunteerism is measured by asking aspirant candidates if they had ever held party office, sat on the national policy forum, attended party conference, participated on a party committee, or worked on a party campaign, with responses collapsed into a single variable scored as "1" if any such activities were undertaken or "0" if not.

32 Interview with a Labour party official.

33 Interview with a Labour party official.

34 On the demand-side, party selectors may prefer those who appear to have time and energy to invest (Norris and Lovenduski, 1995, p. 156).

35 Open-ended survey response from a survey respondent.

36 Interview with a Labour party official.

37 Political experience is measured by asking aspirant candidates if they had ever been elected as a councillor to local government, if they had ever attempted political office in the past, if they had ever held office in an interest group, and/or if they had ever held office in a trade union. Aspirant candidates were asked if prior to their selection attempt they were elected as a councillor to local government, with yes coded as "1" and no coded as "0". They were also asked if they had ever sought candidacy and/or election to local, national, and/or devolved office and/or the European Parliament. The answers to these questions were recoded into a new variable, *prior election attempts*, with "1" indicating prior election attempts and "0" indicating no prior election attempts. As for

holding office in a trade union, aspirant candidates were asked if they had ever held office in a trade union, with "1" indicating yes and "0" indicating no. Lastly, in terms of *holding office in an interest group*, aspirant candidates were asked if they had ever held office in an interest group, student organisation, or women's organisation. The answers to these three questions were combined into a single variable, with "1" indicating they had held office in such groups and "0" indicating they had not.

38 Interview with a Labour party official.

39 Interview with a Labour party official.

40 Interview with a Labour party official.

41 Interview with a Labour party official.

42 Respondents were asked "did somebody ask you to stand for election?", with yes coded as "1" and no coded as "0".

43 In terms of *central party support*, aspirant candidates were asked how positive central party agents were in encouraging them to become candidates, with very positive and positive coded "1" for "received encouragement" and neutral and very negative coded as "0", "did not receive encouragement". Aspirant candidates were also asked if they received good advice from central party agents. The variables – receiving encouragement and positive advice – were recoded into the single variable support: central party agents. Moving to *local party support*, aspirant candidates were asked how positive local party agents were in encouraging them to become candidates. The answers were collapsed into very positive and positive coded "1" for "received encouragement" and neutral and very negative coded as "0", "did not receive encouragement". Aspirant candidates were asked if they received good advice from local party agents. The variables receiving encouragement and advice were recoded into the single variable support: local party agents. In terms of *local councillor support*, aspirant candidates were asked how positive local councillors were in encouraging them to become candidates, with answers collapsed as per the local party support variable. Aspirant candidates were asked if they received good advice from local councillors. The variables receiving encouragement and advice were recoded into the single variable support: local councillors. In terms of *trade union support*, aspirant candidates were asked how positive trade unions were in encouraging them to become candidates, with variables generated as per the local party support variable. Aspirant candidates were also asked if they received good advice from trade unions, with these questions also recoded into the single variable – support: trade unions. As for *interest group support*, aspirant candidates were asked how positive a range of interest groups were in encouraging them to become candidates: women's groups, community groups, religious groups, and business groups. The answers were collapsed into "yes" and "no", with very positive and positive coded "1" for "yes, received encouragement" and neutral and very negative coded as "0", "did not receive encouragement". Aspirant candidates were also asked if they received good advice from these groups. The variables receiving encouragement and advice were recoded into the single variable support: interest groups.

44 Local residency is measured by asking aspirant candidates if they reside in the constituency for which they are seeking a seat, with "yes" coded as "1" and "no" coded as "0".

45 Interview with a Labour party official.

46 Open-ended survey response from a Labour party aspirant candidate.

47 The term "new Labour" was abandoned by the Labour party following its 2010 election loss (BBC, 2010, 3 August). Those surveyed were asked if they frequently, often, or never publicly speak against the Labour party's policies. For measuring central party approval on the NPP, the answers were re-coded as "0" "spoke against the party" and "1" "did not speak against the party". For measuring local party nomination and short-listing, the answers were re-coded as "1" "spoke against the party" and "0" "did not speak against the party". In terms of their position on the *left/right political continuum*,

aspirant candidates were asked "using the scale where '1' means left and '7' means right, where do you place yourself?" *New and old Labour* is measured by asking aspirant candidates if they identify more as new or old Labour. For measuring central party approval on the NPP, old Labour is coded "0" and new Labour is coded "1", whereas for measuring local party support, old Labour is coded "1" and new Labour is coded "0".

48 Interview with a Labour party official.

49 In this study, political ambition is measured by asking aspirant candidates: "on a scale of 1 to 10, with '1' being not at all politically ambitious, '5' being somewhat ambitious, and '10' being very ambitious, where do you place yourself?"

50 In addition, statistical testing reveals no significant relationships between 38 independent variables and the dependent variable – apply to the NPP – in Stage 2. Thus, no one aspirant candidate type who initially applies to the party in Stage 1 is more or less likely to apply to the NPP in Stage 2.

51 Chi-square tests are used on bivariate variables, while Spearman's Rho tests are used for scale variables.

52 Scale variables are treated differently for the idealness score. For *age*, the ideal aspirant candidate is deemed early middle-age, which, as noted earlier, is between 40–55 years old. Thus if the age variable median falls between 40 and 55 years of age, the variable is given a score of "1"; if it does not, it is given a score of "0". In terms of *income*, if the median income is below the 2005 and 2010 UK median household income of 40,000, the variable is given a score of "0"; if it is higher than 40,000, it is given a score of "1" (UK Office of National Statistics). In terms of *membership length*, if the median is below 19 years – the median membership length of Labour party candidates for the 1992 General Election – the variable is given a score of "0" (Norris and Lovenduski, 1995, p. 89). If the median membership length is 19 years or higher, the variable is given a score of "1". In terms of *hours spent on party activities*, if the median is zero hours per week, the variable is given a score of "0"; however, if it is more than this, it is given a score of "1". In terms of being *left or right on the political continuum* – referring back to May's Law – central and local part selectors have different preferences or ideal types. For central party approval on the NPP – if the median score is 4 for centrist, the variable is given a score of "1". If the score is 3 or lower or 5 or higher, the variable is given a score of "0". For local party selectors, if the median is 3 or lower, the variable is given a score of "1", whereas if it is higher than 3, it is given a score of "0". In terms of old and new Labour, for central party selectors, old Labour is given a score of "0", whereas new Labour is given a score of "1", whereas for local party selectors, old Labour is given a score of "1" and new Labour a score of "0". In terms of *political ambition*, if the median is 4 or higher, the variable is given a score of "1"; however, if it is below 4, it is given a score of "0". The variable scores are then added for an overall total idealness score. An attempt was made to test the relationship between aspirant candidate success at the various stages and a similarly calculated idealness score for each case – for example – aspirant candidates with higher idealness scores are more likely to be approved, shortlisted, and selected; however, too many cases were removed from the regression and the model scores were too low. Thus it is unclear what the relationship between success at the various selection stages and the idealness score is. However, while the idealness score does not directly answer the question "why do some and not other types of aspirant candidates secure candidacies", it does provide considerable insight into the qualities of the actual aspirant candidate pool.

53 Interview with a Labour party official.

54 Interview with a Labour party official.

55 Interview with a Labour party official.

56 Interview with a Labour party official.

57 Interview with a Labour party official.

58 Variables marked "*" are statistically related to the dependent variable, which is being shortlisted. Chi-square tests are used to test the extent to which categorical variables are related to the binary dependent variable of shortlisted/not shortlisted. Spearman's Rho tests are used to assess scale variables.

59 The idealness score of 68 percent is the baseline frequency with which idealness scores of the subsequent samples are compared. These comparisons offer a simple way to describe if aspirant candidate samples are more or less ideal than the initial pool of aspirant candidates at Stage 1. The baseline idealness score of 26 out of 38, or 68 percent, reflects the local party selectors' preferences for aspirant candidates who speak out against the party, who are left, and who are old Labour as in Models 2, 3, 4, 5, 6, 7, and 8 (shortlisting and selection models). This score slightly changes to reflect the preferences of central party selectors for aspirant candidates who do not speak out, who are centrist, and who are new Labour as in Model 1 (approval on the NPP). The baseline idealness score for central party selectors is 28 out of 38 or 74 percent, which is also later used for comparative purposes.

60 In terms of *age*, the median aspirant candidate is 44 years, which is only 1 year older than candidates surveyed for the 1992 General Election and is 6 years younger than the median age of British MPs (Keep, 2010, p. 10; Norris and Lovenduski, 1995, p. 88). Looking to sexual orientation, 394 (92 percent) of aspirant candidates are heterosexual compared to 34 (8 percent) who are LGBTQ. Of this 8 percent, 7.5 percent of respondents stated they are gay, 1 percent indicated they are bisexual, and .5 percent indicated they are transgendered. Turning to *first language*, 412 (94 percent) indicated their first language is English, while 28 (6 percent) indicated their first language is "other" – with the most frequently reported being Punjabi, Bengali, Urdu, Welsh, Spanish, Gujarati, and Dutch. Next, education, 398 (83 percent) of the 482 surveyed aspirant candidates have a degree, in comparison to 84 (17 percent) who do not. In terms of employment, of the aspirant candidates, 340 (82 percent) of 415 are in full-time work compared to 75 (18 percent) who are not. In terms of those not in full-time employment, 8 percent indicate they fall into the "other" category, with most identifying as students and self-employed, 2 percent as retired, 1 percent as registered unemployed, and 1 percent as looking after the home. Moving to *class*, a majority of the aspirant candidates, 213 (54 percent) of 394, identify as middle class in comparison to 181 (46 percent) who do not. Not surprisingly, none of the aspirant candidates identify as upper class, which fits a party official's comment that party members have disdain for "show-offs". In terms of *housing tenure*, of the 374 respondents, 300 (80 percent) *own* their main accommodation, compared to 74 (20 percent) who do not. In terms of *non-owners*, 14 percent indicated they rent from a private landlord, 2 percent from a housing association, 1 percent from a local authority, and 3 percent from "other", which is identified as living with a partner or lodging with a parent. Moving next to *dependent children*, 259 (67 percent) of the 384 aspirant candidates who responded to the survey question indicated they do not have children in their care, compared to 125 (33 percent) who do. Next, 352 (90 percent) of 393 aspirant candidates indicate they do not have adults in their care compared to 41 (10 percent) who do. Lastly, 287 or 404 responders (71 percent) recorded having a partner, as opposed to 181 (29 percent) of non-partnered respondents. Of those in a relationship, 52 percent are married to their partner, while 18 percent are not married but cohabitating with their partner. Of the non-partnered, 21 percent indicated they are single, 10 percent divorced, and less than 1 percent reported being widowed.

61 Of those who do not identify as Christian, 43 percent are not affiliated with any religion, whereas 3 percent identify as Muslim, 2 percent as Hindu, 2 percent as Jewish, 1 percent as Sikh, .5 percent as Buddhist, and the rest as "other religion".

62 The average length of party membership is 14 years, ranging from 51 years to less than 1 year. Looking to hours spent on party activities, the average number of hours worked

is 7 hours a week, with some indicating they spend up to 100 hours per week while others spend no time at all. Next, 12 percent of aspirant candidates indicate they were previously and/or currently employed by the British Labour party. Lastly, 90 percent of aspirant candidates volunteer on party related activities, such as holding party office, sitting on the national policy forum, attending party conference, participating on a party committee, and/or working on a party campaign.

63 This reflects the score for local selectors. As noted earlier, the score for central selectors is slightly different given their preferences for aspirant candidates who do not speak out against the party, who are centrist, and who are new Labour. Thus the central party selector score for the political attitudes category is 2 out of 3.

64 Note: "1" indicates absolutely no political ambition, and "10" indicates the highest level of political ambition.

65 Indicated by "*".

66 In binary logistic regression, independent variables are entered to predict the probability of event occurrence, with Exp(B) odds ratios allowing categories within variables to be more meaningfully compared. Logistic regression allows the statistical significance of each entered variable to be tested while holding constant the effect of other included variables.

67 As a reminder, testing for supply-side Stages 1) apply to the party and 2) apply to the NPP also reveal the process is neutral.

68 Supply-side tests for Stage 3) on the NPP and 4) apply to seats reveal the process is neutral – in other words – ideal and non-ideal aspirant candidate types on the NPP are no more or less likely to apply for seats. The median number of seats for which aspirant candidates apply in Stage 4 is 2 – although some aspirant candidates apply for as many as 20. This median score is somewhat surprising. In other countries with single member plurality electoral systems, such as Canada, aspirant candidates are normally limited to seeking one seat at a time. Given the opportunity to seek candidacy in more than one seat, it is reasonable to expect that aspirants may seek more seats to increase their chances at securing a seat. At the same time, there are considerable costs associated with seeking seats, such as travel, which may be prohibitive if applying for more than one seat (Norris and Lovenduski, 1995). Indeed, approximately 18 percent of all aspirant candidates do not apply for seats. Survey respondents' reasons for not applying for seats include lack of resources: "it can be an expensive and time consuming process", and lack of experience and networks: "the process relies on inside knowledge held by some. The selection process is biased towards those who do not have demanding and/or professional jobs outside politics". A comparison reveals, with only a few exceptions, aspirant candidates who do and do not apply for seats are quite similar. In terms of differences, slightly more women and BAME aspirant candidates apply for seats. Moreover, there are slightly more aspirant candidates applying for seats who speak out against the party and who identify as old rather than new Labour. Overall, aspirant candidates with *central party support* are *more likely* to apply to seats than those without such support. To some extent the finding is in line with Fox and Lawless (2010) and Niven (2006), who find party support and encouragement increases the chances of aspirant candidates "staying in the game", which, in this case they do by applying for seats.

69 The language and presentation style of the results for all regression analyses in this study are based on Julie Pallant's (2007) "SPSS Survival Manual".

70 The survey data are more robust than the census data in Chapter 3, which accounts for such inconsistencies.

71 The language used to explain the odds-ratio is taken from Field (2009, pp. 288–289). According to Field: "We can interpret the odds ratio in terms of the change in odds. If the value is greater than 1 then it indicates that as the predictor increases, the odds of

the outcome occurring increase. Conversely, a value less than 1 indicates that as the predictor increases, the odds of the outcome occurring decrease".

72 Winnable seats include safe seats (seats won by the Labour party in the 2001 and 2005 General Elections) and marginal seats (seats with a <10 percent swing) as per Pippa Norris's British Parliamentary Constituency Data Base 1992–2005 and the 6 May 2010 British General Election Constituency Results Release.

73 The higher idealness score is a result of removing unwinnable seats from the sample rather than removing AWS seats from the sample. The AWS sample is explored in more detail in Chapter 7.

74 An aspirant candidate's survey response.

7 Do local party members select "ideal" candidates?

This chapter is similar to Chapter 6 in that it presents the results of logistical regression tests performed on original survey data from British Labour party aspirant candidates to better understand if local party members prefer "ideal" candidates. But this chapter examines data from Stage 7 of the candidate selection process – local selection contests. It also adds an additional set of independent variables concerning the campaign efforts to secure candidacy during these local contests, with those spending more time and money on their campaigns and employing voter mobilisation methods hypothesised as more likely to win candidacies. In total, 8 categories containing a total of 44 variables are included in regression testing: 1) social background; 2) party experience; 3) political experience; 4) political networks; 5) personal support; 6) political attitudes; 7) political ambition; and 8) selection campaign efforts.

The first model presented in this chapter, Model 5, explores data from 334 surveys.[1] Regression results reveal a single statistically significant independent variable: local party members prefer contestants living in the constituency in which the selection contest is held. Models based on a series of sub-samples produce different results. Model 6 includes only surveys of those standing in open contests, removing those participating in AWS seats contests. Regression results shows local residency remains critical to securing candidacy, but so too does sex, with men more likely than women to win candidacy. Model 7 includes only surveys from those standing in open seats (non-AWS) considered winnable for the Labour party. It shows living locally and being a man greatly increases the odds of securing candidacy, but so too does being an elected councillor. These findings all reinforce the ideal candidate theory in that local selectors lean toward those with ideal candidate traits when left unconstrained by rules imposed by central party officials, such as AWS. Finally, regression Model 8 includes a small sample of surveys collected from women standing in AWS seats in order to take a first look into the dynamics of these types of seats. The testing shows only one of the 44 variables proves statistically significant: whether or not the aspirant candidate lives locally, again showing the strong impact of residence on selection process outcomes.

"Idealness scores" are also calculated for each model to reveal the attributes of shortlisted aspirant candidate types in the various seat conditions. The overall idealness scores also reveal aspirant candidates who make it through to the final selection round, Stage 7, are more ideal than those who begin the selection process in Stage 1. Moreover, idealness scores are even higher in contested and winnable seats. Most remarkably, the AWS sample has the highest idealness score of all the samples explored in this study. The idealness scores are a reminder of Holland's argument (1987) that any differences between selected and non-selected candidates likely reflect party selector criteria (p. 53).

Testing selector preferences for ideal candidates during local selection contests

As stated in the introduction, this chapter is very similar to Chapter 6 in terms of theory, methods, and variables. Frequencies and idealness scores from survey data are also presented and discussed for various groups of surveyed aspirant candidates. Chi-square and Spearman's Rho tests are used to whittle down the larger set of independent variables to a smaller set of variables tested using regression to assess their impact on being selected as a Labour party candidate. This section outlines the study variables and samples before moving to analysis in the next section.

The dependent variable used in all Chapter 7 measures is whether shortlisted aspirant candidates report being "selected" or "not selected" during Stage 7 of the party's selection process. In terms of independent variables, the first 38 are identical to those used in Chapter 6 and grouped into seven categories: 1) social background; 2) party experience; 3) political experience; 4) political networks; 5) personal support; 6) political attitudes; and 7) political ambition.[2] An eighth set of independent variables is included in Chapter 7's analysis to capture the possible effects of selection campaign resources and strategies. Little is known about aspirant candidate selection campaign methods and the potential influence they may have upon selection contest outcomes. Considerably more is known about the relationship between election campaign methods, specifically voter mobilisation efforts and electoral success. For example, one of the most comprehensive studies of voter contact mobilisation efforts suggests door-to-door canvassing, phone banks, direct mail, leafleting, automated calling (i.e., robo calling), email, and paid advertising are positively related to electoral success in the US (Green and Gerber, 2008). A study on the selection process in Canada found aspirant candidates who signed up new party members were much more likely to get selected than those who did not (Ashe and Stewart, 2012).

Arguably, shortlisted aspirant candidates who spend more time and money on their selection campaigns and who mobilise party members during their selection campaigns are more likely to get selected than aspirant candidates who spend less time and money and who do not mobilise party members. Mobilising party members and/or signing-up party members involves investing resources such as time and money into selection campaigning (Norris and Lovenduski, 1995, p. 145). Indeed, meeting with party members and contacting potential networks, especially in non-local seats, can be a time consuming and expensive undertaking, as can the production and distribution of campaign materials. In line with this, an aspirant candidate remarked, "it's those with the flashy handouts who win. That takes money".[3] Further, aspirant candidates frequently commented that there should be a set spending limit during the selection process to level out the playing field. Thus, Chapter 7 includes seven selection contest campaign variables: 1) *total hours* worked on the campaign; 2) *total money* spent campaigning; 3) whether the aspirant candidate worked to *sign up members*; 4) if efforts were made to *contact members*, 5) *trade unions*, or 6) *interest groups*; and 7) whether the aspirant candidate employed *social media* during his or her campaign.[4]

The chapter presents results from four regression models numbered 5 through 8. Model 5 includes all 334 surveyed aspirant candidates shortlisted in Stage 6 of the selection process. Model 6 includes 248 surveys only from those competing in open non-AWS seats, thereby eliminating surveys from those who did not face selection contests or compete for AWS seats. Model 7 includes data from 92 surveys of those competing in open non-AWS and winnable seats, thus eliminating AWS and unwinnable seats. Model 8 includes a small sample of 49 surveys of those contesting AWS seats. Results from all models are further discussed in the concluding section.

Model 5: local selection contests

Model 5 explores the entire sample of successful shortlisted aspirant candidates seeking to secure enough votes from local members to become official Labour party candidates. The dependent variable predictor is "selected", and the comparator is "not selected". The model tests 44 variables from the previously described categories.

Frequencies

Table 7.1 displays frequencies describing shortlisted aspirant candidates to better understand who competes in the final selection process stage. In terms of the dependent variable, of the 334 shortlisted survey respondents, 207 (62 percent) indicate they were selected as candidates, with 127 (38 percent) stating they were not selected. These results closely reflect the party census data explored in Chapter 3, which show 40 percent of all shortlisted aspirant candidates failed to get selected.

The independent variables included in Table 7.1 provide a detailed account of what types of shortlisted aspirant candidates participate, and ultimately succeed, in the Labour party's candidate selection process. Looking at the predictor and comparator columns, the sample of all shortlisted aspirant candidates tilts more toward the ideal aspirant candidate type. The overall idealness score for this sample is 71 percent; 3 points higher than the idealness score for those who began the selection process in Stage 1.[5] While ideal aspirant candidates dominate some aspects of the candidate pool, local members are still presented with considerable choice and have the option to choose between ideal and non-ideal candidate types.

Table 7.1 Selection contests

Dependent	PPC Outcome	n	Predictor Selected	#	%	Comparator Not Selected	#	%	Median
		334		207	62%		127	38%	-
Social Background	Sex*	334	Man	222	67%	Woman	112	33%	-
	Race*	334	Non-BAME	292	87%	BAME	42	13%	-
	Ability	334	Non-Disabled	315	94%	Disabled	19	6%	-
	Age	305	-	-	-	-	-	-	42 years
	Sex Orient.	269	Heterosexual	248	92%	LGBTQ	21	8%	-
	Language	308	English	293	95%	Other	15	5%	-
	Religion	241	Christian	105	44%	Other	136	56%	-
	Education	311	Degree	259	83%	No	52	17%	-
	Occupation	291	Instrumental	163	56%	No	128	44%	-
	Income	271	-	-	-	-	-	-	£40–50k
	Employment	282	Full-time	237	84%	No	45	16%	-
	Class	255	Middle	144	57%	No	111	43%	-
	Housing	243	Owner	189	78%	No	54	22	-
	Dependent Children	257	No	176	69%	Yes	81	31%	-
	Dependent Adults	262	No	237	91%	Yes	25	9%	-
	Partner	270	Yes	191	71%	No	79	29%	-
Party Experience	Membership	333	-	-	-	-	-	-	14 yrs
	Hours	265	-	-	-	-	-	-	8 hrs
	Employee*	331	Yes	41	12%	No	290	88%	-
	Volunteer	327	Yes	294	89%	No	36	11%	-
Political Experience	Councillor	332	Yes	155	47%	No	177	53%	-
	Prior Election	332	Yes	267	80%	No	65	20%	-
	Interest Group	330	Yes	223	68%	No	107	32%	-
	Union	330	Yes	139	42%	No	191	58%	-

(Continued)

Table 7.1 (Continued)

		n	Predictor	#	%	Comparator	#	%	Median
Political Networks	Recruited	300	Yes	123	41%	No	177	59%	-
	Local Res.*	315	Yes	134	43%	No	181	57%	-
	Central Party	296	Yes	232	78%	No	64	22%	-
	Local Party	293	Yes	274	94%	No	19	6%	-
	Councillors	278	Yes	141	51%	No	137	47%	-
	Union	296	Yes	184	62%	No	112	38%	-
	Interest Group*	293	Yes	195	67%	No	98	33%	-
Personal Support	Fam/Friends	290	Yes	256	88%	No	34	12%	-
	Employer	282	Yes	121	43%	No	161	57%	-
Political Attitudes	Speak Out	265	Yes	130	49%	No	135	51%	-
	Left/Right	271	-	-	-	-	-	-	Left (3)
	Old/New	260	Old	92	35%	New	168	65%	-
Ambition	Ambition	279	-	-	-	-	-	-	Fairly
Campaign	Total Hours	277	-	-	-	-	-	-	50 hrs
	Total Money	269	-	-	-	-	-	-	£200
	Sign up Members	274	Yes	51	19%	No	223	81%	-
	Contact Members	285	Yes	256	90%	No	29	10%	-
	Contact Unions	277	Yes	109	39%	No	168	61%	-
	Contact Groups	281	Yes	91	32%	No	190	68%	-
	Social Media	285	Yes	105	37%	No	180	63%	-

Note: Chi-square and Spearman's Rho *<.05.

In terms of social background variables, the sample is more ideal in over half of the variables, however, there is a higher percentage of women than in the sample of all aspirant candidates. The likely explanation for this is the central party equality rules in place for women at the preceding stages. Indeed, the percentages of non-BAME aspirant candidates as well as non-disabled aspirant candidates likely results in the first instance from much less robust equality rules and in the second from no rules. As a more general observation, the shortlisted sample facing selection is slightly younger (2 years) than those who set out in Stage 1.

The more dramatic differences between the two samples is within the political network category. In particular, there is a higher percentage of aspirant candidates who are recruited (5 percentage points), live locally (6 percentage points), and who have central party support (8 percentage points) and local party support (6 percentage points). Thus, the aspirant candidates who make it to the final selection round tend to have much stronger political networks than the all aspirant candidate sample. This is not altogether surprising given the emphasis party officials and aspirant candidates alike place on the importance of networks.[6]

Still the relationship between selection and *political networks* is relatively elusive. It is not a quality aspirant candidates are formally required to demonstrate. Yet party officials and aspirant candidates as well as scholars indicate they are amongst the most important criteria to political success (Niven, 2006).[7] For example, a party official notes that when a central party official has a preferred candidate in mind, they:

> may, as an official, talk to [their] friends, maybe sit down and say 'this is what I suggest you need to do'. . . . Or give more general advice, like tips and stuff. Or you've got friends, mates who you think should be selected, who'd do a good job for you. I've certainly sat down and talked to people and have said 'Look, if I were you, I'd do the following' and give them some ideas of candidates.[8]

On the other hand, another party official indicates local party notables also put forward their favourites:

> Well many people, constituency Labour party secretaries etc. go to selection with pre-conceived ideas that it's going to be a local candidate. But sometimes it's not, you can't always tell. Well, sometimes you can, when somebody is so good that if they stood for selection in a seat, they'd probably get it because they're so good.[9]

Additionally, aspirant candidates frequently raised the importance of central and local party networks to selection success. For example, amongst the wide array of benefits that come with strong networks is access to local party membership lists before the central party formally makes them available.[10] Indeed, according to an aspirant candidate: "The 'favoured' candidate was given membership lists, advice and support before the shortlist was declared and so had a head start".[11] Another notes, an aspirant candidate with central party connections won by "us[ing] the membership list to knock on doors before it was officially released".[12] In terms of local networks, an aspirant candidates observes, "local candidates tend to have access to the membership list much earlier than others through various backdoors".[13] Moreover, another aspirant candidate recalls the winning candidate:

> had some councillors already working for her from the inside using the membership list and it was not a level playing field. On the day of selection, she bussed in party members never seen in the constituency, gave them a sandwich and a drink in the nearby pub and asked them to walk across to the selection meeting hall afterwards.[14]

Undeniably, networks work through several other dynamics. For example, stronger networks likely increase an aspirant candidate's chances of being *recruited*. In addition, residing in the constituency likely increases one's *local* networks. Those who receive support, advice, and encouragement from the *central* and *local party*, *councillors*, *trade unions*, and *interest groups* can draw upon a wealth of resources, including endorsements, financial resources, connections, strategy, and financial support.

Table 7.1 also paints a comprehensive picture of campaign resources and efforts, revealing several surprising results. With the exception of contacting party members, overall, very few aspirant candidates actively campaign to win their seats. In terms of resources, the median *total hours* spent (50 hours) and *total money* spent (£200) is, as earlier noted, relatively low compared to other countries with multistage selection processes, such as Canada, where the median total money spent by a set of aspirant candidates in 2009 was three times higher (Ashe and Stewart, 2012, p. 701).[15] The total hours spent ranged from 0 (19 people) to 4680 (1 person), whilst the total money spent ranged from zero (40 people) to £10,000 (2 people). The aspirant candidate who spent 4680 hours campaigning went on to win the seat, as did the two aspirant candidates who spent £10,000. At the same time, 8 winners spent no hours campaigning, and 25 spent no money campaigning. Moreover, while 90 percent of all aspirant candidates contact party members, it is surprising so few directly sign up new members or contact other types of supporters. One explanation for this lack of effort is that they may enter the process after the date to sign up new members expires. They also may be seeking selection in uncompetitive seats for which they do not need to employ any campaign strategies at all – a possibility further tested in later models.

Statistical tests

Table 7.1 also shows results from Chi-square and Spearman's Rho testing. These tests show statistically significant relationships between shortlisted aspirant candidate selection and 5 of the 44 variables: sex, race, paid party work, local

Table 7.2 Model 5 regression results (selected)

Variable Predictor	B	Std Error	Exp (B)
Local Resident (Yes)	1.198	.306	3.314
Constant	.324	.636	1.383

Notes: Nagelkerke Pseudo R2 = .176; p value <.05; N = 284.

residency, and interest group support. As such, the relationship between selection success and these variables is further tested using logistic regression.[16]

As seen in Table 7.2, logistic regression is used to assess the likelihood that certain aspirant candidate types are selected by local party members.[17] In total, 284 cases are included in Model 5, which contains the 5 independent variables found to be statistically significant through the previous Chi-square and Spearman's Rho testing. In terms of model strength, the Nagelkerke Pseudo R-Square score indicates the model explains 17.6 percent of the variance in the dependent variable (getting selected). The model also correctly classifies 68.6 percent of the included cases as either selected or not selected. Only one of the five independent variables included in the model is statistically significant at the .05 level (p value): local resident. The odds ratio of 3.314 indicates that the odds of an aspirant candidate who lives in the constituency getting selected are over three times higher than the odds of an aspirant candidate who does not live in the constituency.

That none of the other variables affect whether shortlisted aspirant candidates are selected indicates the process is mostly fair to all but aspirant candidates who do not reside locally. This finding matches Chapter 6's findings, which showed local residents as more likely to be shortlisted than non-local residents. That sex does not hold is at first puzzling, given the filter tests performed in Chapter 3 show party members disproportionately filter women aspirant candidates out of the process at this stage. However, the initial impression of gender fairness during the local selection contest is likely an effect of AWS, prompting a more thorough dissection of the contest data. Race is not important when controlled for by other variables; being a BAME aspirant candidate who is also local is perhaps "acceptably different" for local party members (Durose et al, 2013). In terms of paid party work, again it appears being local is a more desirable trait amongst local members. This finding reflects the palpable resentment amongst local parties toward Labour party headquarters parachuting in their staffers from London and presents a challenge to the instrumental occupation thesis (Allen, 2012; Cairney, 2007). Further, that aspirant candidates with interest group support are no more or less likely to get selected suggests the importance of this particular type of network – as well as all other networks but being local – is perhaps overstated.

That campaigns do not matter is also surprising but perhaps explains why so few aspirant candidates spend time or money to sign up new members or contact existing members, trade unions, or interest groups or communicate through social media. These results suggest the futility of central party agents supplying underrepresented groups with funds during selection contests. Further, the findings reveal spending limits are likely unnecessary, as spending does not appear to positively or negatively affect an aspirant candidate's selection chances. It also reveals the current patterns of selection preferences are likely entrenched, as no amount of campaigning seems to affect selection process outcomes.

Model 6: local selection contests in open seats

This section develops a model to assess local party member preferences in selection contests held in open seats. This assessment excludes surveys from aspirant candidates shortlisted to compete in AWS seats and those acclaimed as candidates (i.e., they did not face a selection contest). As with Model 5, Model 6 includes 44 independent variables. Frequencies are first explored, followed by Chi-square and Spearman's Rho tests and, finally, logistic regression analysis.

Frequencies

Looking to Table 7.3, 248 surveyed aspirant candidates were shortlisted to compete in open, contested seats. The *predictor variable* "selected" indicates 153 (62 percent) of the shortlisted aspirant candidates were selected as candidates, while the *comparator value* "not selected" shows 95 (38 percent) were not selected. Independent variable measures and hypotheses are the same as in the preceding sections. Overall, the aspirant candidates are *more* ideal than the shortlisted sample who began the process. The overall idealness score is 74 percent – which is again higher (6 percentage points) than in the original pool of aspirant candidates at Stage 1. As anticipated, aspirant candidates shortlisted to compete for seats have a higher idealness score (3 percentage points) than aspirant candidates in the preceding sample for Model 5, which includes non-competitive races.

To highlight, when compared to the sample used in Model 1 in Chapter 6, the idealness score increases across 11 of the 16 social background variables. The percentage of men aspirant candidates increases by 5 percentage points as a result of removing AWS seats from the sample. In addition, the percentage of non-BAME aspirant candidates is higher (4 percentage points). Also, to note, the median age of aspirant candidates is lower – with those shortlisted to compete for seats being three years younger than the all aspirant candidate sample and one year younger than the preceding sample. At the same time, the median income increases to £50–60,000, which is £10–20,000 higher than the preceding samples. Moreover, the percentage of ideal aspirant candidates is higher across all political network variables, most noticeably local (8 percentage points), central party support (6 percentage points), local party support (5 percentage points), and councillor support (5 percentage points). Of interest, a majority of aspirant candidates in this sample speak against party policy, with Iraq, Trident, and ID cards being the top issues. This is the first time the ideal aspirant candidate type makes up a majority here. It may be the case that they perceive that speaking out against the party gives them an edge over their competitors.

Table 7.3 Selection contests in open seats

Dependent	PPC Outcome	N	Predictor Selected	#	%	Comparator Not Selected	#	%	Median
	PPC Outcome	248	-	153	62%	-	95	38%	-
Social Background	Sex*	248	Man	189	76%	Woman	59	24%	-
	Race*	248	Non-BAME	217	88%	BAME	31	12%	-
	Ability	248	Non-Disabled	231	94%	Disabled	17	6%	-
	Age	227	-	-	-	-	-	-	41 yrs
	Sex Orient.	204	Heterosexual	186	91%	LGBTQ	18	9%	-
	First Language	233	English	222	96%	Other	10	4%	-
	Religion	185	Christian	83	45%	Other	102	55%	-
	Education	232	Degree	196	85%	No	36	15%	-
	Occupation*	220	Instrumental	117	53%	No	103	47%	-
	Income*	208	-	-	-	-	-	-	£50–60k
	Employment	214	Full-time	184	86%	No	30	14%	-
	Class	197	Middle class	115	58%	No	82	42%	-
	Housing	186	Owner	142	77%	No	42	23%	-
	Dependent Child	195	No	130	68%	Yes	65	33%	-
	Dependent Adults	199	No	179	90%	Yes	20	9%	-
	Partner	206	Yes	148	72%	No	58	28%	-
Party Experience	Membership*	247	-	-	-	-	-	-	14 yrs
	Hours	209	-	-	-	-	-	-	8 hrs
	Employee*	247	Yes	30	12%	No	217	88%	-
	Volunteer	243	Yes	215	89%	No	28	11%	-
Political Experience	Councillor	247	Yes	115	47%	No	132	53%	-
	Prior Election	247	Yes	198	80%	No	49	20%	-
	Interest Group	245	Yes	166	68%	No	79	32%	-
	Union	245	Yes	100	41%	No	145	59%	-

(Continued)

Table 7.3 (Continued)

		N	Predictor	#	%	Comparator	#	%	Median
Political Networks	Recruited	235	Yes	87	37%	No	148	63%	-
	Local Res.*	240	Yes	108	45%	No	132	55%	-
	Central Party	231	Yes	175	76%	No	56	24%	-
	Local Party	229	Yes	213	93%	No	16	7%	-
	Councillor	216	Yes	114	53%	No	102	47%	-
	Union	232	Yes	139	60%	No	93	40%	-
	Interest Group	229	Yes	145	63%	No	84	37%	-
Personal Support	Fam/Friends	226	Yes	196	87%	No	30	13%	-
	Employer	220	Yes	95	43%	No	125	57%	-
Political Attitudes	Speak Out*	203	Yes	103	51%	No	100	49%	-
	Left/Right	210	-	-	-	-	-	-	Left (3)
	New/Old	199	Old	71	36%	New	128	64%	-
Ambition	Ambition	216	-	-	-	-	-	-	Fairly
Campaign	Total Hours	216	-	-	-	-	-	-	48 hrs
	Total Money Spent	210	-	-	-	-	-	-	£150
	Sign up Members	213	Yes	44	21%	No	169	79%	-
	Contact Members	223	Yes	198	89%	No	25	11%	-
	Contact Unions	217	Yes	77	36%	No	140	64%	-
	Contact Groups	220	Yes	69	31%	No	151	69%	-
	Social Media	223	Yes	79	35%	No	144	65%	-

Note: Chi-square and Spearman's Rho *<.05.

Table 7.4 Model 6 regression results (selected in open seats)

Variable Predictor	B	Std Error	Exp (B)
Local Residence (Local)	1.023	.291	2.782
Sex (Man)	.704	.334	2.021
Constant	-.047	.409	.954

Notes: Nagelkerke Pseudo R2 = .119; p value <.05; N = 183.

Lastly, aspirants shortlisted to compete for a seat are only slightly more likely to sign up members, contact members, and contact trade unions than in the preceding samples. However, only a minority of aspirant candidates use mobilisation methods even when up against other aspirant candidates – with the exception of contacting party members. Counterintuitively, the percentage of aspirant candidates faced with a selection contest actually spend slightly less time and money on their campaigns and are slightly less willing to contact interest groups and use social media.

Statistical tests

As shown in Table 7.3, initial statistical relationship testing reveals 7 of the 44 variables included in the analysis are statistically significant. These are sex, race, income, membership length, party employee, local, and speaking against the party.[18] In light of these test results, the relationship between selection success and these variables is further tested using logistic regression.

Turning to the regression test, in total 183 cases are included in Model 6, which contains the 7 independent variables found to be statistically significant through previous Chi-square and Spearman's Rho testing. In terms of model strength, the Nagelkerke Pseudo R-Square score shows the whole model explains almost 12 percent of the variance in the dependent variable (getting selected). The model also correctly classifies approximately 64 percent of cases as either selected or not selected.

Only two of the seven independent variables make a unique statistically significant contribution to the model. The strongest predictor of selection to open (non-AWS) seats is local residence, with an odds ratio of 2.782. This ratio indicates the odds of an aspirant candidate who lives locally getting selected are 2.782 times higher than the odds of an aspirant candidate who does not live locally, when controlling for all other variables in the model. The odds ratio of 2.021 indicates that the odds of an aspirant candidate who is a man getting selected are over 2 times higher than the odds of an aspirant candidate who is a woman.

As anticipated, the regression results reveal that being a local resident is a trait well worth possessing for those wishing to secure candidacies. Indeed – as an aspirant candidate surmises: "it's difficult to break into the CLP unless the CLP is forced to consider external candidates by the NEC".[19] As well, the results reveal party members prefer men aspirant candidates over women aspirant candidates in non-AWS. This finding reflects a sentiment frequently expressed by women aspirant candidates: "you're the best woman, but . . . with the implication that a man candidate was preferred" and further substantiates the claim that women are disproportionately losing in non-AWS seats (Murray, 2014).[20] As well, it reflects party official fears that women's representation would decrease without AWS – as it did in 2001. Moreover, that the odds are against women winning in non-AWS seats shows why almost half of all women aspirant candidates apply to seats reserved for women. In terms of policy, and as discussed in the concluding chapter, this finding strengthens the case for increasing the number of AWS seats. Notably, the relationship between selection and race, income, length of party membership, party employee, and speaking against the party are not statistically significant in the last stage of the selection process. Whether party member demand for certain aspirant candidate types holds in open (non-AWS) *and* winnable seats is tested in the next section.

Model 7: local selection contests in open and winnable seats

This section focuses on shortlisted aspirant candidates competing for candidacies in open and winnable seats. As such, survey data from those standing in AWS, uncontested, and unwinnable seats are excluded from this sample. As noted, this seat type is more likely to see higher proportions of ideal aspirant candidate types competing and winning than the other seat types on the premise that winning a candidacy in a winnable seat often ensures a seat in parliament.

Frequencies

Looking to Table 7.5, 92 of the aspirant candidates were shortlisted to compete in open and winnable seats. The *predictor variable* "selected" indicates 31 (34 percent) of the shortlisted aspirant candidates were selected as candidates, while the *comparator value* "not selected" shows 61 (66 percent) were not selected. Independent variable measures and hypotheses are the same as in the preceding sections. The overall idealness score is 76 percent – which is higher (10 percentage points) than in the original pool of aspirant candidates in Stage 1, and, as expected, is higher than the aspirant candidates in the preceding sample (2 percentage points).

The aspirant candidates competing for winnable seats are more ideal across a majority of the social background variables. Notably, there is a much higher percentage with university degrees (7 percentage points) and in full-time employment (7 percentage points). As well, they have been party members for longer periods of time (2 years) and spend more hours per week on party activities (3 hours). In terms of political experience, a remarkably higher percentage of aspirant candidates competing for winnable seats are councillors (19 percentage points). Moreover, the percentage of aspirant candidates who are councillors competing for

Table 7.5 Selection contests in open and winnable seats

Dependent		N	Predictor	#	%	Comparator	#	%	Median
	PPC Outcome	92	Selected	31	34%	Not Selected	61	66%	-
Social Background	Sex*	92	Man	65	71%	Woman	27	29%	-
	Race	92	Non-BAME	78	85%	BAME	14	15%	-
	Ability	87	Non-Disabled	95	94%	Disabled	5	5%	-
	Age	87	-	-	-	-	-	-	44 yrs
	Sexual Orient.	76	Heterosexual	71	93%	LGBTQ	5	7%	-
	Language	86	English	83	97%	Other	3	3%	-
	Religion	66	Christian	30	46%	Other	36	54%	-
	Education	87	Degree	78	90%	No	9	10%	-
	Occupation	83	Instrumental	48	58%	No	35	42%	-
	Income	80	-	-	-	-	-	-	£50–60K
	Employment	81	Full-time	72	89%	No	9	11%	-
	Class	70	Middle	40	57%	No	30	43%	-
	Housing	66	Owner	55	85%	No	10	15%	-
	Dependent Children	75	No	46	61%	Yes	29	39%	-
	Dependent Adults	75	No	65	71%	Yes	10	13%	-
	Partner	78	Yes	57	73%	No	21	27%	-
Party Experience	Membership	90	-	-	-	-	-	-	16 yrs
	Hours	76	-	-	-	-	-	-	10 hrs
	Employee	90	Yes	15	17%	No	75	83%	-
	Volunteer	90	Yes	81	90%	No	9	10%	-
Political Experience	Councillor*	92	Yes	58	63%	No	34	37%	-
	Prior Election	92	Yes	77	84%	No	15	16%	-
	Interest Group	91	Yes	60	66%	No	31	34%	-
	Union	91	Yes	34	37%	No	57	63%	-

(Continued)

Table 7.5 (Continued)

		N	Predictor	#	%	Comparator	#	%	Median
Political Networks	Recruited	86	Yes	33	38%	No	53	62%	-
	Local Res.*	89	Yes	34	38%	No	55	62%	-
	Central Party	85	Yes	62	73%	No	23	27%	-
	Local Party	83	Yes	77	93%	No	6	7%	-
	Councillor	78	Yes	44	56%	No	34	44%	-
	Union	85	Yes	57	67%	No	28	33%	-
	Interest Group	82	Yes	62	76%	No	20	24%	-
Personal Support	Fam/Friends	83	Yes	73	88%	No	10	12%	-
	Employer	82	Yes	42	51%	No	40	49%	-
Political Attitudes	Speak Out	71	Yes	28	39%	No	43	61%	-
	Left/Right	74	-	-	-	-	-	-	Left (3)
Ambition	New/Old	67	Old	27	40%	New	40	60%	-
	Ambition	77	-	-	-	-	-	-	Fairly (8)
Campaign	Total Hours*	81	-	-	-	-	-	-	60 hrs
	Total Money*	78	-	-	-	-	-	-	£300
	Sign up Members	77	Yes	18	23%	No	59	77%	-
	Contact Members	83	Yes	74	89%	No	9	11%	-
	Contact Unions	80	Yes	34	43%	No	46	57%	-
	Contact Groups	81	Yes	24	30%	No	57	70%	-
	Social Media	83	Yes	30	36%	No	53	64%	-

Note: Chi-square and Spearman's Rho *<.1.

winnable seats is 16 percentage points higher than in the preceding sample (which includes unwinnable seats). This finding reveals that councillors pragmatically decide to bypass unwinnable seats, reinforcing the pathway to parliament argument (Durose et al, 2013). In line with this, a relatively higher percentage (8 percentage points) of aspirant candidates have prior election experience.

As with the other samples, in this model the idealness scores increase the most across all political network variables, in particular, support from the local party (6 percentage points), local councillors (8 percentage points), trade unions (9 percentage points), and interest groups (12 percentage points). Moreover, support from councillors, trade unions, and interest groups is higher than in the preceding stage. These findings suggest those competing in winnable seats see the strategic value in developing local networks. Notably, a much lower percentage of aspirant candidates speak out against the party in winnable seats compared to all aspirant candidates who begin the process and compared to the preceding stage. This could reflect the central party's closer watch over selection in winnable seats. In terms of political ambition, it is higher in this sample than in any thus far. This is not surprising; winnable seats are by nature more competitive, and aspirant candidates need the drive to win them. In this sample, for the first time a majority (51 percent) of aspirant candidates report receiving support from their employers. Employers are possibly more willing to support aspirant candidates who have a chance at securing a seat and getting elected than those they perceive as "wasting their time". Indeed, there is a degree of kudos that comes with having a former employee sit in parliament.

As anticipated, aspirant candidates competing in open and winnable seats are more ideal insofar that a higher percentage use mobilisation methods during the selection campaigns. For example, compared to the preceding stage, aspirant candidates spend more time (12 hours) and more money (£150), and a higher percentage sign up party members (3 percent) and use social media. However, with the exception of contacting members, still only a minority of aspirant candidates, even in winnable seats, employ campaign tools.

Statistical tests

Six of the forty-four independent variables show a statistically significant relationship with being selected as candidates in open and winnable seats. These include sex, councillor, local resident, total hours spent, and total money spent.[21] As such, the relationship between selection success and these variables is further tested using logistic regression.

As seen in Table 7.6, regression is used to assess the likelihood that certain aspirant candidate types get selected by local party members. In total, 77 cases are included in the model, which contains 5 independent variables found to be significant through previous testing. In terms of model strength, the model score is higher than previous models included in this study, with a Nagelkerke R-Square score of 0.381. Thus, the model as a whole explains 38.1 percent of the variance in the dependent variable (getting selected).

Table 7.6 Model 7 regression results (selected in open and winnable seats)

Variable Predictor	B	Std Error	Exp (B)
Councillor (Yes)	1.664	.727	5.281
Local Resident (Local)	1.619	.620	5.050
Sex (Man)	1.521	.850	4.577
Constant	-3.894	.992	.020

Notes: Nagelkerke Pseudo R2 = .381; p value <.1; N = 77.

Only three of the independent variables made a unique statistically signifi-cant contribution to the model at the .1 level (p value): sex, councillor, and local residency. The strongest predictor of getting selected in open and win-nable seats is experience as a local councillor, with an odds ratio of 5.281. This ratio indicates the odds of an aspirant candidate who has experience as a councillor getting selected are 5.281 times higher than the odds of an aspirant candidate who does not have experience as a councillor. Next the odds ratio of 5.050 indicates the odds of an aspirant candidate who lives in the constituency getting selected are over 5 times higher than the odds of an aspirant candidate who does not live in the constituency. Last, the odds ratio of 4.577 reveals that the odds of an aspirant candidate who is a man getting selected in an open and winnable seat is over 4 times higher than the odds of an aspirant candidate who is a woman.

These findings suggest that, when faced with a choice in open and winnable seats, local party members prefer aspirant candidates possessing particular ideal aspirant candidate traits. First, that party members prefer councillors reflects the literature and, in particular, the relationship between political success and this type of instrumental experience (Allen, 2012; Cairney, 2007). To consider, a selection study on Canadian political parties in British Columbia reveals party members were neither biased for nor against aspirant candidates with or without experience as councillors (Ashe and Stewart, 2012). One possible explanation for this difference is the much stronger relationship between the national British Labour party and local Labour parties than between national/provincial and local party organisations in Canada. Keeping in mind that selections are low informa-tion events: members may not know a great deal about the aspirant candidates. Several aspirant candidates remarked that often the first chance they got to speak to members was at the hustings on the day of the selection – a practice which effectively favours those with already higher profiles.[22] Thus, aspirant candidates with a record of political experience – especially *local* name recognition – are more likely to stand out.

Local members are also more likely to select locally residing shortlisted aspir-ant candidates to winnable seats. This has been the most consistent finding throughout the study and reflects the importance of the local campaign and link between local candidates and their constituents. Finally, party members tend to prefer men aspirant candidates in open and winnable seats. This finding reflects a widely held sentiment amongst the women aspirant candidates surveyed for this study, with one woman noting:

> my experience was of straightforward discrimination by a male dominated local party who refused to consider a female candidate, regardless of how qualified and able she was – no amount of support or training for the candidate could have overcome that prejudice and the end result was absolutely no reflection on the ability of the female candidates.[23]

Overall the finding that local party members prefer men aspirant candidates over women aspirant candidates again reinforces the use of AWS seats and perhaps increasing the number of AWS seats if the party wishes to fulfil its mandate to achieve gender parity. The next section examines the races within AWS seats to better understand the dynamic in races without men aspirant candidates.

Model 8: local selection contests in all women shortlist seats

The statistical tests included in this section are conducted on only those surveys from contests within AWS seats. As such, surveys from those in open (non-AWS) seats or aspirant candidates not facing selection contests are excluded.

Frequencies

Looking to Table 7.7, 49 women aspirant candidates were shortlisted to AWS. The *predictor variable* "selected" indicates 23 (47 percent) of the aspirant candidate women who were shortlisted to AWS were selected as candidates, while the *comparator value* "not selected" indicates 26 (53 percent) were not selected. The rest of this section briefly examines what type of women are selected in AWS contests.

Overall, and importantly, this sample of surveys from women participating in AWS seat contests shows a higher percentage of aspirant candidates fall into the predictor column than in any other sample assessed in this chapter.[24] In other words, this sample has the *highest* idealness score of the eight considered samples. Indeed, the overall idealness score for AWS is 82 percent – 14 percentage points higher than the sample of all aspirant candidates in Stage 1. This finding would seem to stand the "meritocracy" argument used by opponents of quotas on its head (Dahlerup, 2013, p. 11). Instead of the perceived notion of "lower quality" candidates competing in AWS seats, these types of restricted seats attract a "more ideal" set of candidates than open seats.

Note that women competing in AWS are more ideal across a majority of the social background variables. Looking to Table 7.7, there is a higher percentage of non-BAME aspirant candidates (6 percentage points) in the AWS sample than in the all aspirant candidate sample and in the preceding sample (5 percentage points). As well, the median age – 48 years old – is higher (4 years) than the Stage 1 sample and higher than the preceding sample (4 years). Also, all aspirant

Table 7.7 Selection contests in AWS seats

Dependent	PPC Outcome	n	Predictor	#	%	Comparator	#	%	Median
			Selected			Not Selected			
Social	Sex	49	Woman	49	100%	Man	0	100%	-
Background	Race	49	Non-BAME	44	90%	BAME	5	10%	-
	Ability	49	Non-Disabled	48	96%	Disabled	1	4%	-
	Age	46	-	-	-	-	-	-	48 yrs
	Sexual Orient.	41	Heterosexual	41	100%	LGBTQ	-	-	-
	Language	46	English	45	98%	Other	1	2%	-
	Religion	37	Christian	14	38%	Other	23	62%	-
	Education	47	Degree	37	79%	No	10	21%	-
	Occupation	41	Instrumental	29	71%	No	12	29%	-
	Income*	40	-	-	-	-	-	-	£60–70k
	Employment	43	Full-time	30	70%	No	13	30%	-
	Class	39	Middle class	20	51%	No	19	49%	-
	Housing	39	Owner	35	90%	No	4	10%	-
	Children	39	No	33	85%	Yes	6	15%	-
	Adults	39	No	36	92%	Yes	3	8%	-
	Partner*	39	Yes	27	68%	No	13	32%	-
Party	Membership	49	-	-	-	-	-	-	16 yrs
Experience	Hours	35	-	-	-	-	-	-	10 hrs
	Employee	49	Yes	9	18%	No	40	82%	-
	Volunteer	49	Yes	48	98%	No	1	2%	-
Political	Councillor	49	Yes	28	57%	No	210	43%	-
Experience	Prior Election	49	Yes	42	86%	No	7	14%	-
	Interest Group	49	Yes	39	80%	No	10	20%	-
	Union*	49	Yes	28	57%	No	21	43%	-

Category	Variable	n			%			%	
Political Networks	Recruited	44	Yes	24	56%	No	20	44%	-
	Local Res.*	48	Yes	14	29%	No	34	71%	-
	Central Party	43	Yes	37	86%	No	6	14%	-
	Local Party	43	Yes	41	95%	No	2	5%	-
	Councillors	42	Yes	23	55%	No	19	45%	-
	Union	43	Yes	33	77%	No	10	23%	-
	Interest Group	43	Yes	37	76%	No	6	14%	-
Personal Support	Fam/Friends	43	Yes	41	95%	No	2	5%	-
	Employer	43	Yes	15	35%	No	28	65%	-
Political Attitudes	Speak Out	42	No	22	52%	Yes	20	43%	-
	Left/Right	41	-	-	-	-	-	-	Left (3)
	New/Old	41	Old	16	39%	New	25	61%	-
Ambition	Score	42	-	-	-	-	-	-	Fairly (7)
Campaign	Total Hours	42	-	-	-	-	-	-	120 hrs
	Total Spent*	40	-	-	-	-	-	-	£1000
	Sign up Members	41	Yes	5	12%	No	36	88%	-
	Contact Members	42	Yes	42	100%	No	-	-	-
	Contact Union	40	Yes	29	73%	No	11	27%	-
	Contact Groups	41	Yes	20	49%	No	21	51%	-
	Social Media	42	Yes	20	48%	No	22	52%	-

Note: Chi-square and Spearman's Rho * <.1.

candidates who compete in AWS identify as heterosexual, which is higher (8 percentage points) than in the all aspirant candidate sample. Notably, a much higher percentage are employed in instrumental occupations (22 percentage points), and the median income is £60–70,000, which is £20–40,000 more than in the all aspirant sample. To consider, a much higher percentage (22 percentage points) of aspirant candidates seeking AWS do not have dependent children.

Moving to party experience, again, the sample demonstrates a higher percentage of ideal aspirant candidates across all the variables compared to the all aspirant candidate sample in Model 1. Most notably, there is a higher percentage of party employees (6 percentage points) and party activists (8 percentage points). In terms of political experience, there is a strikingly higher percentage of ideal aspirant candidates in all of the political experience variables. For example, the percentage of women who have been councillors is much higher (13 percentage points), as is the percentage who have held trade union office (13 percentage points). The highest percentage increase occurs in the political network category, where a much higher percentage are recruited (20 percentage points), receive support from the central party (16 percentage points), and receive support from trade unions (13 percentage points). At the same time, a much lower percentage are local (18 percentage points). To be sure, a relatively lower percentage (9 percentage points) of aspirant candidates in the AWS sample are local compared to the preceding sample in which AWS are excluded.

In terms of selection campaign variables, women aspirant candidates shortlisted to compete in AWS spend more time (60 hours) and money (£800) than aspirant candidates competing for open and winnable seats in the preceding sample. Moreover, all aspirant candidates contact party members – an 11 percentage point increase from the preceding sample – and an extraordinarily higher percentage contact unions leaders (30 percentage points) and interest groups (19 percentage points). Lastly, a higher percentage of those competing in AWS use social media (12 percentage points) to reach out to potential supporters.

Statistical tests

As seen in Table 7.7, of the 44 included variables, initial Chi-square and Spearman's Rho testing shows 5 to be statistically significant: income, partner, holding office in a trade union, local, and total money spent.[25] As such, these variables are included in regression testing.[26]

Table 7.8 Model 8 (AWS seats)

Variable Predictor	B	Std Error	Exp (B)
Local (Local)	3.012	1.326	20.326
Constant	-4.695	3.091	.009

Notes: Nagelkerke Pseudo R2 = .553; p value <.1; N = 33.

As seen in Table 7.8, logistic regression is performed to evaluate the influence of the previously mentioned variables on the likelihood that aspirant candidates shortlisted to contest AWS are selected as candidates. The model explains 55 percent of the variance in the dependent variable and correctly classifies 75.6 percent of cases. Staying with Table 7.8, only the local resident variable makes a unique statistically significant contribution to the model, with an odds ratio of 20.326 indicating the odds of an aspirant candidate who lives in the constituency getting selected in an AWS seat is over 20 times higher than the odds of an aspirant candidate who does not live in the constituency.

The enormous barrier to non-local women aspirants highlights the difficulty in using AWS to increase candidate pool equity, suggesting non-local women "need not apply". As seen in Table 7.7, most (71 percent) of the women competing in AWS are *not* local residents. Yet this quality would appear to be critical for selection success. Thus, highly qualified non-local women aspirant candidates who might otherwise win in their own local constituencies are being crowded into AWS seats located outside of the constituencies where they live and where they have a much lower chance of winning. With nearly half the women aspirant candidates surveyed in this study indicating they were shortlisted in AWS seats, women are being enticed away from competing in open, non-AWS on the premise that competing in AWS will increase their chances of securing candidacy. Indeed, this is certainly the thinking amongst party officials as well as women aspirant candidates. The women aspirant candidates who compete in AWS have exceptionally high levels of party experience and political experience, and in all other respects they more closely reflect the ideal aspirant candidate type. On another level, this suggests that AWS paradoxically work against the efficient allocation of women aspirant candidates and highly qualified aspirant candidates to other winnable seats.

Conclusion

This chapter performs statistical testing on data collected from original surveys completed by Labour party aspirant candidates to determine why some and not other aspirant candidate types are selected. A total of 44 variables are tested for statistical significance, including information regarding social background, party experience, political experience, political networks, personal support, political attitudes, political ambition, and selection campaign methods. It is hypothesised that ideal aspirant candidate types are more likely to be selected than non-ideal aspirant candidate types. In terms of independent variables, selected aspirant candidates are predicted as having ideal aspirant candidate traits, and therefore will be: men; non-BAME; non-disabled; younger; heterosexual; Christian; degree holders; employed in instrumental occupations; of high income; in full-time employment; middle class; homeowners; dependent-free; and with a partner. Further, it is predicted they will have considerable party and political experience; strong political networks and personal support; be more likely to speak out against the party; be more left than right; be more old than new Labour; have higher levels

Table 7.9 Regression model result summary

Model	5	6	7	8
N	334	248	92	49
Idealness Score	71	74	76	82
Pseudo R2	.176	.119	.381	.553
Sample	All Shortlisted Aspirant Candidates	Shortlisted in Contested Open Seats	Shortlisted in Contested Open and Winnable Seats	Shortlisted in Contested All Women Shortlist Seats
Significant Independent Variables	Local Resident*	Local Resident* Gender*	Local Resident* Gender* Councillor*	Local Resident*

Note: All models are conducted on Stage 7 of the selection process, where local party members select candidates. Thus, the dependent variable in all models is "1", selected, "0", not selected.

(* = supports ideal candidate hypothesis)

of political ambition; and be more willing to spend more effort and money on their selection campaigns.

As shown in Table 7.9, shortlisted aspirant candidates compete under different circumstances. As such, four models are developed using different samples of surveyed aspirant candidates: Model 5 explores all shortlisted aspirant candidates; Model 6 uses a sample of shortlisted aspirant candidates competing in open, non-AWS seats; Model 7 examines surveys from shortlisted aspirant candidates competing in open and winnable seats; and Model 8 takes a first look at AWS seats. Idealness scores show the samples from all models generally contain higher percentages of respondents with ideal aspirant candidate traits than non-ideal candidate traits. Notably, aspirant candidates are generally *more* ideal in seats that are contested than uncontested and even *more* ideal in seats that are contested *and* winnable. Overall, however, aspirant candidates who contest AWS are the most ideal. Importantly, the pool of shortlisted aspirant candidates who are and who are not selected differ, suggesting local party members responsible for selecting candidates prefer some aspirant candidate types over others.

Table 7.9 also summarises findings from the four models included in this chapter to assess party member demand for aspirant candidates during local selection contests. Regression testing finds only 3 of the 44 variables included in the models impact the dependent variable: living locally, being a councillor, and being a man. While party selector demand slightly varies according to seat conditions, the relationship between selection and living locally holds in all seat conditions.

Looking to Table 7.9, *living locally* is statistically significant in all cases, with party members over 3 times more likely to select aspirant candidates who live locally in all seats, 2 times more likely to do so in open contests, over 5 times more likely in open *and* winnable contested seats, and over 20 times more likely in AWS seats. This is clearly the dominant variable in this chapter. However, sex is also important in two models, with men being twice as likely as women to win in open seats and almost four times as likely to win in open *and* winnable seats. Thus, little has changed in this regard since Norris and Lovenduski's 1995 study in which they found a greater demand amongst Labour party members for men aspirant candidates than women aspirant candidates (p. 118, p. 122). Overall, these results provide a glimpse into what would happen should Labour ever decide to remove its AWS seats; women would be disproportionately filtered out of candidacies due to local party member proclivity for selecting ideal candidate types. Being a local councillor shows in only one model, although this finding is so important because it reveals a tendency to lean toward ideal type candidates in the most desirable and openly contested seats.

As noted in Chapter 4, there are long-held tensions between the central and local party members over control of the selection process. However, the findings in this chapter suggest the central party may want to reinforce local party members' preferences for local aspirant candidates for strategic reasons. In other words, reflecting on the importance of the local election and candidate, local party members may have good reason for selecting candidates who live locally, as they may offer a distinct electoral advantage over candidates from other parties who do not live locally (Campbell and Cowley, 2013).

At the same time, the party must balance this preference for local residents with a lack of demand for women aspirant candidates in open seats as shown in Model 6. When AWS are removed from the sample, this study shows the inclusion of AWS seats only serves to make selection processes gender neutral, rather than to boost the number of women holding candidacies. Moreover, when unwinnable seats are excluded from the sample in Model 7, the local preference for men aspirant candidates returns and shows party members do indeed prefer local sons over local daughters – especially in winnable constituencies. However, that Model 8 reveals local party members to be enormously biased toward local aspirant candidates during AWS contests shows that the party will have to change the rules further or make much more effort to encourage women aspirants to stand for office on their home turf rather than parachute into constituencies where they do not reside. This poses a tremendous problem for Labour, as over 70 percent of women seeking AWS seats are non-local. That members are no more or less likely to select non-BAME and non-disabled aspirant candidates over BAME and disabled aspirant candidates suggests other variables are more important to success, such as being a man, living locally, and experience as a councillor. These findings are discussed in more detail in the next chapter.

Notes

1 The regression models in this study are numbered from 1 to 8. Models 1 to 4 are included in Chapter 6 and Models 5 to 8 are included in Chapter 7. The sequence is used to provide continuity in the concluding chapter.

2 Please see Chapter 6 for a complete overview of these variables and their hypothetical relationships to selection process success.
3 Open-ended survey response.
4 In terms of total hours and money, aspirant candidates were asked to indicate how many hours and how much money they spent on their selection campaigns. Aspirants were also asked, "did you sign up any members", with "yes" coded as a "1" and "no" coded as a "0". They were also asked if they contacted any party members, trade unions, or interest groups, with "yes" to these questions coded as a "1" and "no" coded as a "0". Lastly, aspirant candidates were asked if they used social media, with "yes" coded as a "1" and "no" coded as a "0".
5 All idealness scores throughout this chapter are compared to the baseline frequency score of 26 out of 38 or 68 percent for all aspirant candidates who began the process at Stage 1, as assessed in Chapter 6. For reasons of continuity, none of the idealness calculations include the campaign variables.
6 Interview with a Labour party official.
7 Interview with a Labour party official.
8 Interview with a Labour party official.
9 Interview with a Labour party official.
10 According to a Labour party official – and as noted earlier – the membership list is formally made available to all aspirant candidates at the nomination stage for a fee of £20. It is against central party rules to access it in advance of this, and the NEC penalises those who release, access, and use the membership list ahead of its formal release.
11 Open-ended comment from an aspirant candidate surveyed for this study.
12 Open-ended comment from an aspirant candidate surveyed for this study.
13 Open-ended comment from an aspirant candidate surveyed for this study.
14 Open-ended comment from an aspirant candidate surveyed for this study.
15 The median total money spent by aspirant candidates competing for candidacies in a 2009 BC election was $1150 – or £625.
16 As with Chapter 6, "election year" was also tested for its relationship with the dependent variable. Of the 334 total observations, 224 (67 percent) are from the 2010 aspirant candidate pool, while 110 (33 percent) are from 2005. The relationship between election year and selection is not statistically significant, indicating the year in which the survey was conducted has no skewing effect on the sample or subsequent analysis.
17 More specifically, binary regression is used to predict the probability of event occurrence, with Exp(B) odds ratios allowing categories within variables to be more meaningfully compared.
18 The election year variable examines the effect of combining data from the 2005 and 2010 surveys into a single data set. Of the 248 total observations, 166 (67 percent) are from the 2010 shortlisted aspirant candidate pool, while 82 (33 percent) are from the 2005 shortlisted aspirant candidate pool. That there is no statistically significant difference between the election year and the dependent variable indicates the year in which the survey was conducted has no skewing effect upon the sample or subsequent analysis.
19 Open-ended survey response.
20 Open-ended survey response.
21 The effect of combining data from the 2005 and 2010 surveys into a single data set is again tested for this sample. Of the 92 total observations, 69 (75 percent) are from the 2010 shortlisted aspirant candidate pool, while 23 (25 percent) are from the 2005 shortlisted aspirant candidate pool. That there is no statistically significant difference between the election year and the dependent variable indicates the year in which the survey was conducted has no skewing effect upon the sample or subsequent analysis.
22 Open-ended survey comments made by aspirant candidates surveyed for this study.
23 Open-ended survey response by an aspirant candidate.

24 The election year variable examines the effect of combining data from the 2005 and 2010 surveys into a single data set. That there is no statistically significant difference between the election year and the dependent variable indicates the year in which the survey was conducted has no skewing effect upon the sample or subsequent analysis.

25 Given the small sample size, the variables are statistically significant at $p < .1$. Moreover, in some instances there were too few cases to run Chi-square and Spearman's Rho tests (i.e., ethnicity, ability, language, education, housing tenure, dependent children, dependent adults, party employee, party volunteer, past political experience, central party support, local party support, trade union support, interest group support, family support, and membership sign ups).

26 As an observation with regard to AWS, is has been noted in the literature and by some advocacy groups that BAME women aspirant candidate groups are being overlooked for non-BAME women in AWS (Ashe et al, 2010; Operation Black Vote; Fawcett Society). However, the sample size is too small to test this here. In terms of descriptive statistics, BAME women aspirant candidates make up 10 percent of the AWS pool, and 9 percent of all BAME women aspirant candidates are selected – a mere 1 percentage point difference. This indicates local party selectors (i.e., members) are not biased against BAME women in AWS.

8 Conclusion

No legislature reflects the demographic characteristics of the populations they govern. This imbalance is viewed as problematic for a host of normative reasons. While some voters may sometimes prefer certain types of candidates, it would appear the actions of political parties generate much of this representative disproportionality, as parties almost exclusively control what types of people stand as candidates during modern elections. Despite breaking diversity records from one election to the next, women and other groups are still underrepresented, and post-2017 analyses of the British snap election suggest progress has stalled. The reason for this is not a result of voters preferring men or some aspirant types to others but a result of local members selecting too few aspirants from these underrepresented groups to winnable seats. This is even the case for the British Labour party, which was so close in 2015 and 2017 to reaching its target of 50 percent women in its PLP.

The gaps between seat, candidate pool, and population proportions for women and other social groups drive considerable scholarly research, with the debate largely concerned with whether lop-sided candidate pools are a result of an undersupply or a lack of demand for certain types of aspirant candidates. But election results reveal time and time again that parties continue to be the main gatekeepers to selection and election, and future progress will be slow without their intervention (Campbell et al, 2018; Lovenduski, 2016; Kenny, 2013; Kenny and Verge, 2016). Even the diversity records set in the 2017 snap election suggest the promise of an ever upward trajectory is misleading (Campbell et al, 2018). For example, men still make up two thirds of MPs, and the number of women MPs has stalled and in some parties has decreased despite more women holding various leadership positions (Campbell et al, 2018). Parliament is still far from reflecting the make-up of society, and considerably more needs to be done to transform it into a more gender and diversity sensitive place as proposed in Childs' (2016) "The Good Parliament".

This study uses refined analytical methods to better understand supply and demand within the candidate selection process by performing tests on almost 20 years of rare British Labour party data. These methods include using a micro institutional approach to break down the larger selection process into its component stages by which to better examine the impact of party rules and participant behaviour on supply and demand. The study also develops and tests the "ideal candidate type" to examine whether selectors prefer aspirant candidates who more closely resemble past and current MPs. As discussed in the following sections, demand is found to be much more important than supply in terms of understanding disproportionality within the British Labour party's candidate pools. Central party selectors show no preference for the imagined ideal candidate type, whereas local party selectors prefer candidates with certain ideal traits – especially those with local residences. These results indicate Labour, indeed all parties concerned with demographic underrepresentation, should continue and deepen affirmative action efforts such as quotas.

Supply and demand

As shown in Chapters 1 and 2, the underrepresentation of various groups in legislatures is often portrayed as a problem of supply – with too few women, BAME, and disabled people seeking candidacy – and less often as a problem of demand – with party selectors preferring men, non-BAME, and non-disabled aspirant candidates. A *Financial Times* article, "Hostile Press Blamed for lack of Women MPs", goes one step further, assuming undersupply reduces the proportion of women MPs and speculating about the effects of negative reporting (Rigby, 2014). However, some scholars argue the responsibility of underrepresentation lies with political parties, not the press or underrepresented groups. They suggest political parties are the gatekeepers to selection and often have control over who is shortlisted and selected and where, for example, in more or less winnable seats through the use of equality rules (See Dahlerup, 2013, p. 11; Galligan, 2006).

As shown in Chapter 2, many supply-side arguments are problematic due to the data and methods used to test related hypotheses. Conclusions are often drawn using data from participants who ultimately secure candidacies and from only one of many selection process stages. This approach fails to include information from all aspirant candidates, those who win *and* lose candidacy bids, while also ignoring earlier stages of the selection process where disproportional filtering may also occur. Chapter 3 uses Labour party data to track how those who secure or fail to secure candidacies flow through seven stages of this party's candidate selection process – some stages where supply determines the aspirant candidate pool and some where demand is the prime factor.

Test results show four demand-side stages drive the process by which a large pool of initial aspirants is reduced to the final group of party candidates: NPP approval (for 2001, 2005, and 2010) and nomination, shortlisting, and selection (for 2001, 2005, 2010, and 2015). Additional filter tests also eliminate supply-side factors as causing the underrepresentation of women, BAME, and disabled aspirant candidates in the candidate pool, as a sufficient number of these types of candidates come forward to more than fill their expected share of candidacies. Moreover, filtering tests show more women, BAME, and disabled aspirant candidates are disproportionately screened out of the process at demand-side stages than men, non-BAME, and non-disabled aspirant candidates.

Demand and ideal candidates

Almost completely eliminating supply as the main cause of unbalanced candidate Labour party pools prompts a deeper exploration of demand. This study begins with the idea that party selectors prefer "ideal candidates" and will disproportionately select aspirant candidates resembling those who came before. Chapter 2 paints a portrait of selectors' ideal aspirant candidate type. In addition to being a man, non-BAME, and non-disabled person, the ideal aspirant candidate reflects the political norm across 41 other variables. Accordingly, ideal aspirant candidate types tend to be middle-aged, heterosexual, Christian, speak English as a first language, university educated, and employed in a professional, instrumental occupation. Further, they have high incomes, are in full-time employment, and are homeowners. As well, they have a partner but no dependent children or adults. Moreover, they have considerable party and political experience, strong networks, appropriate political attitudes, and political ambition, and they draw upon voter mobilisation methods.

Chapters 6 and 7 use original survey data from 566 Labour party aspirant candidates in tests designed to determine if central and local party selectors more often choose ideal over non-ideal aspirant candidates during Stage 3) approval on the NPP, Stage 6) shortlisting, and Stage 7) selection of Labour's candidate selection process. As shown in Table 8.1, regression testing shows central party selectors in Model 1 are no more or less likely to approve ideal over non-ideal aspirant candidate types to the NPP. This finding shows central party selectors are essentially neutral in terms of what types of aspirant candidates they prefer and reinforces Chapter 5's results showing non-ideal aspirant candidates are much more likely to be disproportionately filtered out at decentralised stages where local selectors dominate the process.

Regression tests performed in Chapters 6 and 7 also reveal local party selectors are not neutral in terms of what types of aspirant candidates they prefer, being more likely to shortlist and select aspirant candidates with ideal traits. As shown in Table 8.1, results from Models 2 to 7 partly reinforce the claim that local party selectors are more likely to select ideal-type candidates – with some models showing local selectors prefer aspirant candidates who are non-disabled people or long-time members. However, some results undermine the ideal candidate thesis, as local selectors sometimes prefer those with lower incomes and who are less left leaning.

That some results are inconsistent between models makes it difficult to generalise. However, three results stand out: living locally, being a man, and holding a local council position. The most prevalent preferences amongst local party selectors are for local aspirant candidates, followed by a preference for men and local councillors. This suggests being local is considerably more important than possessing most of the other traits associated with the ideal aspirant candidate. Further to this – this finding lends some support to the acceptably different argument (Durose et al, 2013). It appears that local party selectors are willing to select otherwise non-ideal aspirant candidates as long as they tick the "local" box. Thus, it is not the other variables associated with being acceptably different that matter, such as education, interest group experience and support,

Table 8.1 Regression modelling summary

Model	1	2	3	4	5	6	7	8
Stage	3	6	6	6	7	7	7	7
N	566	258	226	100	334	248	92	49
R2	n/a	.163	.139	.503	.176	.119	.381	.553
Variables	38	38	38	38	44	44	44	44
Participant Type	Aspirants	Seat Applicants	Seat Applicants	Seat Applicants	Shortlisted	Shortlisted	Shortlisted	Shortlisted
Seat Condition	All	All	Open	Open & Winnable	All	Contested Open Seats	Contested Open and Winnable Seats	AWS Seats
Selector	Central Officials	Local Officials	Local Officials	Local Officials	Local Members	Local Members	Local Members	Local Members
Predictor Category	On NPP	Short listed	Short listed	Short listed	Selected	Selected	Selected	Selected
Comparator Category	Not on NPP	Not Shortlisted	Not Shortlisted	Not Shortlisted	Not Selected	Not Selected	Not Selected	Not Selected
Significant Variables		Local* Ability* Income	Local*	Local* Gender Councillor* Yrs Mber* Left	Local*	Local* Gender*	Local* Gender* Councillor*	Local*

Note: * = supports ideal candidate hypothesis.

instrumental occupation, or party employee. Rather it is being local that makes aspirant candidates acceptably different. This may explain why BAME aspirant candidates are disproportionately screened out at the final selection stage but disappear from the regression.

In terms of sex, the findings in this study reflect those found almost 20 years ago by Norris and Lovenduski (1995). While local selectors appear to prefer women to men during shortlisting in open, non-AWS, and winnable seats, this finding provides a false lead, as it is likely caused by nomination and shortlisting quotas imposed by the central party. Indeed, final candidate selection stage findings show local party members preferring men to women, suggesting quotas serve to plump the number of women contesting seats, only to be thwarted by local members preferring men. This lack of demand for aspirant candidate women amongst local selectors in the party is disconcerting. As noted in Chapters 4 and 5, the party has, to a greater degree than any other British party, put considerable effort into reforming its selection process to increase the percentage of women and even BAMEs in its candidate and PLP pools. Yet in open (non-AWS), the local selectors still prefer men to women, suggesting Labour's culture is still highly masculinised (Lovenduski, 2005). A Westminster speech by Harriet Harman about equality in politics reveals her experiences of sexism in the party and notes, while there is "no longer 'active opposition' to women in parliament there is too much 'passive resistance' and not enough effort to promote equality" (Mason, 2014). This sentiment has been corroborated recently by a senior Labour party official who notes AWS are now a part of the party's culture.[1] Even with AWS and quotas for women in open seats, highly qualified women aspirant candidates are still getting passed over for men.

Indeed, AWS seats were designed to be a fast track policy to increase women's representation, and while these efforts have come close to achieving sex parity in the PLP, some say progress has stalled, with others saying it has come at the expense of increasing the representation of BAME aspirants (Courea, 2019).[2] The party could, if it wished, allocate more winnable seats as AWS, with some party insiders in the lead-up to the 2015 General Election working internally to designate more than 50 percent of targets seats AWS.[3] Still the Labour party is certainly doing more to increase the diversity of its candidate slate than the Conservative and Liberal Democrats. Indeed, in advance of the 2015 General Election, a news headline read: "David Cameron 'open' to all women shortlists on eve of reshuffle: Prime Minister expected to promote a number of women, as he moves to project a modern and diverse face of the Tory party" reflects other parties' recognition that AWS are likely the only way to increase women's representation in the UK and, as noted in Chapter 1, that the Labour party remains a contagion party at least on this front (Seyd, 1999; Mason and Watt, 2014). In 2015, the Conservative party increased the percentage of women MPs, a result that has likely shelved the implementation of sex quotas anytime soon.

Notably, this study finds most of the variables have no effect on selector choice, and no preference patterns emerge for many commonly cited attributes. Indeed, although discussed a great deal, there is no preference for aspirant candidates in instrumental occupations (Cairney, 2007; Allen, 2012). Moreover, as shown in

Chapters 6 and 7, local selectors are not more likely to shortlist or select party employees or those who have political experience with trade unions and interest groups. At the same time, however, they are, as long suspected, more likely to select aspirant candidates who have political experience as local councillors. This finding gives weight to the idea that political success is linked to a new pathway to power – local council remains the main recruiting grounds for higher political office (Durose et al, 2013). Problematically, presently only 32 percent of all councillors in England are women, suggesting gender filtering starts earlier in the candidate supply chain (Trenow, 2014).

In terms of political attitudes, it appears May's Law (1972) does not fully explain political success within the context of selection campaigns. Rather, as shown in Chapter 6, local selectors are more likely, rather than less likely as expected, to shortlist centrist aspirant candidates than those on the left. In terms of selection, local selectors are no more or less likely to select those with or without moderate political attitudes, a finding that differs from Holland's (1987) comparison between winning and losing candidates for the EP. However, this is worth re-evaluating, with more than one third of candidates selected to fight marginals in 2019 snap election closely aligned with the left-wing pressure group Momentum, while nearly half are backed by the trade union Unite – the closet union to Labour (Courea, 2019).

Also, of surprise, aspirant candidates who use voter mobilisation methods are no more or less likely to get selected, even in winnable seats where they are up against competitors. Unlike with parties in the US and Canada, selections in the British Labour party are comparatively low-key affairs, and this seems to be entrenched in all seat conditions. Thus, it is unlikely that increasing party funding for women or other underrepresented groups is going to increase their numbers in the party's candidate pool.

On another note, it is also surprising that aspirant candidates with high or low levels of political ambition are no more or less likely to apply for seats or get shortlisted or get selected. More to this, men and women have the same levels of political ambition: "fairly ambitious". Thus, while political ambition explains why fewer women than men express a desire to run for politics, it does not explain their chances of success once they have formally decided to seek candidacy (Fox and Lawless, 2004).

Lastly, many well-established ideas about party selector preferences do not hold in this study. For example, they do not prefer younger to older aspirant candidates, as was found to be the case amongst Conservative selectors in Norris and Lovenduski's (1995) study. Nor do they prefer those with higher or lower levels of education or those who identify as middle or working class. As well, there is no preference for those with or without children or adult dependents. Nor is there a preference for those with partners – as found in a Canadian study (Ashe and Stewart, 2012). Moreover, as noted, they do not prefer aspirant candidates with professional occupations, in this case, instrumental occupations, whereas in Norris and Lovenduski's (1995) study, Labour party selectors preferred those with professional brokerage occupations.

Multistage approach

This study shows the value of moving beyond examining a single selection process stage and only those who win their candidacy. Stage-by-stage assessments of all participants provide a rich set of results which more completely captures happenings within the secret garden of electoral politics. Chapter 4 describes how single stage studies often misclassify the selection process as "decentralised" on the basis that local selectors play a larger role than central party selectors during the final selection stage. The in-depth review of Labour's selection process reforms suggests the process is instead becoming *more centralised*. Indeed, the central party has become increasingly active in the selection process, especially with regard to implementing equality rules, such as sex and BAME quotas and AWS to counter a lack of local selector demand.

The updated look at Labour's selection process in Chapter 5 provides essential information for testing centralisation hypotheses. Party data are used to test whether non-ideal aspirant candidate types – women, BAME, and disabled aspirant candidates – are more likely to get disproportionately screened out at decentralised stages and processes and less likely to get disproportionately screened out at centralised stages and processes. The argument behind these hypotheses is the central party is more likely than local selectors to work toward the party's overall goal of gender parity as well as increasing the proportion of other underrepresented groups, particularly BAMEs, in part for reasons to do with electoral pragmatism. In other words, it wants to present the voters with a more diverse candidate slate, and it realises that having more women candidates appeal to voters (Russell, 2005). As well, non-ideal aspirant candidates are more likely to do better in highly institutionalised processes where the rules are formalised than in processes left to informal practices (Caul, 1999). As expected, non-ideal aspirant candidates do better at centralised stages and processes where there are equality rules in place to counter a lack of selector demand.

The multistage approach further reveals demand is different in different seat conditions. Looking again to Table 8.1, as noted in Chapters 3, 5, and 6, central party selectors are neutral. However, local party selectors shortlist aspirant candidates with more ideal attributes in more competitive seats. For example, they are more likely to shortlist local aspirant candidates in open seats, but in open and winnable seats, they are more likely to shortlist aspirant candidates who are local *and* who have been party members for longer periods of time. Additionally, they are more likely to shortlist councillors. As shown in Chapter 7, party members are more likely to select aspirant candidates in open seats who are men and who are local. However, in open and winnable seats, they are more likely to select aspirant candidates who are also councillors. This finding is problematic for women aspirant candidates: over half run in AWS and approximately 70 percent are non-local. Thus, most women stand little chance of winning in AWS. Rather, the preference for local aspirant candidates indicates they possibly stand a better chance in their local constituencies – even if they are open, non-AWS. At the same time, the regression results in open, non-AWS show party members prefer local men to local women. In light of this, the number and location of AWS needs to be reconsidered by the party.

As shown in Chapters 6 and 7, the multistage approach lends to comparing "idealness scores" of aspirant candidates at multiple stages of the process. It is proposed that aspirant candidates become "more ideal" as they move through the selection process. Indeed, the overall idealness score for all aspirant candidates who begin the process is much lower than the overall idealness score for aspirant candidates who are shortlisted and selected. Moreover, aspirant candidates who are shortlisted and selected in winnable seats have higher idealness scores than those who are not.

Most remarkably, the idealness scores reveal that aspirant candidates competing in AWS have by far the highest idealness score of any sample, a finding which undermines the meritocracy argument often used against quotas (Dahlerup, 2013). The multistage approach further reveals more than half of all aspirant candidate women are being clustered into less than 10 percent of the constituencies. Additionally, as noted earlier, it shows at which stage and under which conditions women aspirant candidates are being passed over for men. In doing so, it reaffirms the need for more quotas in winnable seats. Indeed, as shown, none of the other alternative variables linked with political success, such as money or interest group networks, in this case women's groups, work. Thus, findings from the multistage approach present a challenge to some scholars who question the utility of quotas over other strategies to increase women's representation (Krook and Norris, 2014).

Policy and future work

Efforts to increase equality for women and BAME aspirant candidates are more robust with each election year. AWS seats guarantee women are shortlisted in a small percentage of winnable seats. In addition, the party has quotas in open, non-AWS to encourage the nomination and shortlisting of more women and BAME aspirant candidates. Nevertheless, women aspirant candidates are filtered out to a greater degree than BAME and disabled aspirant candidates, and thus much more robust measures are needed to address women's underrepresentation. Regression work shows other factors, such as living locally, reduce the impact of the BAME variable upon shortlisting and selection success. Local selectors are no more or less likely to shortlist or select non-BAME over BAME aspirant candidates. Still, equality guarantees for BAME aspirant candidates at the shortlisting stage would increase their overall representation in the candidate pool. Nor are there any equality rules in place for disabled aspirant candidates. These equality rules are something the party should consider, given local selectors are less likely to shortlist disabled aspirant candidates.

In terms of women aspirant candidates, it is problematic that so many women seek selection in AWS seats, especially since they are amongst the most qualified of aspirant candidates in the survey sample. It is quite reasonable for women to converge on AWS seats, as local members are more likely to select men in open, non-AWS seats and even more so in the party's open, non-AWS, and winnable seats. Thus, there is merit to the idea of designating half of all seats as AWS and the other half as All Men Shortlists (Murray, 2014).

AWS seats would seem to be critically an important tool in overcoming the disadvantage women face during candidate selection contests. However, additional change is needed when coupled with the finding that non-local aspirants are at a huge disadvantage when entering AWS races. That nearly half of the women aspirants surveyed indicate they were shortlisted in AWS seats suggests they are being enticed away from competing in open, non-AWS seats to compete in AWS seats in which they do not live and have less of a chance of securing a candidacy. This finding suggests AWS seats, paradoxically, work against the efficient allocation of highly qualified aspirant women to other winnable seats. To remedy this problem, Labour should consider not only increasing the number of AWS seats but also ensuring they are more evenly distributed throughout the country. Given the importance of being local, future studies might be designed to assess different measures of "localness", for example, whether selectors prefer those who were born in the constituency, and/or have lived in the constituency for longer periods of time, and/or work in the constituency.

To come full circle, this study sheds new light on selections such as the 2010 contest between Teresa Pearce and Georgia Gould in the Erith and Thamesmead AWS seat. Regression modelling shows local Labour party members are 20 times more likely to select women who reside locally in AWS contests. This suggests Pearce did not best Gould because Pearce spent more money, or had more party or political experience, or used sophisticated voter mobilisation methods. Pearce likely won because she lived locally. Additionally, if the seat had not been AWS, there is every chance Pearce would have lost to a man candidate if he also lived locally. This single contest illuminates the challenges for central party officials to overcome the preferences of local selectors and how AWS seats are the best way to overcome these challenges.

Finally, it is hoped the methodology presented in this study contributes to the broader understanding of legislative imbalance, as it is flexible enough to be applied to different electoral systems and parties within these systems. The main difficulty with this approach is securing the data needed to perform the required testing. Ideally, winning and losing aspirants would be compared at all identified candidate selection process stages, but if this is not possible, comparisons of these two groups at key stages would deliver a deeper understanding of how rules and participants affect success.

Notes

1 Interview with a Labour party official, 2016.
2 Interview with a Labour party official, 2016.
3 Interview with a Labour party official, 2016.

Appendix: British Labour party candidate survey

Section A: your political background[1]

First, I'd like to ask you some questions about your political background in the lead-up to the 2005/2010 General Election.

1. Were you an incumbent Member of Parliament for the 2005/2010 General Election?

   - Yes
   - No

2. As an incumbent Member of Parliament for the 2005/2010 General Election, did you go through a full selection process? (e.g., did the party units and/or affiliates "trigger" a full selection?)

   - Yes
   - No

   Please enter the name of the constituency for which you were an incumbent MP.

3. Were you selected as a Prospective Parliamentary Candidate for the 2005/2010 General Election?

   - Yes
   - No

   If yes, please enter the name of the constituency.

4. As a Prospective Parliamentary Candidate for the 2005/2010 General Election, did you compete against other nominees for the candidacy at a selection contest?

   - Yes
   - No

5. Some aspirants for political office apply to the National Executive Committee to get on the National Parliamentary Panel, while others

do not. Thinking back to your selection experience for the 2005/2010 General Election, please indicate the situation that applied to you (please tick one).

- I applied to the National Parliamentary Panel and was accepted
- I was automatically included on the National Parliamentary Panel by recommendation of a nationally affiliated organisation
- I applied to the National Parliamentary Panel, but was not accepted
- I did not apply to the National Parliamentary Panel
- I ran as an "independent", that is, if I applied to seats I did so without being on the National Parliamentary Panel

6. Why didn't you apply to the National Parliamentary Panel for the 2005/2010 round of selections? (please enter in)
7. Please enter in the explanation, if any, given to you by the National Executive Committee for not getting on the National Parliamentary Panel.
8. Did you apply to any seats for the 2005/2010 General Election?

- Yes
- No

9. Please enter in why you did not apply to any seats in the lead-up to the 2005/2010 election.
10. How many open seats did you apply to in the lead-up to the 2005/2010 election? (please tick all that apply)

- Open Seats: 0, 1, 2, 3, 4, 5, 6, 7, 8, 9, 10, 11, 12, 13, 14, 15 or more

11. How many all women short–list seats did you apply to in the lead-up to the 2005/2010 election? (please tick all that apply)

- All Women Shortlist Seats: 0, 1, 2, 3, 4, 5, 6, 7, 8, 9, 10, 11, 12, 13, 14, 15 or more

12. In thinking about the 2005/2010 round of selections, for how many seats were you nominated by party units and/or affiliates? And for how many seats were you interviewed by a Constituency Labour Party's General Committee? (please tick)

- Seats Nominated: 0, 1, 2, 3, 4, 5, 6, 7, 8, 9, 10 or more
- Seats Interviewed: 0, 1, 2, 3, 4, 5, 6, 7, 8, 9, 10 or more

13. For how many seats were you shortlisted by a Constituency Labour Party's Shortlisting Committee in the lead-up to the 2005/2010 selection?

- Number of seats shortlisted: 0, 1, 2, 3, 4, 5, 6, 7, 8, 9, 10 or more

14. Was the LAST seat for which you sent in an application for the 2005/2010 General Election located in the constituency where you lived?

    • Yes
    • No

15. And what was the name of the LAST seat for which you applied to in the 2005/2010 election?

16. In thinking about the LAST seat you applied to in the lead-up to the 2005/2010 General Election, were you nominated by any party units, affiliated branches, and/or other affiliated organisations?

    • Yes
    • No

17. In thinking about your LAST selection attempt in the lead-up to the 2005/2010 election, approximately how many eligible nominating bodies were there? (i.e., party units, affiliated branches, and/or other affiliated organisations)

18. And for your LAST selection attempt in the lead-up to the 2005/2010 election, approximately how many of these nominating bodies nominated you?

19. Thinking back to your LAST seat application for the 2005/2010 election, were you shortlisted by a Constituency Labour Party's Shortlisting Committee? (please tick one)

    • No, not shortlisted
    • Yes, shortlisted to an open seat
    • Yes, shortlisted to an ALL Women Shortlist seat

20. For your LAST selection attempt in the lead-up to the 2005/2010 election, did you face a selection contest? That is, did you compete against other nominees at a selection/hustings meeting where members cast votes to decide upon a prospective parliamentary candidate?

    • Yes
    • No

21. This question asks you to think about your LAST selection contest. Please describe your opponents, those nominees who competed against you for the candidacy. . . (please tick)

    Not including yourself, how many nominees were on the final shortlist?

    • 0, 1, 2, 3, 4, 5, 6, 7, 8, 9, 10 or more

Not including yourself, how many nominees were women?

- 0, 1, 2, 3, 4, 5, 6, 7, 8, 9, 10 or more

Not including yourself, how many nominees were ethnic minorities?

- 0, 1, 2, 3, 4, 5, 6, 7, 8, 9, 10 or more

Not including yourself, how many nominees were women ethnic minorities?

- 0, 1, 2, 3, 4, 5, 6, 7, 8, 9, 10 or more

22. Next, please describe your MAIN OPPONENT, the nominee who posed the greatest challenge to you in your LAST selection contest for the 2005/2010 General Election (tick yes or no)

- Woman
- Ethnic minority
- Good speaker
- Experienced
- Local
- A celebrity
- Strong networks
- Party insider
- Well organised campaign
- Well financed
- Educated
- Married

23. Now, how would you describe yourself during the candidacy for the 2005/2010 General Election? (tick yes or no)

- Good speaker
- Experienced
- Local
- A celebrity
- Strong networks
- Party insider
- Well organised campaign
- Well financed
- Educated
- Union sup0ported

Section B: your campaign to get selected

In this next section, I'd like to ask you a few questions about the type of resources you had for your LAST selection attempt in the lead-up to the 2005/2010 General Election.

24. Approximately HOW MANY WEEKS did you spend campaigning on your LAST selection attempt for the 2005/2010 General Election?

25. Approximately HOW MANY HOURS PER WEEK did you spend campaigning on your LAST selection attempt for the 2005/2010 election?

26. And approximately HOW MUCH MONEY did you spend campaigning in total on your LAST selection attempt for the 2005/2010 election? (please write in pounds sterling)

27. For your LAST selection attempt for the 2005/2010 General Election, did you do any of the following? (tick yes or no)

    • Telephone party members
    • Mail information to party members
    • Sign up new local party members
    • Knock on doors
    • Meet with union leaders
    • Meet with business leaders
    • Meet with community groups
    • Meet with faith based groups
    • Meet with women's organisations
    • Meet with ethnic based groups
    • Email party members
    • Write in a blog
    • Text message party members
    • Had a personal website
    • Other
    • If "other", please enter in.

28. For your LAST seat application in the lead-up to the 2005/2010 election, did you apply to a seat (tick yes or no):

    • Close to Westminster
    • Where you knew party members
    • Because you were asked to
    • Because you thought you could win it
    • Because it was a safe seat
    • For the experience
    • Because it was an All Women Short–list seat
    • Other
    • If "other", please enter in.

29. Some people receive a lot of advice from those around them during their selection attempts, while others receive some or no advice. Did any of the following people give you A LOT, SOME, or NO ADVICE during your LAST

selection attempt for the 2005/2010 election? (please tick all that apply) (Answer Options: A lot, Some, None)

- Labour Party Executive members
- Local constituency secretary/procedures secretary
- Retiring incumbent MP
- Other MPs
- Local councillors
- Party leaders
- Party activists
- Party members
- Party staff
- Labour Women's Network
- Other
- If "other", please enter in.

30. And did any of the following people give you A LOT, SOME, or NO ADVICE during your LAST selection attempt for the 2005/2010 election? (please tick all that apply) (Answer options: A lot, Some, None)

- Union leaders
- Union activists
- Community activists
- Faith based activists
- Ethnic group activists
- Other women's organisations

31. For your LAST selection attempt in advance of the election, did any party officials ask you anything you felt was inappropriate?

- Yes
- No
- If "yes", please explain in the provided space.

32. And for your LAST selection attempt in advance of the election, did any party officials make negative comments about you?

- Yes
- No
- If "yes", please explain in the provided space.

33. In thinking about your LAST selection experience for the election, do you recall any irregularities in the process?

- Yes
- No
- If "yes", please explain in the provided space.

Section C: your political experience

34. In what year did you first join the British Labour Party? (enter the year)

35. Prior to the 2005/2010 General Election, had you ever. . . (Answer Options: Yes, No)

   - Been a candidate for local government
   - Been a candidate for the European Parliament
   - Been a candidate for the Scottish Parliament or Welsh Assembly
   - Been elected to local government
   - Been elected to the European Parliament
   - Been elected to the Scottish Parliament or Welsh Assembly

36. Prior to the 2005/2010 General Election, had you ever. . . (Answer Options: Yes, No)

   - Held local, regional, or national Party office
   - Served on a local or national public body
   - Held office in a local or national pressure group
   - Held office in other community groups
   - Held office in a professional body
   - Held office in a student organisation
   - Held office in a trade union
   - Held office in a women's organisation
   - Held an executive or board position
   - Been a member of a pressure group
   - Other
   - If "other", please enter in.

37. Prior to the 2005/2010 election, had you ever. . . (Answer Options: Yes, No)

   - Been employed by the British Labour Party
   - Served on the Party's National Policy Forum
   - Been a conference delegate
   - Sat on a party committee
   - Worked on a national or local campaign, or a European Parliament campaign
   - Other
   - If "other", please enter in.

38. Approximately HOW MANY HOURS IN AN AVERAGE WEEK did you devote to party activities? (please enter)

39. Prior to the 2005/2010 General Election, had you ever been. . . (Answer Options: Yes, No

   - Nominated by party units, affiliated branches, or organisations
   - Trade union sponsored

- Shortlisted
- Selected
- Elected

Section D: your experience of selection

Next, I would like to ask you a few questions about your overall selection experience for the 2005/2010 General Election.

40. Did someone ask you to stand for Parliament for the 2005/2010 General Election?

   - Yes
   - No
   - If "yes", what was the role of the person(s)? If more than one person asked you, please list their roles.

41. What was the single most important reason why you first wanted to stand for Parliament? (please enter in)

42. Some people receive encouragement from those around them when they decide to stand for public office, while others experience indifference or disapproval. How positive or negative were the following people in encouraging you to become a candidate for the 2005/2010 election? (Answer Options: Very positive, Positive, Neutral, Very Negative, Not applicable)

   - Your spouse or partner
   - Other family members
   - Personal friends
   - Women's groups/networks
   - Community groups
   - Religious groups
   - Business associates
   - Trade unionists
   - Party members
   - Party agents
   - Your employer

43. Were the following activities easy or difficult for you in your candidacy attempt? (Answer Options: Very easy, Fairly easy, Fairly difficult, Very difficult, Not applicable)

   - Finding out about the application process
   - Getting good advice from party officials
   - Feeling qualified to put your name forward
   - Working up the courage to put your name forward

- Producing an effective application form
- Selecting seats
- Getting a preliminary interview
- Getting shortlisted
- Presenting yourself for an interview
- Getting support from party members
- Having enough money to cover interview expenses
- Having enough time to campaign

44. Where would you most like to be ten years from now? (Answer Options: Yes, No)

   - A member of the British Parliament
   - A member of the British Government
   - A member of Cabinet
   - A member of the European Parliament
   - A member of the Scottish Parliament or Welsh Assembly
   - A member of the Greater London Authority
   - In the House of Lords
   - Working for an international body or organisation
   - Head of a non-profit body or organisation
   - Head of a private company or public agency
   - Retired from public life
   - Other
   - If "other", please enter in.

45. On a scale of 1 to 10, with "1" being not at all politically ambitious, "5" being somewhat ambitious, and "10" being very ambitious, where do you place yourself?

   Your level of political ambition

Section E: your political attitudes

In this section, I would like to ask you a few questions about your political attitudes on economic and social issues in the lead-up to the 2005/2010 General Election.

46. In political matters, some talk of being "left" and "right". Using the following scale, where "1" means left and "7" means right, in advance of the election, where would you have. . .

   - Placed yourself
   - Your constituency party
   - Your parliamentary party
   - Your party leader
   - Your party's voters

47. People look at the world in different ways, through different lenses. In the lead-up to the election, did you primarily view political issues through a gender, race, class, or nationalist lens? (Answer Options: Yes, No)

    • Gender
    • Race
    • Class
    • Nationalist
    • Neutral, no lens

48. Some say "Old Labour" is more left of centre on economic policies than "New Labour". In advance of the election, where would have. . . (Answer Options: Old Labour, New Labour, Don't know)

    • Placed yourself
    • Your constituency party
    • Your parliamentary party
    • Your party leader
    • Your party's voters

49. In advance of the election, how often did you publicly speak against your party's official policies? (please tick one) (Answer Options: Always, Frequently, Sometimes, Never)

    I spoke against my party's policies. . .

50. If you spoke against your party's policies, which ones did you speak against? (please enter)

Section F: your personal background

Finally, I'd like to ask you some questions about yourself and your circumstances in the lead-up to the 2005/2010 round of selections.

51. In what year were you born?

52. Are you

    • Female
    • Male

53. What was your marital status during the 2005/2010 round of selections? (please tick one)

    • Married
    • Widowed
    • Divorced/separated

- Cohabitating with a member of the opposite sex
- Cohabitating with a member of the same sex
- Single
- Separated

54. In the lead-up to selections for the 2005/2010 General Election, did you have any children in your care who were aged. . . (Answer Options: None, One child, Two children, Three children, More than three)

   - Under five years old
   - Five to fifteen years old

55. In the lead-up to the 2005/2010 General Election, did you have dependent adults in your care?

   - Yes
   - No

56. Prior to the selections, what was your highest educational qualification? (please tick one)

   - Primary school
   - Secondary school
   - Other further education
   - University or polytechnic degree
   - Post–graduate qualification

57. If you are a graduate, please indicate if your first degree was from Oxford, Cambridge, or other. (please tick one)

   - Oxford
   - Cambridge
   - Other
   - Not applicable

58. From the list, what type of school did you last attend full–time? (please tick one)

   - Grammar
   - Independent fee-paying
   - Direct grant or grant aided
   - Comprehensive
   - Secondary modern or technical
   - Other

59. In what year did you complete your formal education? (please enter year)

60. In the lead-up to the 2005/2010 election, were you. . . (Answer Options: Yes, No)

    - A member of a trade union?
    - A member of a staff association?

61. For your LAST selection, were you sponsored by a trade union?

    - Yes
    - No
    - Not applicable
    - If "yes", please enter in which union.

62. Which of these best describes what you were doing prior to the selections? If you were an MP, which best describes your position immediately prior to being elected? (please tick one)

    - In full–time employment (30+ hours per week)
    - In part-time employment (10–29 hours per week)
    - Registered unemployed
    - Wholly retired from work
    - In full–time education
    - Looking after the home
    - Other
    - If "other", please enter in.

63. In the lead-up to the selections, in which sector were you employed? (please tick one)

    - Small business
    - Large business
    - Central government
    - Law
    - Local government
    - Education
    - Health service
    - Nationalised industry
    - Other
    - Not applicable
    - If "other", please describe.

64. If you were employed immediately prior to the round of selections, please describe your occupation and employer. If an MP, please describe your occupation and employer immediately prior to being elected in (2005/ 2010).

    - Occupation
    - Employer

65. Have you ever performed on stage as an actor, musician, singer, or dancer?

   - Yes
   - No

66. Immediately prior to the selections, did you think of yourself as belonging to the working class, middle class, or upper class? (please tick one)

   - Working class
   - Middle class
   - Upper class
   - None of these

67. In your main accommodation, did you or your household. . . (please tick one)

   - Own the property
   - Rent from your local authority
   - Rent from a private landlord
   - Rent from a housing association
   - Other
   - If "other", please enter in.

68. What is your ethnic group? (please tick one)

   - White British
   - White Scottish
   - White Welsh
   - White British Other
   - White Irish
   - White Other
   - Mixed Black Caribbean
   - Mixed White Asian
   - Asian British
   - Asian Indian
   - Asian Pakistani
   - Asian Bangladeshi
   - Black British
   - Black Caribbean
   - Black African
   - Any other ethnic group?
   - If "other", please enter in.

69. Is English your first language?

   - Yes
   - No
   - If "no", please enter in your first language.

70. What is your religion? (please tick one)

    - None
    - Christian (write denomination below)
    - Buddhist
    - Hindu
    - Jewish
    - Muslim
    - Sikh
    - Other religion
    - If Christian or "other", please enter in your denomination.

71. Around the time of selections for the (2005/2010) election, what was your household's income in pounds sterling? (please tick one)

• 0–5,000	• 110,000–120,000
• 5,000–10,000	• 120,000–130,000
• 10,000–20,000	• 130,000–140,000
• 20,000–30,000	• 140,000–150,000
• 30,000–40,000	• 150,000–160,000
• 40,000–50,000	• 160,000–170,000
• 50,000–60,000	• 170,000–180,000
• 60,000–70,000	• 180,000–190,000
• 70,000–80,000	• 190,000–200,000
• 80,000–90,000	• +200,000
• 90,000–100,000	

72. Where were you living when you were 14 years old?

73. Which of the following applied to you in advance of the election?

    - Heterosexual
    - Gay
    - Lesbian
    - Transgendered

74. Do you consider yourself to be an ethnic minority?

    - Yes
    - No

75. Do you have a physical disability?

    - Yes
    - No

76. Do you have a current personal website?

   - Yes
   - No
   - If "yes", please enter in the URL: Http://

77. Would you be willing to help the project further with a brief interview?

   - Yes
   - No
   - If "yes", could you please provide the best way to get in touch with you (email or telephone number)?

Note

1 The survey was sent separately to aspirant candidates seeking selection for the 2005 and 2010 General Elections. With the exception of the election year (i.e., 2005/2010), the survey questions are the same.

Bibliography

Allen, P. (2012) 'Linking Pre-Parliamentary Political Experience and the Career Trajectories of the 1997 General Election Cohort', *Parliamentary Affairs*, 1–23.

Allen, P., and Cutts, D. (2018) 'An Analysis of Political Ambition in Britain', *The Political Quarterly*, 62(1), 121–130.

Ashe, J. (2017) 'Enough Come Forward, (Still) Too Few Chosen', *Canadian Journal of Political Science*, 50(2), 597–613.

Ashe, J., Campbell, R., Childs, S., and Evans, E. (2010) ' "Stand by Your Man": Women's Political Recruitment at the 2010 UK General Election', *British Politics*, 5(4), 455–480.

Ashe, J., and Stewart, K. (2012) 'Legislative Recruitment: Using Diagnostic Testing to Explain Underrepresentation', *Party Politics*, 18(5), 687–707.

BBC. (2009) 'Labour Ballot Box "Tampered With" ', Saturday, 18 April, http://news.bbc.co.uk/2/hi/uk_news/politics/8005377.stm

BBC. (2010) 'The Rise and Fall of New Labour', 3 August, www.bbc.com/news/uk-politics-10518842

BBC. (2013) 'Why Aren't More Disabled People Becoming Politicians?' 15 February, www.bbc.com/news/uk-england-21464655

Best, H., and Cotta, M. (2000) *Parliamentary Representatives in Europe, 1848–2000: Legislative Recruitment*. Oxford: Oxford University Press.

Bille, L. (2001) 'Democratizing a Democratic Procedure: Myth or Reality? Candidate Selection in Western European Parties 1960–1990', *Party Politics*, 7(3), 363–380.

Bird, K. (2005) 'The Political Representation of Visible Minorities in Electoral Democracies: A Comparison of France, Denmark and Canada', *Nationalism and Ethnic Politics*, 11(4), 425–465.

Bird, K. (2011) 'Patterns of Substantive Representation Among Visible Minority MPs: Evidence from Canada's House of Commons', in K. Bird, T. Saalfeld, and A. Wüst (eds.), *The Political Representation of Immigrants and Minorities: Voters, Parties and Parliaments in Liberal Democracies*. London: Routledge.

Bird, K. (2014) 'Ethnic Quotas and Ethnic Representation Worldwide', *International Political Science Review*, 35(1), 12–26.

Bittner, A., and Thomas, M. (2017) *Mothers and Others*. Vancouver: UBC Press.

Bjarnegård, E., and Kenny, M. (2014) 'Gender, Institutions and Political Recruitment: A Research Agenda', Unpublished conference paper, *ECPR Joint Sessions of Workshops*, Salamanca, Spain, 10–15 April.

Black, J. (2017) 'The 2015 Federal Election: More Visible Minority Candidates and MPs', *Canadian Parliamentary Review*, 40(1), 1–8.

Bochel, J., and Denver, D. (1983) 'Candidate Selection in the Labour Party: What the Selectors Seek', *British Journal of Political Science*, 13, 45–69.

Bowleg, L. (2008) 'When Black + Lesbian + Woman ≠ Black Lesbian Woman', *Sex Roles*, 59, 312–325.

Budge, I., and Farlie, D. (1975) 'Political Recruitment and Dropout: Predictive Success Over Five British Localities', *British Journal of Political Science*, 5(1), 33–68.

Cairney, P. (2007) 'The Professionalisation of MPs: Refining the "Politics Facilitating" Explanation', *Parliamentary Affairs*, 1–22.

Campbell, R. (2011) 'The Politics of Diversity', in P. Cowley and C. Hay (eds.), *Development in British Politics 7*. London: Palgrave, pp. 196–214.

Campbell, R., Childs, S., and Hunt, M. (2018) 'Women in the House of Commons', in C. Leston-Bandeira and L. Thompson (eds.), *Exploring Parliament*. Oxford: Oxford University Press, pp. 231–238.

Campbell, R., and Cowley, P. (2013) 'What Voters Want: Reactions to Candidate Characteristics in a Survey Experiment', *Political Studies*, 1–23.

Campbell, R., and Lovenduski, J. (2005) 'Winning Women's Votes? The Incremental Track to Equality', in P. Norris and C. Wlezien (eds.), *Britain Votes 2005*. Oxford: Oxford University Press.

Caul, M. (1999) 'Women's Representation in Parliament: The Role of Political Parties', *Party Politics*, 5(1), 79–98.

Charlton, M., and Barker, P. (2013) 'Should Representation in Parliament Mirror Canada's Diversity?' in M. Charlton and P. Barker (eds.), *Crosscurrents: Contemporary Political Issues*. Toronto: Nelson.

Cheng, C., and Tavits, M. (2010) 'Informal Influences in Selecting Female Political Candidates', *Political Research Quarterly*, 64(2), 1–12.

Childs, S. (2004) *New Labour's Women MPs: Women Representing Women*. New York: Routledge

Childs, S. (2007) 'Representation', in V. Bryson and G. Blakeley (eds.), *The Impact of Feminism on Concepts and Debates*. Manchester: Manchester University Press, pp. 73–91.

Childs, S. (2008) *Women and British Party Politics: Descriptive, Substantive and Symbolic Representation*. New York, NY: Routledge.

Childs, S. (2016) *The Good Parliament*. Bristol: University of Bristol.

Childs, S., and Cowley, P. (2011) 'The Politics of Local Presence: Is There a Case for Descriptive Representation?' *Political Studies*, 59(1), 1–19.

Childs, S., and Dahlerup, D. (2018) 'Increasing Women's Descriptive Representation in National Parliaments: The Involvement and Impact of Politics and Gender Scholars', *European Journal of Politics and Gender*, 1(1–2), 185–204.

Childs, S., and Krook, M. L. (2008) 'Critical Mass Theory and Women's Political Representation', *Political Studies*, 56(3), 725–736.

Childs, S., and Lovenduski, J. (2013) 'Political Representation', in G. Waylen (ed.), *The Oxford Handbook of Gender and Politics*. Oxford: Oxford University Press, pp. 489–513.

Childs, S., Lovenduski, J., and Campbell, R. (2005) *Women at the Top*. London: Hansard Society.

Collins, R. (2009) 'Labour's General Secretary, Ray Collins' Speech to the 2009 Labour Party Annual Conference', http://www2.labour.org.uk/ray-collins-speech-conference

Conway, M. (2001) 'Women and Political Participation', *Political Science and Politics*, 34, 231–233.

Courea, E. (2019) 'Labour Selects Just Six BME Candidates Across 99 Target Seats', *New Statesman*, 26 February, www.newstatesman.com/politics/elections/2019/02/labour-selects-just-six-bme-candidates-across-99-target-seats

Cross, W. (2004) *Political Parties*. Vancouver: UBC Press.

Dahl, R. (1961) *Who Governs?* New Haven, CT: Yale University Press.

Dahlerup, D. (2006) 'Women, Quotas and Politics', in D. Dahlerup (ed.), *Women, Quotas and Politics*. London: Routledge.

Dahlerup, D. (2013) 'Introduction', in D. Dahlerup (ed.), *Women, Quotas and Politics*. London: Routledge.

Darcy, R., Welch, S., and Clark, J. (1994) *Women, Elections, and Representation*. 2nd ed. Lincoln: University of Nebraska Press.

Denver, D. (1988) 'Britain: Centralised Parties and With Decentralised Selection', in M. Gallagher and M. Marsh (eds.), *Candidate Selection in Comparative Perspective*. London: Sage Publications.

Disability Living Foundation (2019) *Key Facts* https://www.dlf.org.uk/content/key-facts

Dolan, K. (2010) 'The Impact of Gender Stereotyped Evaluations on Support for Women Candidates', *Political Behavior*, 32(1), 69–88.

Durose, C., Richardson, L., Combs, R., Eason, C., and Gains, F. (2013) 'Acceptable Difference: Diversity, Representation and Pathways to UK's Politics', *Parliamentary Affairs*, 66, 246–267.

Epolitix. (2014) 'Profile: David Miliband', http://centrallobby.politicshome.com/latestnews/article-detail/newsarticle/profile-david-miliband/

Epstein, L. (1980) *Political Parties in Western Democracies*. New Brunswick, NJ: Transaction Books.

Erickson, L. (1993) 'Making Her Way in', in J. Lovenduski and P. Norris (eds.), *Gender and Party Politics*. London: Sage Publications.

Erickson, L. (1997a) 'Canada', in P. Norris (ed.), *Passages to Power*. Cambridge: Cambridge University Press.

Erickson, L. (1997b) 'Might More Women Make a Difference? Gender, Party, and Ideology Among Canada's Parliamentary Candidates', *Canadian Journal of Political Science*, 30(4), 663–688.

Erickson, L., and Carty, R. K. (1991) 'Parties and Candidate Selection in the 1988 Canadian General Election', *Canadian Journal of Political Science*, 24(2), 331–349.

European Parliament. (2014) 'Results', www.results-elections2014.eu/en/country-results-fr-2014.html

Evans, E. (2012) 'Selecting the "Right Sort": Patterns of Political Recruitment in British By-Elections', *Parliamentary Affairs*, 65, 195–121.

Everitt, J., and Camp, M. (2014) 'In Versus out: LGBT Politicians in Canada', *Journal of Canadian Studies*, 48(1), 226–251.

The Everyday Sexism Project. (2019) http://everydaysexism.com/

The Fawcett Society. (2019) 'Sex and Power, 2018', https://www.fawcettsociety.org.uk/Handlers/Download.ashx?IDMF=ea2cb329-e6e0-4e0f-8a0b-5022f99bc915

Field, A. (2009) *Discovering Statistics: Using SPSS*. London: Sage Publications.

Fowler, L. (1993) *Candidates, Congress and the American Democracy*. Ann Arbor, MI: University of Michigan Press.

Fox, R., and Lawless, J. (2004) 'Entering the Arena? Gender and the Decision to Run for Office', *American Journal of Political Science*, 48, 264–280.

Fox, R., and Lawless, J. (2010) 'If Only They'd Ask: Gender, Recruitment, and Political Ambition', *The Journal of Politics*, 72(2), 310–326.

Freidenvall, L. (2016) 'Intersectionality and Candidate Selection in Sweden', *Politics*, 36(4), 355–363.

Gallagher, M. (1988a) 'Introduction', in M. Gallagher and M. Marsh (eds.), *The Secret Garden: Candidate Selection in Comparative Perspective*. London: Sage Publications, pp. 1–19.

Gallagher, M. (1988b) 'Conclusion', in M. Gallagher and M. Marsh (eds.), *The Secret Garden: Candidate Selection in Comparative Perspective*. London: Sage Publications, pp. 237–283.

Gallagher, M., and Marsh, M. (1988) *The Secret Garden: Candidate Selection in Comparative Perspective*. London: Sage Publications.

Galligan, Y. (2006) 'Bringing Women in: Global Strategies for Gender Parity in Political Representation', *University of Maryland Journal of Law Race, Religion, Gender & Class*, 6(2), 319–336.

Galligan, Y. (2013) 'Gender and Politics in Northern Ireland: The Representation Gap Revisited', *Irish Political Studies*, 28(3), 413–433.

Galligan, Y., and Clavero, S. (2008) 'Prospects for Women's Legislative Representation in Post-socialist Europe: The Views of Female Politicians', *Gender & Society*, (11 February), 1–23.

Gerring, J. (2004) 'What Is a Case Study and What Is It Good for?' *American Political Science Review*, 98(2), 341–354.

Gould, M. (2011) 'Helping More Disabled People Get Into Parliament', *The Guardian*, Wednesday, 4 May, www.theguardian.com/society/2011/may/04/disabled-people-electoral-representation

Green, D. P., and Gerber, A. S. (2008) *Get out the Vote: How to Increase Voter Turnout*. Washington, DC: Brookings Institution Press.

The Guardian. (2001) 'Labour Pains', Thursday, 29 March, www.theguardian.com/politics/2001/mar/29/labour.bookextracts

The Guardian. (2010) 'Parliamentary Representation: Opening up the House', Monday, 11 January, www.theguardian.com/commentisfree/2010/jan/11/commons-mp-expenses-equality-women

Harris, J. (2009) 'Caught in the Grip of a Clique', *The Guardian*, Sunday, 19 April, https://www.theguardian.com/commentisfree/2009/apr/19/labour-ballot-box-postal-voting

Hazan, R. Y., and Rahat, G. (2006) 'Candidate Selection: Methods and Consequences', in R. Katz and W. Crotty (eds.), *Handbook of Party Politics*. London: Sage Publications, pp. 109–121.

Hector, G. (2012) 'The Decline of Working Class MPs?' *Huffington Post*, 18 July, www.huffingtonpost.co.uk/gordon-hector/the-decline-of-working class-mps_b_1682274.html

Helm, T. (2009) '120 Labour MPs Plan to Stand Down at Next General Election', *The Observer*, Sunday, 9 August, www.theguardian.com/politics/2009/aug/09/labour-mps-quit-election

Hills, J. (1983) 'Candidates, the Impact of Gender', *Parliamentary Affairs*, 34, 221–228.

Hinsliff, G. (2009) 'Labour "Machine" Parachutes Ideal Candidates Into Safe Seats', *The Observer*, Sunday, 11 October, www.theguardian.com/politics/2009/oct/11/labour-selection-parachute-candidates-row

Holland, M. (1981) 'The Selection of Parliamentary Candidates: Contemporary Developments and the Impact of the European Elections', *Parliamentary Affairs*, 34(1), 28–46.

Holland, M. (1986) *Candidates for Europe*. Aldershot: Gower.

Holland, M. (1987) 'British Political Recruitment: Labour in the Euro-Elections of 1979', *British Journal of Political Science*, 17, 53–70.

Huddy, L., and Terkildsen, N. (1993) 'The Consequences of Gender Stereotypes for Women Candidates at Different Levels and Types of Office', *Political Research Quarterly*, 46(3), 503–525.

Hughes, M. (2013) 'Diversity in National Legislatures Around the World', *Social Compass*, 7, 23–33.

Hughes, M., Paxton, P., and Clayton, A. (2019) 'Global Gender Quota Adoption, Implementation, and Reform', *Comparative Politics*, 51(2), 219–238.

Hunt, A. L., and Pendley, R. E. (1972) 'Community Gatekeepers: An Examination of Political Recruiters', *Midwest Journal of Political Science*, 6(3), 411–438.

Institute for Democracy and Electoral Assistance (IDEA). (2019) 'Gender Quotas Database', https://www.idea.int/data-tools/data/gender-quotas

Inter-parliamentary Union. (2014) 2019 'Percentage of Women in National Parliaments', https://data.ipu.org/women-ranking?month=10&year=2019

Jacob, H. (1962) 'Initial Recruitment of Elected Officials in the U.S.: A Model', *Journal of Politics*, 24, 703–716.

Judge, D. (1999) *Representation: Theory and Practice in Britain*. London: Routledge.

Katz, R. (2001) 'The Problems of Candidate Selection and Models of Party Democracy', *Party Politics*, 7, 277–296.

Katz, R., and Mair, P. (1992) *Party Organisations: A Data Handbook on Party Organisations in Western Democracies: 1960–90*. London: Sage Publications.

Katz, R., and Mair, P. (2002) 'The Ascendancy of the Party in Public Office: Party Organisational Change in Twentieth Century Democracies', in R. Gunther, J. Montero, and J. Linz (eds.), *Political Parties: Old Concepts New Challenges*. Oxford: Oxford University Press.

Keep, M. (2010) 'Characteristics of the New House of Commons', *House of Commons Library Research*, www.parliament.uk/business/publications/research/key-issues-for-the-new-parliament/the-new-parliament/characteristics-of-the-new-house-of-commons/

Kenny, M. (2013) *Gender and Political Recruitment: Theorizing Institutional Change*. Basingstoke: Palgrave.

Kenny, M., and Verge, T. (2016) 'Opening up the Black Box: Gender and Candidate Selection in a New Era'. *Government and Opposition* 51, 351–369.

Kenyon, P. (2010) 'Skimming Through Life in the Labour Party, and Churning the Cream', http://petergkenyon.typepad.com/

King, G., and Zeng, L. (2001) 'Logistic Regression in Rare Events Data', *Political Analysis*, 9(2), 137–163.

Kittilson, M. C. (2006) *Challenging Parties, Changing Parliaments: Women and Elected Office in Contemporary Western Europe*. Columbus, OH: Ohio State University Press.

Kittilson, M. C. (2010) 'Women's Representation in Parliament: The Role of Political Parties', in M. L. Krook and S. Childs (eds.), *Women, Gender, and Politics: A Reader*. Oxford: Oxford University Press, pp. 159–166.

Kornberg, A., and Winsborough, H. H. (1968) 'The Recruitment of Candidates for the Canadian House of Commons', *The American Political Science Review*, 62(4), 1242–1257.

Krook, M. L. (2009) 'Beyond Supply and Demand: A Feminist-Institutionalist Theory of Candidate Selection', *Political Research Quarterly*, 63(4), 707–720.

Krook, M. L., and Norris, P. (2014) 'Beyond Quotas: Strategies to Promote Gender Equality in Elected Office', *Political Studies*, 62, 2–20.

Kenyon, Peter. (2010) 'Special Selections Panel', https://petergkenyon.typepad.com/peterkenyon/special-selections-panel/

Labour Party. (1997) 'New Labour, New Life for Britain', www.politicsresources.net/area/uk/man/lab97.htm

Labour Party. (2001) 'The National Rules of the Labour Party'.

Labour Party. (2003) 'Labour's Future: NEC Guidelines for Selection of Parliamentary Candidates'.

Labour Party. (2006) 'Labour's Future: NEC Guidelines for Selection of Parliamentary Candidates'.

Labour Party. (2008) 'The NEC Procedural Rules on Selection of Parliamentary Candidates'.

Labour Party. (2014) 'How We Work', www.labour.org.uk/how_we_work

Lawless, J., and Fox, R. (2005) *It Takes a Candidate: Why Women Don't Run for Office.* New York, NY: Cambridge University Press.

Lewin, K. (1947) "Frontiers in Group Dynamics: Concept, Method and Reality in Social Science; Social Equilibria and Social Change", *Human Relations*, 1(1), 5–41.

Lovenduski, J. (2005) *Feminizing Politics.* Cambridge: Polity Press.

Lovenduski, J. (2016) 'Feminist Political Science, Institutionalism and the Supply and Demand Model of Political Recruitment: Some Reflections', *Government and Opposition* 51, 513–528.

Lovenduski, J., and Norris, P. (1989) 'Selecting Women Candidates: Obstacles to the Feminisation of the House of Commons', *European Journal of Political Research*, 17, 533–562.

Lundell, K. (2004) 'Determinants of Candidate Selection: The Degree of Centralisation in a Comparative Perspective', *Party Politics*, 10(1), 25–47.

Mackay, F. (2001) *Love and Politics.* London: Continuum.

Mackay, F., Kenny, M., and Chappell, L. (2010) 'New Institutionalism Through a Gender Lens: Toward a Feminist Institutionalism?' *International Political Science Review*, 31(5), 573–588.

Mansbridge, J. (2010) 'Should Blacks Represent Blacks and Women Represent Women? A Contingent "Yes" ', in M. L. Krook and S. Childs (eds.), *Women, Gender and Politics: A Reader.* New York, NY: Oxford University Press, pp. 201–214.

March, J., and Olsen, J. (1989) *Rediscovering Institutions.* New York, NY: Free Press.

Mason, R. (2014) 'Harriet Harman Savages Gordon Brown Over Sexism and Inequality: Former Deputy Leader of Labour Claims She Was Marginalised for Being Female and Gives "Examples of Sexism" in Parliament', *The Guardian*, 14 July, www.theguardian.com/politics/2014/jul/08/harriet-harman-gordon-brown-inequality-labour-sexism

Mason, R., and Watt, M. (2014) 'David Cameron "Open" to All-women Shortlists on Eve of Reshuffle: Prime Minister Expected to Promote a Number of Women, as He Moves to Project a Modern and Diverse Face of the Tory Party', *The Guardian*, 14 July, www.theguardian.com/politics/2014/jul/14/david-cameron-open-to-female-only-shortlists-tories

Matland, R., and Studlar, D. (1996) 'The Contagion of Women Candidates in Single-Member District and Proportional Representation Electoral Systems: Canada and Norway', *The Journal of Politics*, 58(3), 707–733.

May, J. D. (1973) 'Opinion Structure of Political Parties: The Special Law of Curvilinear Disparity', *Political Studies*, 21(2), 135–151.

McDermott, M. L. (1997) 'Voting Cues in Low-Information Elections: Candidate Gender as a Social Information Variable in Contemporary United States Elections', *American Journal of Political Science*, 41(1), 270–283.

McDermott, M. L. (1998) 'Race and Gender Cues in Low-Information Elections', *Political Research Quarterly*, 51(4), 895–918.

McDonald-Gibson, C., and Lichfield, J. (2014) 'European Election Results 2014: Far-right Parties Flourish Across Europe', *The Independent*, Sunday, 25 May, www.independent.co.uk/news/world/europe/european-election-results-2014-farright-parties-flourish-across-europe-in-snub-to-austerity-9434069.html

McGuinness, F. (2012) 'Membership of UK Political Parties', *Library of House of Commons*, 3 December.

McKenzie, R. T. (1963) *British Political Parties: The Distribution of Power Within the Conservative and Labour Parties*. New York, NY: St Martin's Press.

Mishler, W. (1978) 'Nominating Attractive Candidates for Parliament: Recruitment to the Canadian House of Commons', *Legislative Studies Quarterly*, 3(4), 581–599.

Murray, R. (2013) 'Quotas, Citizens, and Norms of Representation', *Politics and Gender*, 9(3), 304–309.

Murray, R. (2014) 'Time for All-Men Shortlists?' *PSA Blog Political Insight*, www.psa.ac.uk/insight-plus/blog/time-all-men-shortlists

Niven, D. (1998) *The Missing Majority*. Westport, CT: Praeger.

Niven, D. (2006) 'Throwing Your Hat out of the Ring: Negative Recruitment and the Gender Imbalance in State Legislative Candidacy', *Politics and Gender*, 2, 473–489.

Norris, P. (1993) 'Conclusions: Comparing Legislative Recruitment', in J. Lovenduski and P. Norris (eds.), *Gender and Party Politics*. London: Sage Publications.

Norris, P. (1997a) 'Introduction to Theories of Recruitment', in P. Norris (ed.), *Passages to Power: Legislative Recruitment in Advanced Democracies*. Cambridge: Cambridge University Press.

Norris, P. (1997b) 'Conclusions: Comparing Passages to Power', in P. Norris (ed.), *Passages to Power: Legislative Recruitment in Advanced Democracies*. Cambridge: Cambridge University Press.

Norris, P. (2014a) 'The British Parliamentary Constituency Data Base 1992–2005', https://sites.google.com/site/pippanorris3/research/data

Norris, P. (2014b) 'The May 6th 2010 British General Election Constituency Results Release', https://sites.google.com/site/pippanorris3/research/data

Norris, P., Carty, R. K., Erickson, L., Lovenduski, J., and Simms, M. (1990) 'Party Selectorates in Australia, Britain and Canada: Prolegomena for Research in the 1990', *The Journal of Commonwealth and Comparative Studies*, 28(2), 219–245.

Norris, P., and Lovenduski, J. (1989) 'Women Candidates for Parliament: Transforming the Agenda?' *British Journal of Political Science*, 19(1), 106–115.

Norris, P., and Lovenduski, J. (1993) 'If Only More Candidates Came Forward: Supply Side Explanations of Candidate Selection in Britain', *British Journal of Politics*, 23, 373–408.

Norris, P., and Lovenduski, J. (1995) *Political Recruitment: Gender, Race, and Class in British Parliament*. Cambridge: Cambridge University Press.

The Office for Disability Issues. (2014) 'Official Statistics: Disability Facts and Figures' http://odi.dwp.gov.uk/disability-statistics-and-research/disability-facts-and-figures.php#gd

Office for National Statistics. (2019) 'UK Censuses Data', www.ons.gov.uk

One in Five. (2019) 'The One in Five Campaign', www.oneinfive.scot/

Operation Black Vote. (2019) 'Home', www.obv.org.uk/

Ostrogorski, M. (1902) *Democracy and the Organisation of Political Parties*. London: MacMillan.

Pallant, J. (2007) *SPSS Survival Manual*. Berkshire: McGraw-Hill.

Patzelt, W. (1999) 'Recruitment and Retention in Western European Parliaments', *Legislative Studies Quarterly*, 24, 239–279.

Pearson, K., and McGhee, E. (2013) 'What It Takes to Win: Questioning "Gender Neutral" Outcomes in US House Elections', *Politics and Gender*, 9, 439–462.

Phillips, A. (1991) *Engendering Democracy*. Cambridge: Polity Press.

Phillips, A. (1995) *The Politics of Presence*. New York, NY: Clarendon Press.

Phillips, A. (1998) 'Democracy and Representation: Or, Why Should It Matter Who Our Representatives Are?' in A. Phillips (ed.), *Feminism and Politics*. New York, NY: Oxford University Press.

Pitkin, H. F. (1967) *The Concept of Representation*. Berkeley, CA: University of California Press.

Powell, W., and Dimaggio, P. (1991) *The New Institutionalism in Organisational Analysis*. Chicago, IL: University of Chicago Press.

Prewitt, K. (1970) 'Political Ambitions, Volunteerism, and Electoral Accountability', *American Political Science Review*, 64, 5–17.

Pruysers, S., and Cross, W. (2016) 'Candidate Selection in Canada: Local Autonomy, Centralization, and Competing Democratic Norms', *American Behavioral Scientist*, 60, 781–798.

Pugh, M. (2010) *Speak for Britain! A New History of the Labour Party*. London: Random House.

Puwar, N. (2004) 'Thinking About Making a Difference', *British Journal of Politics and International Relations*, 6, 65–80.

Quota Project. (2013) 'Global Database of Quotas for Women', www.quotaproject.org/

Rahat, G. (2007) 'Candidate Selection: The Choice Before the Choice', *Journal of Democracy*, 18(1), 157–170.

Rahat, G., and Hazan, R. Y. (2001) 'Candidate Selection Methods: An Analytical Framework', *Party Politics*, 7, 297–322.

Rahat, G., and Hazan, R. Y. (2007) 'Political Participation in Party Primaries: Increase in Quantity, Decrease in Quality?' in T. Zittel and D. Fuchs (eds.), *Participatory Democracy and Political Participation: Can Democratic Reform Bring Citizens Back in?* London: Routledge, pp. 57–72.

Randall, V. (1982) *Women and Politics*. London: Macmillan.

Ranney, A. (1965) *Pathways to Parliament: Candidate Selection in Britain*. London: Macmillan.

Ranney, A. (1981) 'Candidate Selection', in D. Butler, H. Penniman, and A. Ranney (eds.), *Democracy at the Polls*. Washington, DC: American Enterprise Institute, pp. 75–105.

Reynolds, A. (2017) 'The UK Elected a Record Number of LGBTQ People to Parliament', *Pink News*, 9 June, www.pinknews.co.uk/2017/06/09/the-uk-just-elected-a-record-number-of-lgbtq-people-to-parliament/

Riddell, P. (1993) *Honest Opportunism: The Rise of the Career Politician*. London: Hamish Hamilton.

Rigby, E. (2014) 'Hostile Press Blamed for Lack of Women MPs', *The Financial Times*, 25 April.

Ruedin, D. (2009) 'Ethnic Group Representation: A Cross-National Comparison', *The Journal of Legislative Studies*, 15(4), 335–354.

Ruedin, D. (2013) *Why Aren't They There? The Political Representation of Women, Ethnic Groups and Issue Positions in Legislatures*. Colchester: ECPR Press.

Rule, W. (1985) 'Congressional Women: Their Recruitment, Treatment, and Behavior by Irwin N. Gertzog', *The American Political Science Review*, 79(2), 527–528.

Rush, M. (1969) *The Selection of Parliamentary Candidates*. London: Nelson.

Rush, M., and Cromwell, V. (2000) 'Continuity and Change: Legislative Recruitment in the United Kingdom 1868–1999', in H. Best and M. Cotta (eds.), *Parliamentary*

Representatives in Europe, 1848–2000: Legislative Recruitment. Oxford: Oxford University Press, pp. 463–492.

Russell, M. (2005) *Building New Labour: The Politics of Party Organisation*. New York, NY: Palgrave MacMillan.

Saggar, S. (2013) 'Bending Without Breaking the Mould: Race and Political Representation in the United Kingdom', *Patterns of Prejudice*, 47(1), 69–93.

Sanbonmatsu, K. (2002) 'Political Parties and the Recruitment of Women to State Legislatures', *Journal of Politics*, 64(3), 791–809.

Sanbonmatsu, K. (2014) 'Gender Stereotypes and Vote Choice', *American Journal of Political Science*, 46(1), 20–34.

Saner, E. (2009) 'I Signed It: Then the Man Said: "Have You Met Georgia? She's Very Nice"', *The Guardian*, Saturday, 18 April.

Scarrow, H. A. (1964) 'Nomination and Local Party Organisation in Canada: A Case Study', *The Western Political Quarterly*, 17(1), 55–62.

Scarrow, S., Webb, P., and Farrell, D. (2000) 'From Social Integration to Electoral Contestation: The Changing Distribution of Power Within Political Parties', in R. J. Dalton and M. P. Wattenberg (eds.), *Parties Without Partisans: Political Change in Advanced Industrial Democracies*. Oxford: Oxford University Press, pp. 129–153.

Schnattschneider, E. E. (1942) *Party Government*. New York, NY: Holt, Rinehart and Winston.

Seligman, L. (1961) 'Political Recruitment and Party Structure: A Case Study', *American Political Science Review*, 55, 77–86.

Seyd, P. (1999) 'New Parties/ New Politics: A Case Study of the British Labour Party', *Party Politics*, 5(3), 383–405.

Seyd, P., and Whiteley, P. (1992) *Labour's Grass Roots: The Politics of Party Membership*. London: Oxford University Press.

Shah, P. (2013) 'It Takes a Black Candidate: A Supply-Side Theory of Minority Representation', *Political Research Quarterly*, 67(2), 1–14.

Shepherd-Robinson, L., and Lovenduski, J. (2002) *Women and Candidate Selection in British Political Parties*. London: Fawcett Society.

Sigelman, C. K., Sigelman, L., Walkosz, B. J., and Nitz, M. (1995) 'Black Candidates, White Voters: Understanding Racial Bias in Political Perceptions', *American Journal of Political Science*, 39(1), 243–265.

Skard, T., and Haavio-Mannila, E. (1985) 'Women in Parliament', in T. Skard and E. Haavio-Mannila (eds.), *Unfinished Democracy: Women in Nordic Politics*. Oxford: Pergamon Press, pp. 51–80.

The Speaker's Conference Final Report on Parliamentary Representation. (2010) www.publications.parliament.uk/pa/spconf/239/23902.htm

Squires, J. (2012) 'Gender and Minority Representation in Parliament', *Political Insight*, April, www.politicalinsightmagazine.com/?p=488

Stratton, A. (2010) 'Labour's Election Line-up Too Male Dominated, Harriet Harman Says', *The Guardian*, Monday, 5 April, www.theguardian.com/politics/2010/apr/05/labour-campaign-male-dominated-harman

Thomas, S. (1994) *How Women Legislate*. Oxford: Oxford University Press.

Tolley, E. (2019) 'Who You Know: Local Party Presidents and Minority Candidate Emergence', *Electoral Studies*, 58, 70–79.

Tremblay, M. (2007) "Democracy, Representation and Women: A Comparative Analysis", *Democratization*, 14(4), 533–553.

Tremblay, M., and Pelletier, R. (2001) 'More Women Constituency Presidents: A Strategy for Increasing the Number of Women Candidates in Canada?' *Party Politics*, 7(2), 157–190.

Trenow, P. (2014) 'Sexism and Unsociable Hours: Why Less Than a Third of Councillors Are Women', *The Guardian*, 2 June, www.theguardian.com/local-government-network/2014/jun/02/sexism-women-local-government-councillors

Trimble, L. (1997) 'Feminist Politics in the Alberta Legislature', in J. Arscott and L. Trimble (eds.), *The Politics of Presence*. Toronto: Harcourt Brace and Co.

UK Parliament. (2010) 'Speaker's Conference on Parliamentary Representation: Final Report', www.parliament.uk/business/committees/committees-a-z/other-committees/speakers-conference-on-parliamentary-representation/

University of Twente. (2014) 'Gatekeeping', www.tcw.utwente.nl/theoriesenoverzicht/Theory

Wagner, A. (2019) 'Avoiding the Spotlight: Public Scrutiny, Moral Regulation, and LGBTQ Candidate Deterrence', *Politics, Groups and Identities*. Published Online 16 April, 1–17; https://www.tandfonline.com/doi/abs/10.1080/21565503.2019.1605298.

Wängnerud, L. (2015) *The Principles of Gender-Sensitive Parliaments*. New York, NY: Routledge.

Ware, A. (1996) *Political Parties and Party Systems*. Oxford: Oxford University Press.

Welch, S. (1985) 'Are Women More Liberal Than Men in the US Congress?' *Legislative Studies Quarterly*, 10(1), 125–134.

Index

Note: Page numbers in *italics* indicate figures and page numbers in **bold** indicate tables. Numbers with a letter n indicate these are found in the notes section.

2005, 2010 survey of aspirant candidates **122**

2009 special selections panel 71

2010 British General Election: address disparity 25

2010 General Election: increase in women candidates 5; interview data 43; selection process stages 45, **46**, 47–48

2015 General Election: interview data 43; selection process stages 45, **46**, 47–48

2015 selections: filtering sex, race, disability 56–57, **57**

all black shortlists (ABS): Diane Abbott implement 52; equality guarantees not implemented 78; more quotas and guarantees 106; policy measures needed 104

Allen, Peter 38, 116

all women list (AWS): 2001, no quotas for women 99; 2005 General Election 13–14; centralisation effect on women **102**, 102–103; clustering into AWS seats 144; competing in AWS use social media 174; crowded into AWS seats outside their area 175; disproportionately filtered, final stage 106; equality quotas/guarantee 4, 13–14, 25, 32, 55, 70–71, 73, 77, 78, 95, 97, 99, 106, 134, 159, 186, 187; Erith and Thamesmead 15, 188; first used 1989 19n7–20n7; higher percentile identify heterosexual 174; reduced pool in 2001 166; reduced pool in 2015 51; reform implementing 68; representation decrease without 103, 166; women ghettoised into AWS 141

Ashe, Jeanette 36

behavioural factors: influencing selection process **11**, 11–12; party selector preferences 14

Bercow, John 22

Best, Heinrich 35

Bird, Karen 2, 5, 64, 204

Bittner, Amanda 38, 204

Bjarnegård, Elin 30, 31, 40, 204

Black, Asian, minority, or ethnic (BAME): centralisation effect on BAME candidates 103–104, **104**; disproportionately filtered, all stages 106; equality quotas 4, 9, 13, 32, 62, 72, 73, 76–77, 78, 85, 95, 97, 99, 106, 134, 159; equality rhetoric and promotion strategies 77; multistage assessment, Labour selection process **100**, 100–101; percent elected 20n11; preference for non 16; surplus/deficit test, disproportionately filters 52, 54, **55**

Blair, Tony (1994–2007) 69

Bochel, John 64

British Conservative party: fewer women, BAME candidates 4; fewer women candidates 14

British Labour party: centralised, party selection process 66–69; central party interference 66; focus on demand-side problems 58; founded for working people 68; ideal candidate successful 16; multistage selection process 87–98; non-local women "need not apply" 175; no undersupply of women candidates 51; outcomes, rules centralised 85; reforms, effects 68–72, **69**; representative democracy 68; selection process 4, 45–53 **46**, **50**, 63; selection process,

participants and rules 87–98, **88**; selection stages and filtering 45, 47–58, **54**, **55**, **56**, **57**; seven selection stages 42, 45–46; studies classify decentralised 64
British MP's: occupation, gender 36–37
British Parliament: few disabled 5; LGBTQ diverse 6

campaign: hours, money, success 160; mobilisation methods, social media 169; spending limits 156; women in AWS, use social media 174
Campaign for Labour Party Democracy (CLPD) 69
Campbell, Rosie. 37
candidate: access to membership lists 80n7, 92, 116, 160; application to NPP 88; approval NPP 88–91, 124; aspirant/final pool 3; candidate surplus/deficit test **50**; compare, at multiple stages 34; comparison, win/lose 28–29; disabled 22, 52, 78, **101**, 101–102; ideal qualities 1–3, 10, 12, 14–16, 22–23, 30, 33–34, 36, 38, 110–121; identify as Christian 141; local preferred 15, 18–19, 37–38, 110, 119, 144, 145, 154, 161, 165; man 2 times more likely selected 165–166; multistage approach, selection process 86; nomination rules, stage 5 92–94; nominations required 3; NPP vetting system 71; "other" 111; party application, stage one 87; recruitment, selection process *6*, 6–9, *8*, 34, 51–52; requirements of 75–76; seat application, stage 4 91–92; selection, stage seven 96–97; set spending limits 156; shift in type 37; shortlisted, if no children 117; shortlisting, stage six 94–96, 142; survey of aspirants **122**; university education 37, 115; using voter mobilisation 154, 169
Candidates' Code of Conduct 75
census data: interviews with party officials 43; Labour party data 43–53
centralisation: impacts participant success 101–105, **102**, **104**, **105**; measured 105
centralised: participants and rules 61–62; rules constrain choice 61–62; selection outcomes 85
centralised vs decentralised 12–13, 42, 61–62, 86–87
central party: involvement, preferential treatment of underrepresented 86; not biased against particular candidate 146;

wields control over candidate selection 63
central party agents: do not filter non-ideal candidate 144; futile funding underrepresented selection 162; *versus* local party agents 61–63; preferential treatment of underrepresented 86
Cheng, Christine 33, 34, 39, 205
Child, Sarah: "The Good Parliament" 22, 180
Chi-square and Spearman Rho testing 113, 123, 124, 130, 133–134, 138, 151n58, 155, 161, 162, 165, 174, 179n25
Clause IV 68
CLP Executive Committee (EC) 68
comparison, candidate win/lose 28–29
Constituency Labour party (CLP): composition of 59n12, **74**, 74–75; discontent with central party intrusion 61; seats, trade union members and socialists 68
Conway, Manon 11
Cotta, Maurizio 35
Cowley, Phillip 37
Cromwell, V. 64, 65
Cross, William 63, 206, 211
culture of masculinity 33

Dahl, Robert 32
Dahlerup, Drude 19n4, 64, 171, 181, 187, 205, 206
data sources 42–43
decentralised: selection process, disabled candidates 101, **101**; stages, filter disproportionately 85
demographics 180
Denver, David 64, 65
descriptive representation 22–24
Disability Rights UK 22
disabled: British Parliament, very few 5; effect of centralisation on disabled candidates 104–105, **105**; multistage assessment, Labour selection process **101**, 101–102; no quotas or guarantees 78, 97–98, 101, 134, 144; in politics 22; underrepresented in candidate pool 52
discrimination: party rules to counter selector 10; selectors judgements shaped by 15, 32; structural 24, 29
diversity: candidate slate 4, 78; records set in 2017 snap election 180
Durose, Catherine 30, 32, 33, 37, 38, 111, 113, 117, 144, 148, 161, 169, 182, 185, 206

empirical theorists: macro level studies 26, 27, 62; meso level studies 26, 27, *27*, 62; micro level factors *27*, 27–29, 62; underrepresentation 26
Epstein, Leon 63
equality. *see also* all women list (AWS); Black, Asian, minority, or ethnic (BAME): guarantee, 2010 British General Election 25; rules, objective to increase underrepresented 76–77
Erickson, Linda 12, 24, 34, 39, 206, 210
Erith and Thamesmead: Teresa Pearce 15, 188
Evans, Elizabeth 38

Fawcett Society 22
filtering: physical ability 54–55, **56**; race, BAME 54, **55**; sex 53, **54**
Fowler, Linda 11
Fox, Richard 14, 119; *US Citizen Political Ambition Study* 38
Freidenvall, Lenita 5, 206
frequencies: 14 percentage drop, women aspirants 135, 143; higher percent BAME, open, winnable seats 138, **139–140**; Model 8 shortlisted AWS candidates 171, **172–173**, 174; open seats 162, **163–164**, 165; shortlisted candidates, final selection 156, **157–158**, 159; shortlisting 130, **131–132**, 133; stage 1 candidates, NPP approval 124, **125–126**, 127; Stage 4 shortlisted 130, **131–132**, 133

Gallagher, Michael 64, 65, 67
gatekeeper theory 33
General Committee (GC): shortlist formed 8; working class held seats 68
Gould, Georgia: runner-up 1, 15–16, 188

Hazan, Reuven 9, 13, 26, 86, 207, 211
Hills, J. 29
Holland, Martin 64, 65, 155, 185
homo politicus model 2
Hughes, Melanie 64, 208

ideal aspirant candidate theory 110–121, 154; "ideal candidate" defined 110
illusion of decentralisation 63
institutional approach: *centralised* vs *decentralised* 12–13

justice: descriptive underrepresentation 24

Katz, Richard 7, 26, 62, 207, 208
Kenny, Meryl 3, 12, 29, 30, 31, 33, 34, 40, 113, 180, 204, 208, 209

Kittilson, Miki Caul 12, 26, 39, 63, 208
Krook, Mona Lena 30, 31, 39, 187, 205, 208, 209

Labour Party Rule Book (1999–2010) 73, 76
Labour Representation Committee (LRC) 67
"ladders of recruitment" 34, 35
Lawless, Jennifer 14, 119; *US Citizen Political Ambition Study* 38
legislative imbalance: unbalanced candidate pools 2, 6, 182
legislative recruitment 6, 26–27, *27*
lesbian, gay, bisexual, transgendered, queer (LGBTQ) 3; record selection 20n13
Liberal Democrats: lower diversity, candidate 4
Liverpool Walton 1, 66
local party agents: *versus* central party agents 61, 63; key selector, later stages 9; prefer men aspirant candidate 171; rights, restrictions 75; shortlist women in non-AWS, winnable seats 146
longlisting 7
loser data: supply or demand 34–35
Lovenduski, Joni 64, 65, 111, 116, 184, 185
lower house: social elite 1

Mackay, Fiona 12, 30, 31, 209
macro level studies: evaluating candidate selection 62; opportunity structures 26, 27
Mansbridge, Jane 23
marginalised: not ideal candidate 2
Marsh, Michael 64
May's Law of Curvilinear Disparity 120, 145, 185
McDermott, Monika L. 33
McGhee, E. 38
McKenzie, R.T. 64
media commentary: rhetoric present 77
membership lists access 80n7, 92, 116, 160
meso level studies: evaluating candidate selection 62; party selection processes 26–27, *27*
#MeToo 3
micro level factors: evaluating candidate selection 62; process factors *27*, 27–29
monopolise representation 5
multiple stages 7, 8, *8*, 34
multistage 3, 7, 8, 12
Murray, Rainbow. 30, 32, 38, 60, 111, 141, 145, 166, 188, 210

Nagelkerke Pseudo R-Square score 161, 165
National Executive Committee (NEC):
2017 snap election 8–9; application
submitted to 8; authority to modify
selection rules 59n11; equality
guarantees 78; Erith and Thamesmead
15; rejects candidates 71; screened
candidates 74; supervisory powers 64;
takes directives from PLP 73
National Parliamentary Panel (NPP):
2010 General Election 17; candidate
endorsement critical 124; eliminate 8,
43, 45, 49; failed AWS goals 58; lacked
resources 49; members key to reforms
69; NPP approval: variables, statistics
125–126; power shifts to local GC 70;
reason to reinstate, AWS 106; removing
decentralises process 72; supplied pre-
endorsed qualified women 49; vetting
system, pre-approve candidates 71, 90
NEC Guidelines for the Selection of
Parliamentary Candidates 45
*NEC Guidelines for the Selection of
Parliamentary Candidates*
(2003–2006) 73
NEC's Special Selections Panel (SSP):
took over shortlisting 66
Niven, David 14
nomination stage: longlisting stage 20n15
Norris, Pippa. 64, 65, 111, 116, 184, 185
Norway Politics 67

"oligarchical control . . ." 63
one member one vote (OMOV) 65, 68
open seats: frequencies 162–165, **163–164**,
165; and winnable, frequencies 166–
169, **167–168**
Operation Black Vote (OBV) 22, 78
Ostrogorski, M. 64

Parliamentary Labour Party (PLP): AWS
increased participation 20n19
party application 7–8, *8*
party elite 120
party rules: 2015 changes 8, 97; British
Labour party 42, 45, 97–98; central,
implements 9; *centralised*, transparent
12, 61, 62; equality 13, 159; greater
participation, constrain selection 63;
selection 6
party selection process: 11 statistically
significant variables **133**; candidate
requirements 87, **88**; centralisation,
British Labour 66–73; *centralised* vs
decentralised 12–13, 28, 42, 61–62;

central party agents vs local party
agents 61; deficit not undersupply
51–52; disproportionately filters out
women 51–52; equity rules, constrain
selector behaviour 63–64; final selection
filters disproportionately 57, **57**; key
participants and rules 73–79; "ladders
of recruitment" 34; local aspirants, men
19, 38; meso level studies 26–28, *27*;
multiple stages 34; multistage analyses
28–29; "oligarchical control . . ." 63;
one candidate "acclaimed" 20n16;
quotas, improve balance 64; rules
constrain choice 61–62, 63; selection
process 1, 6, *6*; social imbalance 2–6,
16–17, 38; Stage 7 imbalance 56,
57; supply/demand 32; unbalanced
candidate pools 2, 6, 182; women,
BAME, dis-abled filtered out 52–53
party selector perceptions 10, 15, 30
party selectors: gatekeepers 33; key
selector 9
Pearson, K. 38
perceptions 14
Phillips, Anne 5, 24, 29
Pitkin, Hannah: *The Concept of
Representation* 24
political elite: party selectors determine 33;
social characteristics 32
political inequalities: failure, liberal
democracy 23; *structural
discrimination* 24
political success: network 159
Procedures Secretary: application step one 49
prospective parliamentary candidate
(PPCs) 43
Pruysers, Scott 63, 211
Puwar, Nirmal 111

quasi-autonomous non-governmental
organisation (QUANGOs) 37
quotas: disabled 78, 97–98, 101, 134, 144;
equality for women, BAME 4, 12, 19,
25, 32, 52, 101, 103, 104, 106, 114,
184, 186–187; fast track representation
balance 64; key reforms **69**, 70–73, 78,
86, **88**, **93**; lack of 94–99

Rahat, Gideon 9, 12, 13, 26, 61, 62, 63, 73,
79, 86, 207, 211
Randall, Vicky 29
Ranney, Austin 63, 64
recruitment: strong network, increase 160;
supply and demand model 9–14, 17,
22–23, 25–26, 29; three levels 27, *27*

reforms: 1980 Electoral College 70; 1980 mandatory reselection 69; 1989 women on shortlists 70; 1993 all women shortlists 70; 1993 One Member One Vote 70; 1996 quotas for women 70; 1998 approval on the NPP 71; 2002 all women shortlists 71; 2009 special selections panel 71; 2010 quotas for BAME 72; key reforms **69**; post-2012 removal of the NPP 72
regression: Model 2 results **133**; Model 3 results **138**; Model 4 results **142**; Model 5 results **161**; Model 6 results **165**; Model 7 results **170**; Model 8 results **174**; models, explore independent variables 110, **112**; model summary **143**, **176**, **183**; not used to test variables 35; relationship between NPP approval and variables 130; shortlisting 130, **131–132**, **133**, **136–137**, **138**; survey data from aspirant candidates 2005, 2010 121–123, **122**; test, shortlist ideal candidate 145; used, traits seat conditions 19
representative democracy 68
representativeness 23
Ruedin, Didier 5, 211
rule books 42, 45
rules: 2015, changes 8, 97; selection process, centralised 85
Rush, M. 64
Russel, Meg 64, 65–66, 68, 69

Saggar, Shamit 114
Sanbonmatsu, Kira 40, 41, 146, 211, 212
Scarrow, Harold 34, 62, 212
Scottish National Party: lower diversity candidates 4
seat application 8
"secret garden" 7, 42
selection contests: stereotype theory 33
selection process: multiple stages, rules, participants 7–8, *8*
selector preferences: candidate with no children 117; electors use racial stereotypes 114; English first language, "Britishness" 115; ideal aspirant candidate traits **112**; for "ideal candidates" 111–121, 175; occupation 115–116; party experience 117; political ambition 121; political attitudes 120; political experience, networks 118–119;

shortlisted, variables, statistics **131–132**; women, discrimination 113
seven selection campaign variables 156–165
sex quotas: return to 103, 106; women, BAME, disabled 32, 94, 184, 186
Seyd, Patrick 4, 120, 184, 212
#SheShouldRun 3
shortlisted: Stage 7 selected or not 155
shortlisting 7–8, *8*; demands plays strong role 146; local residents preferred 145, 161; in open, winnable seats 138–142, **139–140**, **142**; variables, statistics 130, **131–132**, **133**, **136–137**, **138**
Smith, John (1992–1994) 69
socialist societies 68
social justice: women's 3
Squires, Judith 5, 6, 115, 212
Standardized Notice of Shortlisting by CLP 95
Statement of Candidate's Qualities 92
statistical information 45–53, **46**, **50**, 121–124, **122**, **125–127**
statistical tests: AWS seats **174**, 174–175; open and winnable seats 169; open seats, Model 5 160–162, **163–164**; shortlisting, Stage 4 130–142, **131–132**
stereotype theory 33
Stewart, Kennedy: selector bias 36
stratification hypotheses 32
structural discrimination 24, 29
substantive representation 23–24
supply and demand: 2010 British General Election 25; analogy, underrepresentation 26; behavioural approach 14; caused by demand-side factors 42; data on winners vs losers 35; develop multistage method 36; efforts needed, gender equality 145; institutional factors **11**, 11–12, 16; main paradigm 9–10; micro level investigation 26, 29, 34; selection processes, outcomes 29; stages apply 35; women, BAME, new pathway 37

term limits 27
The Speaker's (6th) Conference on Parliamentary Representation: rectify disparity 25
Tolley, Erin 5, 33, 39, 114, 212
trade unions 68; recommended applicants endorsed 90
Trimble, Linda 212

underrepresentation: approach, data 25–26; *behavioural factors* 12; central party favors 12–13, 28; descriptive 22–24; investigative approach 26; studies, defined 26–29; supply/demand 10; women, marginalised 2, 3, 9, 13

under-supply: factors 30

US Politics: decentralised candidate selection process 63; primary system, regulate candidate selection 62; stereotype theory 33; voter bias 38; voter mobilisation, door-to-door, successful 155

US women candidates: negative selection process 14

voter mobilisation: electoral success in US 155; more time, money, winner 154

Wängnerud, Lena 24, 213

Ware, Alan 26, 61, 63, 64, 67, 213

women: candidate disadvantages 38; candidates, key participant and rule values 97–98, **98**; centralised party 28, 62; clustering into AWS seats 144; disproportionately filtered, final stage 106; new pathway 37; selection process filters out 51–52; women's representation globally 19n7

Women's Action Committee (WAC) 69